ENGLISH FURNITURE 1800-1851

EDWARD T. JOY

ENGLISH FURNITURE

1800-1851

SOTHEBY PARKE BERNET PUBLICATIONS

WARD LOCK LIMITED · LONDON

© Edward T. Joy 1977

ISBN 085667 031 6

First published in Great Britain 1977
by Sotheby Parke Bernet Publications
Russell Chambers, Covent Garden, London WC2E 8AA
in association with Ward Lock Limited
116 Baker Street, London W1M 2BB,
a member of the Pentos Group.

Edition for the United States of America
available from
Biblio Distribution Center for
Sotheby Parke Bernet Publications
81 Adams Drive
Totowa, New Jersey 07512

House editor Sue Unstead
Designed by Trevor Vincent

Printed in Great Britain
by Balding & Mansell Ltd, Wisbech.

CONTENTS

INTRODUCTION

'The slightest observation of the domestic life of the middle and humbler classes will shew that, within the last thirty years, there has been a manifest improvement in the appearance of the household furniture of this country. . . . The general introduction of mahogany, and the comparative cheapness of furniture made externally of this beautiful material (principally in consequence of the extreme thinness into which veneers can be cut) have introduced a more elegant description of furniture even into the commonest houses. In this, there is a national benefit. A taste for comforts and elegancies, universally diffused throughout society, not only calls into action a great deal of mechanical ingenuity, and employs considerable capital, but it gives even to the humblest a sort of self-respect, inferior, indeed, to purer motives, but still operating to produce something of independence, and a desire to maintain the possession of these comforts and trifling distinctions, by honest industry. But the general adoption of articles of luxury, such as well-made furniture, by the bulk of the people, has a natural tendency to make the wealthy desirous of procuring articles not so accessible to the many; and, in this way, there is a constant demand not only for new patterns in furniture, but for new materials of which such furniture should be made. Our commerce with all the known world has enabled the dealers in wood constantly to introduce new sorts; and even our native timber, such as oak and elm, by the ingenuity of the workman, has been converted into the most beautiful and the most expensive of the articles of common use by which the rich are surrounded.'[1]

This paragraph makes a good summary of what we have come to regard as the main features of English furniture-making in the mid-Victorian period. There are references to the general diffusion of furniture among the general population and its improved quality and appearance, mainly through the cheaper process of veneering in mahogany; to the universal taste for 'comforts and elegancies'—the eighteenth century would have reversed the order of these two words—and to the use of machinery, to which so many of these benefits are due. The reaction of the wealthy to this increased production of furniture was a constant search for new styles, new shapes and new materials, hence the great variety of new timbers imported from abroad and the use of new processes for treating native timbers. There is the touch of moral approbation rarely absent

Chair, *c.* 1845, of curvilinear outline with Berlin woolwork upholstery. The rounded forms are typical of the mid-Victorian search for comfort.

from the Victorian scene when improvements reach the right quarters; a hint of the fruits of 'self-help'. The abundance of household goods which do so much to instil a spirit of independence and self-respect among the lower classes are regarded as incentives towards, and due rewards for, honest toil. The passage catches the spirit of pious optimism which was prevalent at the time of the Great Exhibition of 1851, and something of the exhilaration engendered by the sense of rapid material achievement, and the consequent confident and almost breath-taking belief in progress which could lead the Rev H. Wellesley to write in the *Quarterly Review* in October 1844 that 'the century we live in is not more remarkable for its railways and marvels of science, than for a re-action from preceding barbarism in matters of taste'.[2]

Yet the opening paragraph was written before the end of the Georgian period, while George IV was still on the throne, and almost a decade before Victoria became queen in 1837. It is taken from a series with the very Victorian title of *The Library of Entertaining Knowledge*, in the volume devoted to trees and fruits, which was first published in 1829, to be followed immediately by a second edition in 1830. The paragraph summarizes the progress of a whole generation, going back to 1800. It makes the obvious point that those changes which are so often taken now as typically Victorian were already at work at the beginning of the nineteenth century and indeed, in most cases, they were deeply rooted in the eighteenth century. This makes nonsense of the idea of 1830 as a vital terminal date in the development of English furniture; its selective and artificial character has helped to conceal important changes which would tend to make 1851, if one wants a date at all, the real landmark. Certainly much too much emphasis has been placed on machinery as the major cause of change; the factors which conditioned the ruling taste of the nineteenth century in furniture were in full swing before the impact of mechanization.[3]

The two most powerful influences on the development of English furniture in the first half of the nineteenth century were the cult of the Picturesque and the Industrial Revolution. The first brought Romanticism, indiscipline, historicism and eclecticism; the second brought new materials, an eagerness for experiment, a striving for novelty and a search for comfort. These changes were accomplished against the background of an unprecedented rise in the country's population and the concluding stages of the Classical tradition, which had been the established canon of taste for some two centuries. The population of England and Wales had been increasing remarkably since the middle of the eighteenth century, when it reached about six and a half millions, and was to double in size–from approximately nine to eighteen millions–between the first official census of 1801 and that of 1851. Here was the ever-widening market for furniture and the reason for the vast increase in output. The implications of this rise are examined further in Chapter 6, Patent Furniture.

The term 'Picturesque' was applied originally to a landscape or building which recalled the paintings of Lorrain, Salvator Rosa and Poussin.[4] It was a term which long remained imprecise, and indeed its definition had been the subject of involved and often wearisome controversies. An important new stage with more precise definition was reached in the 1790s through the writings of Sir Uvedale Price (1747–1829) and Richard Payne Knight (1750–1824). Price in his *Essay on the Picturesque*, 1794, defined his subject as an aesthetic category, distinct from the Sublime and the Beautiful as defined by Burke thirty-eight years previously.[5] Knight published his views in his didactic poem, *The Landscape*, 1794, which, though primarily concerned with landscape gardening, and including an attack on Capability Brown's smooth and artificial style, emphasized the numerous elements of surprise, variety and intricacy contained in the concept of the Picturesque. As in architecture the picturesque love of asymmetry of form and variety of texture produced the *cottage orné*, the Italianate house and the castellated mansion; so it was bound to influence the interior of the house and the appearance and arrangement of its furniture.

There were, of course, repercussions from the Romantic movement which had many features in common with the Picturesque. As late as 1868 G. A. Sala attributed the revival of interest in medieval and Renaissance art to the novels of Sir Walter Scott, not to Pugin or Ruskin.[6] The Romantic movement underlay the conception of the 'Olden Time', which was immensely popular in the 1840s and 1850s, and the taste for 'Merry England', that embraced the Elizabethan and Jacobean as well as the medieval periods and was the inspiration of the famous Eglinton Tournament of 1839. Like so many other revivals of the time it mixed a genuine regard for scholarship with sentiment derived from association, and with escapism.[7]

The most important factor was the Industrial Revolution. This half-century saw the transition of England from a predominantly agricultural society to an industrial one, the first industrialized country in the world. The furniture craftsman and designer, usually one and the same person, had always been trained to relate furniture directly to the needs of society, a relatively straightforward task in the static social conditions of the eighteenth century, when fashionable taste was dictated by a cultured minority within the well-defined framework of the Classical tradition. But in the rapidly changing social conditions of the time the problems facing the furniture designer were completely novel. The arbiters of fashion, still the wealthy classes but now infused with new blood, gradually adopted a new criterion – comfort. The very novelty of the situation ruled out any speedy solution to the problem of developing the kind of furniture that would suit the new social structure. The architects and craftsmen who were reaching the peak of their skill and experience when George IV died in 1830 had all been reared on Classical principles, though many were willing enough to experiment in other styles. The influences which prompted historical revivals were a further brake on adaptation. No other country faced these problems; none, therefore, could offer any solution. To dismiss the first fifteen years of Victoria's reign, as has been done, as marking 'the lowest ebb ever reached in the whole history of English furniture design' is perhaps to do less than justice to the immensity of the problem, even if one did not suggest, with good reason, that the fifteen years after 1918 were still worse.[8]

There had in fact been pioneer attempts in the early nineteenth century to solve the problem. Some of the most notable achievements of the period lay in the fusion of fine craftsmanship, the legacy of the Sheraton era, with the mechanical skill of industry. This alliance between the cabinet-maker and the engineer, often resulting in furniture of pure functional precision in the 'patent' furniture of the time, is a much neglected subject. It is in this direction that one must look to find the roots of modern design.[9] On the other hand the fruits of industry –better living conditions, increasing national wealth, material output– which were within the reach of more and more people in spite of the areas of social distress, encouraged insistence on comfort and ostentation. There was a dichotomy in furniture development between the vernacular–the simple and functional–and the fashionable–the ornate and exhibitionist.

It is unfortunate that the functionalism of early nineteenth-century patent furniture was destroyed by the very technological developments that had made it possible, i.e. the multiplication of mechanized ornament, employed for its cheapness and speed of production. From this it was an easy step to the Victorian theory that to apply 'art' (ornament) to 'manufacture' (any standard piece of furniture) would result in good design.

In common with much European furniture English styles in a way reflected the wave of nationalist sentiment which was a feature of the post-Napoleonic period. Cultural traditions were emphasized, and a new lease of life was given to the vernacular style, in building and interior decoration as well as in furniture. This was a further impulse to the revival of Tudor, Elizabethan and Jacobean styles in English furniture. The Gothic style was the subject of a shift of emphasis towards the Perpendicular period, which was considered to be a peculiarly English contribution to architecture and decoration.

New figures appeared on the English furniture scene. The professional furniture designer was to be more truly a figure of the second half of the century, but his coming importance was forecast in such men as Ludwig Gruner.[10] By 1851 the historian of antiquarian furniture, the dealer in antique furniture and the manufacturer of reproduction furniture were all well established, no doubt considerably helped in their various activities by the new railways.[11] The furniture craftsman given most prominence was the upholsterer. His became a fashionable title, synonymous with that of 'decorator', which was now adopted by many fashionable firms. 'Decorator to Her Majesty' was that of H. W. & A. Arrowsmith early in the queen's reign. This period could justly be called 'the age of the upholsterer', the origin of which can be traced to France under Napoleon. After 1815 upholstery became perhaps the controlling material in furniture design. Seating furniture–chairs, settees, couches –lost their precise outlines under bulky upholstery, while other heavily cushioned furniture inspired by oriental influence, such as ottomans and divans, occupied the central places in rooms.[12] Sprung upholstery, coupled with the Rococo revival, hastened this process in England.

Regency armchair, *c.* 1820, of bergère type in rosewood; padded arms on scrolled supports and U-shaped cushioned seat; tapered moulded legs on brass castors.

Regency rosewood armchair, *c.* 1820, pull-out padded foot-rest beneath the seat. Re-upholstered in buttoned green leather.

Two examples of the effect of heavily buttoned upholstery on dining-room chairs of the mid-century.

The Industrial Revolution was in many ways the acceleration of forces which had already begun to work and was not a revolution in the sense of a sudden fundamental change. The structure of the furniture industry, for instance, though subject to striking growth in the nineteenth century, retained essentially its eighteenth-century form. Its existing framework was ready and able to cope with the fresh demands, and there was no question of the factory system taking its place.[13]

The changes which had occurred in furniture-making by 1851 raise the vexed question of patronage. Who finally dictated taste, employed the most important upholsterers and cabinet-makers and encouraged the historical revivals, the multiplicity of styles and the growing trend towards elaboration of ornament? The view usually put forward is that the court and aristocracy, who in the eighteenth century had had such a secure control over standards of taste, surrendered their lead in the nineteenth to the *nouveaux riches* from industry and trade. These parvenus, it is claimed, lacked the traditional training in matters of taste of the established upper classes and imposed their own debased standards. This view hardly bears close examination. The most natural procedure for newcomers to society is to conform to the manners of the aristocracy. Victorian novels give many instances of the new families who send in their cards to their established neighbours and wait anxiously for acceptance. The court and aristocracy seem to have continued to exert their leadership in fashion. This is certainly true of George IV and the Prince Consort. The best-known families took the lead in sponsoring new styles; the Duke of Rutland, for example, with the Louis Quatorze,[14] and the Duke of Devonshire and the Earl of Shrewsbury with A. W. N. Pugin's Gothic.

The clue to patronage lies in the search, common now to the old and new rich alike, for comfort. The Georgian country house built for the man of taste was a 'temple of art', the collector's showpiece, open for display to all approved visitors. In contrast the Victorian country house –it could be a totally new one or an older one modernized–emphasized privacy and a comfortable home life for family and friends.[15] Comfort was the prime consideration in this period. It confirmed the importance of the upholsterer, it conditioned the form of furniture and it led to a completely new arrangement of the contents of the house.

The half-century under review is fortunate in having, among the welter of pattern books, three particularly valuable documentary sources, each of which in its own way makes a valuable commentary on the furniture of its time. The three sources are Ackermann's *The Repository of Arts, Literature, Commerce, Manufacturers, Fashions and Politics*, 1809–28; John C. Loudon's *Encyclopaedia of Cottage Farm and Villa Architecture and Furniture*, 1833; and the *Art-Journal Illustrated Catalogue* of the Great Exhibition, 1851.

Rudolf Ackermann (1764–1834), born in Stolberg, Saxony, settled in London, where he opened a print shop in the Strand in 1795, and subsequently became well known as a fine-art publisher and bookseller, being credited with the establishment of lithography as a fine art in England. Between 1809 and 1828 he published in monthly parts the *Repository of Arts*, most numbers of which included a section on 'Fashionable Furniture' with a colour plate of furniture and interior decoration and explanatory text; the total of 189 such plates, together with the background furniture in the numerous coloured plates of ladies' costume, provides a unique single guide to Regency taste. A feature of the *Repository* is the presentation of the furniture of a single firm, sometimes in successive plates and over a period of years. The earliest issues make frequent references to Morgan and Sanders of Catherine Street, Strand. The designs of George Bullock are shown in several issues between 1816 and 1824 (continuing after his death in 1818). These designs, which include the first recorded publication of a piece of furniture in the 'Elizabethan' style, have preserved Bullock from oblivion, and subsequent research has revealed him as one of the most important and representative figures of the time. A detailed study of his work is made in Chapter 3. In 1819 and 1820 furniture designs are replaced by window draperies designed by John Stafford, the Bath upholsterer. In April 1822 the firm of Snell of Albermarle Street are referred to as specialists in French furniture and in March 1825 illustrations appear of the carved, painted and gilt drawing-room chairs made by Morel and Hughes for the Duke of Northumberland, which today are at Syon House.[16]

Classical taste predominates in the earlier issues when George Smith was responsible for some of the designs and, according to the commentary, 'a much lighter style evinces itself in modern works of art . . . for which we are indebted to the Grecian school' (May 1809). But the *Repository* was catholic in its tastes and, in addition to Gothic pieces, illustrated much 'patent' furniture, designed for compactness and incorporating mechanical devices, including Morgan & Sanders' 'metamorphic library chair' (July 1811) and Pocock's 'reclining patent chair' (February 1813). Pocock is another very typical figure of his day, and his work will merit further scrutiny below (Chapter 6). As early as 1812, the year of Napoleon's Moscow campaign and of the publication of Percier and Fontaine's *Recueil de Décorations Intérieures*, the *Repository* is quick to illustrate, in four successive numbers from June onwards, pieces in French Empire style. These designs are continued at intervals after the peace of 1815, a secretaire-bookcase being described in April 1822 as 'after the style so exquisitely perfected by M. Persée, the French architect to Buonaparte'. The Egyptian style also has a brief showing in 1812 and 1813, probably through French influence, and

Walnut armchair with the typical curved outline of the mid-century.

Games table, incorporating requisites for several games; typical of the portable, elegant and well-equipped furniture of the early 19th century.

despite previous criticism of the style by the *Repository*. Between 1821 and 1824 a few designs are contributed by John Taylor, who later published two small and undistinguished volumes on furniture.

A significant shift of emphasis occurs in 1825, when the *Repository's* concluding issues give an enthusiastic reception to the fashionable Gothic style. Twenty-seven plates of Gothic furniture, published between October 1825 and October 1827, form the longest run of illustrations devoted to a single fashionable style that the *Repository* ever published. They coincide with George IV's refurnishing, partly in Gothic style, of the royal apartments at Windsor Castle. The designs, by Pugin, were published separately in 1827 as *Gothic Furniture*; they form a comprehensive study of the 'unreformed' Gothic of the late Regency (see Chapter 3).

Five years after the final issue of the *Repository* there appeared Loudon's *Encyclopaedia of Cottage, Farm and Villa Architecture and Furniture*, a different publication in every way.[17] John C. Loudon (1783–1843), the son of a Scottish farmer, came to London as a young man and, throughout his working life, displayed incredible energy as a landscape gardener, architect, compiler of books and editor of encyclopedias and magazines, all in spite of being dogged by ill-health and serious financial worries. He had those qualities of intense application and unwavering belief in social and scientific progress through self-help—it is significant that his last book was entitled *Self-Instruction to Young Gardeners*—which we recognize as typically Victorian virtues, although he lived for only six years in Victoria's reign. The *Encyclopaedia*, his best-known book, is by far the most comprehensive and informative treatise on furniture that had ever been published in England. It was also one of the most popular and was reissued in 1835, 1836, 1839, 1842, 1845, 1846, 1847, 1850, 1857, 1863 and 1867, making eleven issues altogether with some insignificant revisions—a striking testimony to the strong conservative element in Victorian taste. It reached a wide public in America as well as in England. Originally some 1,100 pages long, it was increased to over 1,300 pages with the addition of a supplement in 1846, edited by his widow, Jane; with its small print, it is a truly monumental work. Most of the work was concerned with buildings, but there is plenty on furnishings and equipment even here to add to the sections on furniture. The latter form a valuable social document, for not only do they cover, as the title indicates, all types of furniture for all classes (in sharp distinction to the *Repository's* emphasis on upper-class fashions), but they also mark the first attempt to consider in detail the impact of the Industrial Revolution on domestic furniture. Hence the attention paid, among many other subjects, to mechanical devices, invalid furniture and to new materials such as cast iron, gas piping and wire springs.

The most frequently quoted passage in the *Encyclopaedia* is that which sets out the four fashionable styles of the day, viz. Grecian, Gothic, Elizabethan and Louis Quatorze.[18] The historical attributions of these revivals are often muddled, but Loudon is hardly to blame for this in view of the backward state of the study of art history. His summary has been accepted as accurate enough and is borne out by modern research. He has come in for a certain amount of criticism for his 'neutrality' in considering these fashionable styles, but in fact he makes his own opinions clear on many occasions and is as ready to condemn as he is to praise.

In the preliminary skirmishes of what has become known as the 'Battle of the Styles' one is left in no doubt as to what side Loudon is on. He dislikes the Louis Quatorze revival as 'unsuitable to the present advancing state of the public taste'. His preference is obviously for the Grecian (or 'modern') taste, which is well illustrated, though the Classical ornament now lacks the precision which Thomas Hope gave it. But even his admiration for the Grecian is tempered with criticism, which shows his perception of forces at work and is worth noting in detail; he is writing of hall chairs for a villa:

'With respect to the taste of these chairs, we object to the front legs, as being too much ornamented for those behind. Who, on being shown the front legs, while the back legs were concealed, would ever expect to find the latter united in the same whole with the former? Certainly no one would do so who understood the principle of unity of style in composition. The reason why cabinet-makers are in the habit of bestowing so much work on the straight legs of chairs and benches, and so little on those which are curved, is that the straight legs are readily ornamented at a cheap rate in the turning lathe; whereas, all the ornament that is bestowed on the curved legs must be carved by hand, at a great expense. The question is, how far the designer of a chair is justified in deviating from the principle of unity, for the sake of displaying more ornament than he would otherwise be able to show. Ask a cabinet-maker, and he will tell you at once, that his customers prefer the ornamented chair, and care nothing about the unity, or the want of unity, of style. Their great object is to get a display of rich workmanship, at as cheap a rate as possible. Our readers, we are sure, will agree with us, that this taste on the part of the purchaser is of a vulgar and grovelling kind, and ought to be corrected. This can only be done by enlightening the minds of the public in general on the subject of taste; and this is one of the grand objects of our work.'

More could be quoted on these lines. The design of bed pillars is criticized for 'the deviation from simplicity'. This was due to the great demand for cabinet furniture and the desire for novelty, so that the

Fancy chair with interlaced wicker back and cane seat; a light type intended for dressing-rooms and bedrooms. 'They may be considered as not inelegant'–Loudon, *Encyclopaedia*, 1833.

upholsterer, striving to satisfy his customer, 'has only called forth mechanical changes or combinations of forms'.

Yet Loudon fails lamentably on occasions to use his stated principles as a yardstick. He is full of praise for the Gothic style, which he illustrates essentially in the combination of forms–the addition of Gothic components to current un-Gothic structures–that he condemns elsewhere. A general view of a drawing-room furnished in the Gothic style is held to be above criticism, 'for every reader, we think, must be pleased with it'. The chairs in a Gothic library, like every other piece of furniture in it, are in the most perfect unity of style, for 'there is not that discrepancy between the hind and fore legs, that there is in the designs for chairs in the modern style'. The stiffness, which he admits he sees in these Gothic chairs, belongs to the style.

Loudon advocates the staining and graining of wood, a common practice of the time, sometimes with the intention of imitating another wood; he carries this to its strangest conclusion in his illustration of a cast-iron chair in Etruscan taste with detailed instructions for painting it in imitation of oak. But in many respects he must be given credit for illustrating numerous examples of simple and attractive furniture of all kinds, and for his interest in functional forms, particularly for cottage and farmhouse pieces. One prime consideration is comfort, dispensed, as it were, through a kindly providence as a reward for honest toil. 'A sofa', he writes, 'is a piece of furniture which affords a great source of comfort to its possessor; and therefore the cottager ought to have one as well as the rich man.' He stresses the need to design furniture that will not harbour dust and will thus be easier to keep clean. For this reason, and at variance with the views expressed above, he is against furniture in the 'enriched Gothic style', as this will greatly increase the labour of servants when 'all, from the highest to the lowest are beginning to recognize their equal natural right of enjoyment'.

Loudon warns readers against a growing practice of his time, the results of which are all too apparent in surviving pieces, of making up antique furniture from old fragments. He names London firms who specialize in producing furniture of this sort. He is strangely quiet about Gothic furniture, but makes particular reference to the practice in connection with Elizabethan pieces, with an interesting aside on the export trade:

'As London has a direct and cheap communication with every part of the world by sea, the American citizen or the Australian merchant, who wishes to indulge in this taste . . . may purchase real antiques at much less expense than he could have the articles carved by modern artists.'

The *Art-Journal Illustrated Catalogue* of the Great Exhibition,

1851, which illustrates the chief exhibits, is far more critical of the standard of design than the three-volume *Official Descriptive and Illustrated Catalogue* and other contemporary publications which adopt a laudatory and uncritical attitude.[19] The Great Exhibition, the most famous ever held in England, was preceded by others in Manchester in 1846, in London between 1845 and 1849, when annual exhibitions were held by the Society of Arts, and in Birmingham in 1849. The furniture shown at the Crystal Palace in 1851 (this exhibition, unlike the others, was an international one) gave a completely misleading impression of the ordinary furniture of the time. It brought to a head the elaboration which had been a growing feature of the decoration of furniture, and to this were added novelty, inventiveness and exhibitionism. The *Official Catalogue*, more readily available than pattern books of the time, was for long accepted as representative of early Victorian taste. Yet the everyday products of Gillows and Hollands, to take the two firms whose order books have survived, were quite different from their specially commissioned exhibition pieces. Hollands, for instance, exhibited an elaborately carved combined chimney-piece and bookcase, now at Flintham Hall, Nottinghamshire, designed by T. R. Macquoid in Cinquecento style, which contrasts strongly with the furniture which they were supplying during the same period to Osborne House and numerous government departments. Contemporary pattern books, as well as surviving pieces, further confirm the unrepresentative character of the Exhibition furniture, which offered Loudon's 'display of rich workmanship', particularly carving, but not 'at as cheap a rate as possible'. The cabinet furniture was expensive, and overloaded with an abundance of naturalistic ornament which carried symbolism to extremes never reached before. No real attempts at a radical reform in design or ornament, with the exception of Pugin's Gothic, were apparent among English designers.

To correct the impressions conveyed by the *Official Catalogue*, we have the objective view of the *Art-Journal Illustrated Catalogue* for, though this is not lacking in enthusiastic descriptions of many of the illustrated exhibits, it has at the end of the work a valuable essay by R. N. Wornum on 'The Exhibition as a Lesson in Taste', which won the prize of 100 guineas offered by the editors. Wornum (1812–77) had spent some years visiting museums and art galleries in Europe and had lectured on art in the government's design schools. He was later to be appointed Keeper of the National Gallery in 1854 and to publish the best-selling *Analysis of Ornament* in 1856.

To the vast majority of the six million visitors the Great Exhibition was a source of delight and amazement, and their visit the event of a lifetime. William Morris refused to go round, declaring the Exhibition to be 'wonderfully ugly'. There can have been very few indeed who acted as he did. Wornum's value to us is his ability to bring a keen analytical mind on all the exhibits, adopting an attitude of neutrality in the 'Battle of the Styles', which he reviews in the beginning of his essay. His main target is the use of ornament.[20]

His strongest criticism is reserved for the Louis Quatorze and Louis Quinze styles, particularly the latter, which he castigates as 'a mere mass of vagaries of indescribable forms'. From the start he is highly suspicious of French influence on English design, while freely acknowledging the superiority of French carving, and, though this appears surprising in view of the high cost of most English exhibits, he makes the fundamentally telling point that 'while England has been devoting nearly all its efforts to the mere comfort of the million, France has expended its energies, for the most part, over luxuries for the few'. He is astonished to find so little Classical ornament; what there is stands out, surrounded by endless specimens of 'the prevailing gorgeous taste of the present day'. He also has distinct reservations about the Medieval Court, 'the copy of an old idea; old things in an old taste'. He regarded the current Cinquecento—the revival of sixteenth-century Italian ornament—as the best-understood style of the day and for this reason he could praise the chimney-piece-bookcase exhibited by Hollands.

With reference to ornament, particularly carved ornament, Wornum puts his finger on the weakest spot in the whole conception of Victorian design. The predominant naturalist ('horticultural') ornament has led to the serious artistic fault of 'using our imitations from nature as principals in the design instead of mere accessory decorations, substituting the ornament itself for the thing to be ornamented'. This confusion of design and ornament bedevilled Victorian thinking. It lay at the root of that truly Victorian idea of 'art-manufactures'—a term which Wornum himself used at the beginning of his essay—by which 'art' (i.e. ornament) added to 'manufacture' (i.e. a basic form of furniture, such as a sideboard, or of any other commodity) equalled good design. As Wornum points out, 'art', in the sense of the carved ornament which he saw at the Exhibition, showed 'want of definite design and disregard of utility . . . overloading of detail . . . a disagreeable inequality of execution, one part destroying the effect of the other'. It must have been a shock to the comfortable, preconceived notions of many viewers to find Wornum highly critical of one of the most admired exhibits, the 'Kenilworth Buffet', so-called from its carved panels showing scenes from Scott's novel, *Kenilworth*, made by Cookes & Son of Warwick and regarded as a *tour de force* of the Warwick school of carving.[21] This sideboard, now in Warwick Castle, is described by Wornum as massive and handsome but impaired by the dramatic treatment of the figures and the consequent loss of symmetry, 'for which we have only a very feeble expression of a doubtful idea'.

The famous 'Kenilworth Buffet' with its mass of anecdotal carving, exhibited in 1851 by Messrs Cookes and Sons of Warwick.

It is easy to see Wornum's deficiencies as a critic. He ends his essay by asserting that the time had gone by for the development of any particular or national style, but makes no attempt to fill the vacuum. He misses the implications of Pugin's Gothic, and makes no reference to what we now regard as exciting *avant-garde* functionalism, seen, for example, in Thonet's chairs (admittedly these passed practically unnoticed by everybody). His was, for a time, a voice crying in the wilderness, for the confusion between design and ornament did not cease after 1851 but was to be perpetuated in commercial productions until the end of the century and even beyond. Nevertheless his public widened with his *Analysis of Ornament*, which reached its eighth edition in 1893. He was soon joined by Richard Redgrave RA, whose review of the Paris Exhibition of 1855 condemned the 'beauty' (or 'art') added to English furniture as 'too often a useless piece of ornamental lumber'.[22] And Wornum's lessons were learnt by the increasing number of reformist furniture designers in the second half of the century.

Sofa, *c.* 1820, in Classical taste, rosewood inlaid
with brass decoration.

Above Mahogany circular table, *c.* 1810, on
quadrupedal support, the top crossbanded and
inlaid with anthemion and acanthus scrolls in
ebony.

Right Regency Pembroke table, rosewood,
inlaid with brass anthemion.

[20]

CHAPTER 1
THE REGENCY

As the nineteenth century opened English furniture was entering upon the second main phase of the Neo-Classical style, which had been the dominant European fashion since the mid-eighteenth century. By 1800 archaeological discoveries, stimulated by the excavations of Herculaneum from 1738 and Pompeii from 1748, had established a growing corpus of information on Classical antiquities, which turned designers into the direction of a more accurate adherence to the forms of ancient furniture. In England this change coincided with the end of Robert Adam's light and delicate treatment of Classical decoration (Adam himself died in 1792), and the new approach was given a philosophical formulation by Archibald Alison's *Essays on the Nature and Principles of Taste*, first published in 1790, which reached its sixth edition in 1825. Alison indulged in a great deal of emotive writing on sublimity and beauty, related to current theories of the Picturesque, but he established the chief features of ancient furniture, in relation to his theories of beauty, as the use of straight or angular lines and delicate forms ('strong and massy furniture is everywhere vulgar and unpleasing'), relatively low height and plain surfaces. He accepted the association of ideas to justify the 'imitation of those models which have been lately discovered in Italy' because this would 'occupy our imagination by leading to those recollections of Grecian or Roman taste'. He had to commit himself to justify the Chinese and Gothic styles for the same reasons; the former recalled 'eastern significance and splendour', the latter 'Gothic manners and adventure'.[1]

The first published designs of furniture which bridged the two phases of Neo-Classicism were Sheraton's. His *Cabinet-Maker and Upholsterer's Drawing Book* of 1791–4, reissued in 1794 and 1802, was his masterpiece, the true foundation of the 'Sheraton style', for it carried Hepplewhite's interpretation of Adam's Classical themes a stage further by stressing extreme delicacy of form. In this sense it looked back to Adam for inspiration, but in one important respect it foreshadowed an important development of the early nineteenth century; this was in its range of compact, portable, multi-purpose furniture which often incorporated mechanical devices. And though the appearance of furniture was to change, some of Sheraton's mannerisms were to continue in the new phase; reeded chair and table legs, for example, splayed claw feet on tables and, on some cabinet pieces, the short (*toupie*) foot.

This display table illustrates many Regency features: rosewood veneers, mirror back, S-scroll supports, tapered reeded legs, joined lotus-leaf ornament on the legs, and brass gallery and columns.

Mahogany armchair, c. 1810, reeded rectangular top rail and turned cross bar; scrolled arm supports and sabre legs.

Mahogany dwarf bookcase, c. 1810. Furniture of low height was fashionable during the Regency; it followed Classical precedents and also left wall space for hanging pictures.

Rosewood armchair and single chair. c. 1815, mounted with gilt metal in Empire taste; cross bar pierced with a gilt metal roundel; gilt enrichment on the front seat rail and sabre legs.

Mahogany 'Wellington' chest, c. 1835, stamped brass ring handles.

Armchair and single chair, *c.* 1815, painted and parcel gilt, rectangular backs with stuffed panels and lotus decoration above and below; tapered legs with fluted decoration.

Armchair, single chair and footstool, *c.* 1810–20, the frames painted black and parcel gilt; the chairs have reeded cresting-rails with cross bars centring in an oval panel; sabre legs.

Right Secretaire cabinet or bookcase, *c.* 1805, mahogany and rosewood; lower stage has a fall front; metal trellis work on cupboard doors.

Below Tortoiseshell worktable, *c.* 1820, shallow domed lid enclosing drawers, with a removable lid above the pouch; square pillar support on a concave-sided platform.

Secretaire cabinet, *c.* 1810, satinwood and burr yew crossbanded in rosewood, decorated with brass stringing and gilt metal anthemion mounts; the upper stage surmounted by a gilt metal fret gallery; fitted secretaire drawer above the lower cupboards.

Rosewood cabinet, *c.* 1810, frieze inlaid with fruitwood stringing, plinth inlaid in similar fashion; cupboard doors flanked by free-standing ring-turned columns. The low height (3 ft 1 in) and short width (2 ft 10 in) are typical features of Regency furniture.

Etagère, *c.* 1815, rosewood with parcel-gilt decoration, reeded supports; drawer below the bottom shelf.

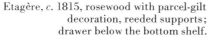

Right Gentleman's dressing cabinet, *c.* 1820, mahogany, the top cross-banded with tulipwood; a rising mirror panel at the back; gilt metal beading round the front three panels, and moulding of acorns and oak leaves on the frieze and base.

Below Mahogany break-front cabinet, *c.* 1810, centre section with three dummy shelves of leather book spines flanked by leaf-carved reeded balusters and enclosing a cupboard fitted to hold bottles; each side section with three open shelves and matching balusters.

Two 'Herculaneum' chairs from Sheraton's *Cabinet Dictionary*, 1803.

The new archaeological approach to furniture was clearly heralded in Sheraton's *Cabinet Dictionary* of 1803, more a practical compendium than a pattern book.[2] Features that are distinctly Regency in character are the Grecian couch, one of the most typical of all Regency pieces, animal monopodia (i.e. with miniature head and body and single, life-size foot), lion-paw feet and lion masks, curved front chair legs which anticipate the concave (or 'sabre' form), and simulated bamboo legs of chairs and tables. Sheraton's final work, the unfinished *The Cabinet-Maker, Upholsterer and General Artist's Encyclopaedia*, 1804–6, never came to grips with the new style; its designs bordered on the fantastic and suggested a disordered mind. It made, however, one innovation; it is the first pattern book in England to illustrate the Egyptian taste with its use of sphinx heads and feet as capitals and bases of pilasters. The new style was to develop through two men of ability and influence, Henry Holland and Thomas Hope, the latter being responsible for the design of the most archaeologically exact furniture ever made in England.

'Regency' is now the accepted title for the English version of the intensive Classical revival which characterized the last phase of Georgian furniture and interior decoration.[3] The title is misleading, for the style had clearly emerged in the eighteenth century and owed much to *le goût Etrusque*, which developed in France towards the end of Louis XVI's reign (1774–92). Thus it obviously outstrips the chronological limits of the political Regency (1811–20) of George, Prince of Wales. On the other hand the style is rightly centred in the Prince for, from the time when he came of age in August 1783 until his death in 1830, he proved to be a distinguished patron of the arts, although very extravagant and

Painted and gilt chair, *c.* 1805, sabre legs and lion's paw feet.

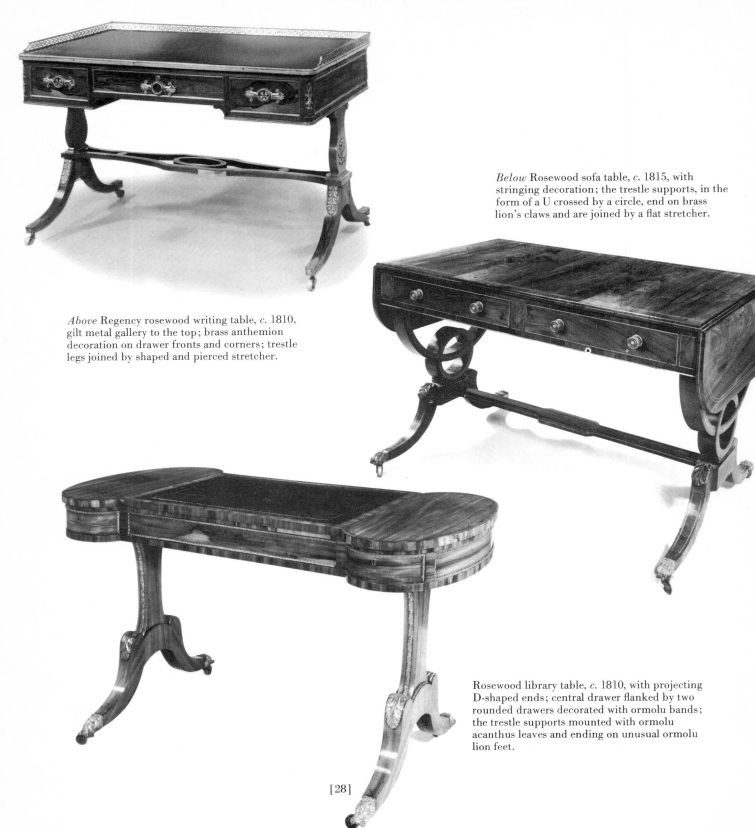

Below Rosewood sofa table, *c.* 1815, with stringing decoration; the trestle supports, in the form of a U crossed by a circle, end on brass lion's claws and are joined by a flat stretcher.

Above Regency rosewood writing table, *c.* 1810, gilt metal gallery to the top; brass anthemion decoration on drawer fronts and corners; trestle legs joined by shaped and pierced stretcher.

Rosewood library table, *c.* 1810, with projecting D-shaped ends; central drawer flanked by two rounded drawers decorated with ormolu bands; the trestle supports mounted with ormolu acanthus leaves and ending on unusual ormolu lion feet.

Mahogany library table, *c.* 1820, ormolu
anthemion decoration on the drawer fronts;
turned trestle supports on scroll feet mounted
with acanthus leaves and joined by a turned
stretcher.

Sofa table, *c.* 1815, calamander crossbanded with
satinwood and decorated with ebony stringing;
trestle supports with double stretchers.

Mahogany card table, *c.* 1815, folding top crossbanded with rosewood on spirally fluted pillar
supported by a platform on four curved and
reeded legs decorated with carved acanthus.

[29]

unpopular in the process. It was in the rebuilding and refurnishing of Carlton House as his official London residence from 1783 that this new version of Classicism was launched in England. This version had from the first a strong French flavour. It was a tradition of the Georges that the Prince of Wales always quarrelled with his father and in 1783 the Prince, in opposition to his father's strong Tory and anti-French proclivities, chose his friends from influential leaders of the Whig party and adopted decidedly pro-French sympathies. These sympathies could be cultivated now that the Treaty of Versailles in 1783 had ended the American War of Independence and re-established peace with France.

For his architect and designer the Prince chose the gifted Henry Holland, who in addition to his work at Carlton House carried out important commissions for the coterie of distinguished Whigs surrounding the Prince–the Duke of Bedford at Bedford House, Bloomsbury and at Woburn Abbey, Lord Palmerston at Broadlands, Lord Spencer at Althorp and Samuel Whitbread at Southill. Through this patronage Holland was to become the pioneer of Graeco-Roman detail in English interior decoration and furnishing.[4]

Top Bedroom chair, *c.* 1815, with triple turned splats, painted with green leaves on a cream ground; *above* Regency dining-chair, mahogany, cresting-rail carved with gadrooned motifs, back filling of gadrooned leaves supporting a cabochon and front legs of sabre form. Stamped with maker's initials 'H.H.', *c.* 1820.

Rosewood card table, *c.* 1840. Classical Regency decoration has been coarsened as can be seen in the heavily carved paw feet.

This rosewood card table of *c.* 1840 shows lingering Regency influence in the paw feet, lotus decoration at the base of the pillar support, and anthemion carved on the frieze.

Combined work and games table, rosewood, *c.* 1850. While the top retains much of earlier lightness, the heavy scrollwork on the standards is typical of mid-century developments.

Lotus-leaf carving decorates the standards of this rosewood centre table, *c.* 1850.

Four circular tables of about the mid-century. *Right* Rosewood centre table with marble top with carved Classical decoration on rim and base.

Increasing heaviness is evident in this rosewood breakfast table of *c.* 1830.

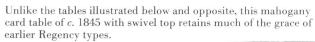

Unlike the tables illustrated below and opposite, this mahogany card table of *c.* 1845 with swivel top retains much of the grace of earlier Regency types.

Loo table (named after a popular card game), of the type fashionable *c.* 1850. The unusual top has inset metal plaques in a blue velvet ground.

Rosewood breakfast table; late Grecian carving on the base and a heavy Vitruvian scroll on the frieze.

Sofa and elbow chair from a set carved and painted in imitation of patinated bronze, scimitar legs of chair fluted and gilt and arm rests terminating in claws. Made for Carlton House, 1807.

HENRY HOLLAND

Holland (1745–1806) was the son of a successful master-builder of Fulham who was closely associated with Lancelot (Capability) Brown, the landscape gardener. The young Holland became in turn assistant and partner to Brown, whose daughter, Bridget, he married in 1773; and as the man responsible for the architectural side of Brown's practice he came into direct contact with the latter's important and influential clients. After a period of financially successful building speculation in what was to become the Sloane Street area of London, Holland gained his introduction to the Whig aristocracy when he was commissioned to build Brooks's Club, St James's Street in 1776–8. This was the noted Whig centre under the patronage of the Prince of Wales. The association with the club's members marks the beginning of the French influence which was to be so notable a feature of Holland's later architectural style and interior decoration. Holland never made the tour abroad which was regarded as part of an architect's professional training to study Classical ruins and Renaissance buildings, and he had no direct contact with French architects. He did not visit France until October 1785, shortly before the Revolution. He almost certainly gained his knowledge of French styles from his study of French architectural writings, such as those of Peyre, Patte and Gondoin, and from his contacts with the French craftsmen and designers employed at Carlton House and elsewhere. He also saw a great deal of fashionable French furniture which was brought to England from 1783 onwards.

The Prince spent enormous sums collecting magnificent French furniture for Carlton House. He employed agents to buy fine pieces in Paris and after the outbreak of the French Revolution in 1789 he took advantage of the exceptional opportunities which then arose to buy more furniture from dispossessed and impoverished *émigrés*, or from the Revolutionary government in France when they sold off stocks of furniture confiscated from wealthy opponents of their régime. Until the beginning of war between England and France in 1793 the Prince had employed the two most important agents in France, Dominique Daguerre and his partner Martin-Eloy Lignereux.[5] Daguerre was not a cabinet-maker (though often described as one) but a dealer (*marchand-mercier*) on a grand scale. As *marchand privilégié de la cour* he had supplied furniture to Louis XVI from his shop in the fashionable rue Saint Honoré. As well as sending large quantities of furniture to the Prince for Carlton House he ran a very profitable export trade to England. William Beckford's *Letters from Paris* reveal that English visitors to Paris were spending considerable sums on furniture at Daguerre's shop, while the Baroness d'Oberkirch in her *Mémoires* describes a large crowd at the shop on 25 May 1784 admiring a beautifully made sideboard which was to be sent to England for the Duke of Northumberland.[6] It is clear that the latest furniture made in France at that time was coming into the possession of English collectors on a considerable scale. Daguerre settled in London and continued his partnership with Lignereux in Sloane Street, still supplying costly furniture to Carlton House. In 1795, when a commission was set up on the occasion of the Prince's marriage to settle his debts, Daguerre put in a claim for £15,500, which was paid over to him gradually during the next seven years.

Already in 1789 a bill headed 'Carlton House' mentioned the sum of £1,659 for 'carving and gilding done by S. Nelson by order of Mr. Degare'. Nelson had been employed by Robert Adam at Shelburne House and Kenwood and had also carved and gilded picture frames at Spencer House. Among the finest pieces supplied by Daguerre to the Prince were a set of sixteen chairs which were signed by Georges Jacob, the most celebrated *menuisier* of the immediate pre-Revolutionary era, and which carried also the label '*Monsieur Daguerre, Fauteuil courant pour le Sallon*'. There were in addition four carved settees by Jacob, also with Daguerre's label. These pieces by Jacob are now in Buckingham Palace, though the word '*Sallon*' on the label presumably referred to the Drawing-Room at Carlton House. The chairs, carved and gilt,

Carved and gilt armchair by Georges Jacob *c.* 1787; in Buckingham Palace, probably originally in Carlton House.

have square backs and tapered legs with stopped fluting. The frames of the backs and the rails of the seats have a minutely carved decoration, while the concave arm supports are decorated with carved acanthus leaves and beading. The cresting rail in each case forms a flat straight line, a prominent feature of Jacob's chairs, as is the small section of fluting on the back uprights between the back of the chair and the rear seat rail. The four carved and gilt settees have eight legs and enclosed arms; in this case the top rail has delicately carved leaves in the centre, a feature also found occasionally on Jacob's chairs. The simple form of this seat furniture, and the concentration on surface ornament, emphasize the essential linear character of Jacob's work.[7]

Although Jacob also produced case furniture, he was pre-eminently a specialist in chairs, in the making of which he proved to be one of the most original craftsmen of eighteenth-century France. Some time before 1784 he made a set of studio furniture for the artist, J. L. David, in this instance to David's design. None of this set has survived, but some pieces appear in David's picture *Les Amours de Paris et Hélène*, painted in 1788.[8] David, himself a pioneer in the archaeological movement in painting, had based his designs for the furniture on details from Graeco-Roman monuments and decorations on Etruscan vases. (These vases, it must be pointed out, were actually Greek and not Etruscan.) The pieces made for the studio were in mahogany decorated with gilt bronze. Jacob may well have been the first French craftsman to use mahogany for chair-making, an indication, it would seem, of his interest in contemporary developments in England, where mahogany had been in fashion for so long. He also made a number of lyre-back chairs just prior to the Revolution and, as these were entirely English in conception, and the only French chairs of the eighteenth century with pierced splats in English taste, it is clear that the traffic in ideas in furniture design between England and France was by no means one-way.

Also in mahogany was the famous set of seating furniture and tables in Etruscan taste which Jacob made in 1787 for Marie Antoinette's dairy at Rambouillet. The chairs had tapered legs with fluted spiral decoration and cresting boards scrolled backwards in Roman fashion. The stools were of the type known as *ployants* and were based on Classical folding stools with cross-frame supports. Jacob described the set as '*de forme nouvelle du genre étrusque*'.[9] He made them from designs by Hubert Robert, the artist who specialized in painting architectural ruins. In all essential respects Jacob's furniture for David's studio and for Rambouillet anticipated the fashionable Classical taste of the Empire by some twenty years.

The very distinct French atmosphere at Carlton House is confirmed in the George IV accounts preserved at Windsor Castle.[10] Between September 1783 and May 1786 Guillaume Gaubert was recorded as being in charge of the craftsmen working in the house under Holland's general direction. 'By order of Mr. Gaubert' appeared on the furniture bills which were certified jointly by Gaubert and Holland, who in some instances reduced the charges. John Edwards, upholsterer, for example, had his original charges of £1,126 13s. 5d. for work carried out between October 1783 and January 1784 reduced to £1,078 4s. 5d. Very little is known about Gaubert. In 1785 Horace Walpole in a letter to Lady Ossory describes a visit to Carlton House and says that 'Gobert, who was a cook . . . designed the decorations'. This apparent slighting of the originator did not stop Walpole on the same occasion from expressing his admiration for the new style with its 'august simplicity . . . rather classic than French', adding 'How sick one shall be after this chaste palace of Mr. Adam's gingerbread and sippets of embroidery'. Gaubert appeared in the Commissioners' Reports on the Prince's debts as 'William Gaubert of Panton Street, Maker of Ornamental Furniture', his claim amounting to £1,133 19s. 8d. for 'ornaments at Carlton House'.[11]

Among the French furniture craftsmen and decorators working at Carlton House were Jean Dominique, 'founder', L. A. Delabrière, painter and decorator, and Francis Hervé, 'French chair-maker', the latter's bill amounting to £1,275 17s. 7d. in 1786. Delabrière, who was to be responsible for some of the most exquisite interior decoration at Southill, appears as 'Labrière' in a list of French craftsmen connected with the London firm of Sheringham. A little more information about the latter, otherwise a very shadowy concern, can be gleaned from the papers of J. B. Papworth, who while training as an architect 'was urged to spend some time in the study of Internal Decoration (and Fresco work) as then practised, it having been lately introduced from France by Mr. Sheringham of Great Marlborough Street, and was making its way into general use. (Sheringham brought over 1788–90 Labrière, Boileu, Dumont le Romain and Boulanger, to decorate Carlton House, under the architect, Henry Holland)'.[12]

For his mastery of Graeco-Roman detail, which was an essential part of his style, Holland had again to rely upon information from outside sources, for he himself never travelled in the Mediterranean. His agent here was Charles Heathcote Tatham (1772–1842), who entered Holland's office when he was almost nineteen.[13] He was the brother of Thomas Tatham, the cabinet-maker who supplied furniture to Carlton House. In May 1794 Holland sent C. H. Tatham to Italy for three years at his own expense to supply him with drawings of Classical ornament for Carlton House. The result was the publication in 1799 of *Etchings of Ancient Ornamental Architecture Drawn from the Originals in Rome and Other Parts of Italy*. This important and successful publication had further editions in 1803, 1810 and 1836, and also a German

Details from C. H. Tatham's *Etchings of Ancient Ornamental Architecture*, 1799, the important contribution to the assimilation of Graeco-Roman decoration in England.

edition at Weimar in 1805. Tatham published other works, including *Etchings Representing Fragments of Grecian and Roman Architectural Ornaments*, 1806. In these works lay the inspiration of so many of the precisely accurate pieces of furniture as well as the details of decoration – the cross-frame stools, circular tables on three monopodia supports, lion masks with rings, terminal figures as cabinet supports, chimera monopodia, acanthus leaves as the base of table or candelabrum – which became the stock features of the new classical style and included motifs from Egyptian antiquities. Among the letters written by Tatham to Holland from Italy reference is made in June 1795 to the Grecian style which 'is gaining ground in England'. The Architectural Publication Society's *Dictionary of Architecture*, edited by Wyatt Papworth, states in its section on *Furniture* that the influence of Percier and Fontaine in France 'was paralleled by that of Tatham. To him perhaps more than to any other person, may be attributed the rise of the 'Anglo-Greek style'. The *Dictionary* adds that 'it was said in 1822 "the English is more chaste than the French-Greek and has advanced so rapidly during the last ten years that the French have adopted much of it" '.[14]

A chimney-piece with mirror in the Ball Room at Wilton Park, Buckinghamshire, executed from a design by Tatham in 1803–5, incorporates the motif of winged lion with torch which Holland had employed at Southill. This rare example of Tatham's work is bolder in execution than Holland's and represents a maturer development of English Neo-Classicism.[15]

The exact part played by Holland personally in the design of the furniture in his houses has been the subject of a great deal of speculation and has not so far been completely determined. There is no collection of his furniture designs which can match in any way that left by Robert Adam. The Library of the Royal Institute of British Architects contains two sketchbooks by Holland which have miscellaneous drawings for Woburn Abbey, Carlton House, Debden, Althorp, Southill and other places, but these are concerned primarily with architectural ornament. There are some details of furniture ornament and a few sketches of furniture pieces, including 'two bookcase tables glasses and ornaments for the piers in the Library' at Southill (these are the present bookcases with coved corners and mirrors, the latter surmounted by a panel decorated with a design of griffins taken from a plate in Tatham's *Ancient Ornamental Architecture*); an 'ornamental stand to support a lamp'; a wardrobe; bookcases in the Library at Woburn Abbey; and 'pier tables with glass over' in the same room.

The two sketchbooks as a whole indicate, as was the case with Robert Adam, the architect's concern with the wall decoration of his rooms. The few furniture designs are of pieces intended to stand against the wall and are in fact, with the exception of the lampstand, permanent fixtures. But

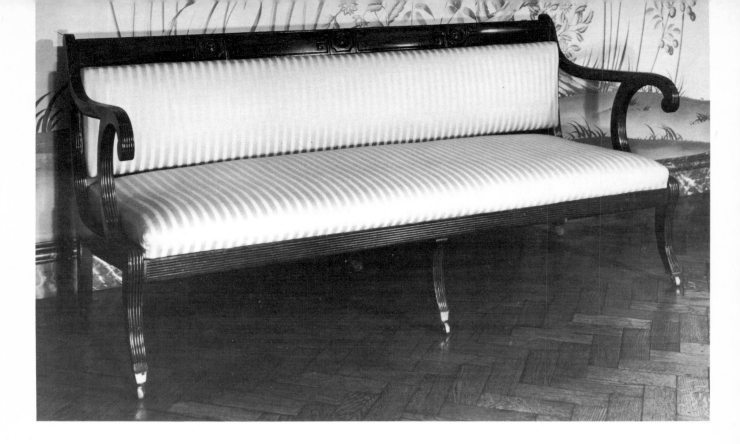

though there are so few of his own designs, Holland is generally credited with the overall control of the style of the furniture in his houses.[16] A letter in the Bedford archives, written by Holland in January 1796 to the Duke of Bedford, states: 'On the articles of furniture, was anyone to examine the endless number of drawings I have made, and witness the trouble I have had, they would not envy me my charge on that account.' This would appear to indicate responsibility by Holland for furniture apart from wall fixtures, as also does the record of payment of £200 to him in 1801 as 'commission on furniture'. And in spite of the dearth of clear-cut documentary evidence this responsibility can reasonably be accepted.[17]

The question of Holland's part has arisen in particular over the furniture which originally stood in the Chinese Drawing-Room at Carlton House, and which is illustrated in the second edition of Sheraton's *The Cabinet-Maker and Upholsterer's Drawing Book*, 1794. This room had a chimney-piece with flanking Chinese figures, ebony chairs decorated with ormolu, and two fine pier tables, not quite a matching pair, also of ebony and ormolu. These tables are of superb craftsmanship; one has Chinese figures as supports, the other has straight legs. Their importance lies in the fact that they are clearly *avant-garde* pieces of the new Regency style. They have straight fronts and curved ends, with curved shelves below, a shape that was to become established for this and similar

Opposite
Top Settee, mahogany with scroll arms and scimitar legs, reeded decoration. Similar to hall seats provided by Henry Holland for the Royal Pavilion, Brighton in 1802 and probably made by Elward, Marsh and Tatham, Mount Street, London.
Bottom Commode in the Chinese Drawing-Room, Carlton House, No. 41, Plate 2, Sheraton's *Drawing Book*, 1791.

Left Pier table, ebony and ormolu, Chinese figures as supports; attributed to Weisweiler, *c.* 1780. Now in Buckingham Palace, formerly in Carlton House.

Pier table, ebony and ormolu, attributed to Weisweiler. Straight legs, as illustrated in Sheraton's *Drawing Book*, 1791 (*see* p. 40). Now in Buckingham Palace, formerly in Carlton House.

Armchair, one of a set of four, in carved and gilt oak, probably made to Henry Holland's design for William Lee Antonie, Colworth, Bedfordshire, *c.* 1796–9; similar to chairs in 'Etruscan' taste made for Samuel Whitbread (Antonie's friend) at Southill.

types of furniture for a long time to come. Their design has often been ascribed to Holland, but, as has been noted, no drawings or bills for them exist. There is good reason to credit the pier tables, which are now in Buckingham Palace, to Adam Weisweiler, the great French *ébéniste* who served Marie Antoinette. He was fond of working in ebony, which was not used in any Holland designs, and his furniture had other features, such as the bronze terminal figures and tapered feet *en toupie* with spiral decoration, which appear on the Carlton House pieces. His name is also linked with those of Daguerre and Lignereux, who supplied one of his bookcases to Lord Spencer at Althorp, and who probably also supplied the pier tables. In this context it is worth recalling that when the Daguerre-Lignereux partnership flourished in France, it seems to have supplied much of Weisweiler's furniture to the French royal palaces, including Saint-Cloud.[18]

Southill, Bedfordshire, the home of Samuel Whitbread, is Holland's acknowledged masterpiece.[19] In spite of the definite French character of the furnishing, there is neither a slavish copying of French models nor an attempt to pursue a strict archaeological rendering. The furniture was a skilful adaptation to an English milieu and has the great advantage of surviving in its original setting. Only three pages of Holland's sketch books deal with Southill and only one of these is concerned with furniture, as described above.

For a number of years the expenditure on furniture for the house was considerable, rising to over £2,000 in 1798 (after a modest start in 1796–7), and thereafter remaining high until the maximum of nearly £4,000 was reached in 1802. There was then a decline to only £100 in 1807, the year after Holland's death. It rose again to almost £1,000 annually until Samuel Whitbread's death in 1815. This was followed by a detailed inventory of the contents of the house in 1816. This is, of course, of great value for a study of the furniture, but perhaps of greater interest is a letter of 1800, written by the Reverend Samuel Johnes, describing a visit to the house while it was still in process of building. This gives details of the contents of Mrs Whitbread's room and boudoir, which were then already furnished. The former contains a rosewood commode and a pair of chiffoniers *en suite*, designed by Holland. The commode, partly ebonized, has ormolu mounts and a large brass rosette, in which is a cameo of a woman's head, in the centre of the front. The chiffoniers, like the commode, have drawer fronts with ebonized crossbandings which emphasize the ormolu mounts. In addition they have tapered octagonal columns which are fluted and partly gilded and their curved ends have fluted shelves. All three pieces have small vase-shaped feet. The chiffoniers resemble the open-ended commodes made in France by Weisweiler and Beneman just prior to the Revolution, but they are here given an English touch by the addition of a small, two-shelved bookcase on their marble tops. The low height of these pieces (if we exclude the superimposed bookcases on the chiffoniers), their rectangular form and emphasis on straight lines, with some concessions to curves to enliven the plan, and their use of dark and glossy wood as a foil to the bright metal mounts, are all characteristic of the new Regency style. In the same room a rosewood writing desk with a tambour top has a curved interlaced stretcher directly inspired by French originals and a form which was much favoured by Weisweiler. Less French in inspiration are two writing tables, one of rosewood on two cross-frame supports formed by lion monopodia, bronzed to imitate Roman furniture, the other of mahogany on carved and fluted legs ending on lions' paws which are linked in the form of an H.

Mrs Whitbread's boudoir, which measures only 9 ft 6 in by 15 ft 10 in, is accounted one of Holland's finest achievements in interior decoration. The painting of the walls and ceiling in Pompeian style is the work of Delabrière, who worked for Holland at Carlton House. He had been associated with the Comte d'Artois, the future Charles X, who was a friend of the Prince of Wales and for whom the charming pavilion, Bagatelle, was built in 1780 at the edge of the Bois de Boulogne. Delabrière also painted some of the pieces of furniture in the boudoir. But the best-known piece here is the china cabinet, which is very French in inspiration, but was supplied by the London firm of Marsh and Tatham. This cabinet, in rosewood and ebony, has ormolu mounts, fluted feet *en toupie* and a decorated panel set in the plinth above the plate-glass doors, all of which are again very typical of Weisweiler's work of the same period.

The most celebrated examples of Holland's mature style in the opening years of the nineteenth century can be seen in the Drawing-

Opposite
Top Drawing-Room, Southill, showing the great sofa of Classical design with a rectangular tablet on the back.

Bottom Drawing-Room, Southill. The single-headed couch on the right, upholstered in rose-red silk on a gilded frame, is based on antique Roman models.

Right Rosewood writing table in Mrs Whitbread's room, Southill; bronzed cross-frames of lion monopodia in imitation of ancient Roman furniture.

Below Southill, Bedfordshire: Mrs Whitbread's room. On the left is the rosewood commode designed by Henry Holland, with a large rosette in the front; in the window recess is the writing table illustrated above.

Room at Southill, which was furnished after 1800. Here the seat furniture represents well-developed anglicized versions of Louis XVI Classicism. A large gilt sofa of Classical design, some 9 ft 6 in long, has a framework of sunk panels with bolt-head decoration in the lower seat frame and a rectangular tablet surmounting the back. Smaller gilt and carved sofas, couches with one end raised and chairs with the same bolt-head decoration are all clearly inspired by French versions of Classical models. The chairs are typical examples of *le goût Etrusque*, with the marked sweep back of their rear legs, tapered and fluted front legs—the features of which had been foreshadowed some years earlier in the Neo-Classical designs associated with Robert Adam—and, in particular, the pronounced scrolling of both the arm rests and the backs, the latter taking an S-form (or crozier, *en crosse*). These chairs resemble those made for David by Jacob in 1788.

In the Drawing-Room there is also a circular monopodium table of kingwood with a massive triangular base and rich ormolu mounts, its gilt fluted frieze interrupted by large gilt metal lion masks with rings in their mouths. This table is *en suite* with a kingwood writing table supported on two standards, i.e. single wide supports at each end which are panelled and pierced. These two pieces are stylistically later than the seat furniture and probably belong to the second main period of spending on the house, from 1808 until Whitbread's death in 1815. Both were to become established types for many years. The writing table is an early example of the use of standards—a common early Victorian form of table support.

Mahogany side table with four carved lion legs, in the Dining-Room, Southill.

THOMAS HOPE

In the year after Holland's death there appeared the textbook which ushered in the full archaeological phase of English Neo-Classical furniture. This was *Household Furniture and Interior Decoration executed from Designs by Thomas Hope*, 1807. The author, Thomas Hope, whose life span (1768–1831) coincided closely and fittingly with the chronological limits of European Neo-Classicism, has always been considered the apostle of the severest forms of the Classical revival in England. This is true to a point, but to view this as Hope's only role is, as will be shown, to ignore his wide eclecticism, which clearly foreshadowed early Victorian developments.[20]

Hope, a member of a wealthy Amsterdam banking family, was a rich connoisseur who was able to make a magnificent collection of antiquities which bore testimony to his strongly held personal beliefs based on detailed study and first-hand experience. The next generation of great collectors, such as Meyrick and Bernal, though cultured men, were to rely to an increasing extent on antique dealers to make their collections for them. Hope's grand tour was far more thorough and extensive than that of his contemporaries, for he spent eight years, following his eighteenth birthday in 1786, travelling throughout the Mediterranean area to make drawings of antiquities. His travels took in Sicily, Turkey, Greece, Egypt, Syria, Spain and Portugal. Early in 1795 he was in England, whither his family had fled after the French invasion of Holland, and from that time England was to remain his home.

Hope's tours had taken him to the birthplaces of Classical antiquity. Interest in these areas was stimulated during the French Wars by the fact that the customary route to Italy was no longer available for those who wished to make the grand tour or pursue professional studies. The eastern Mediterranean, however, remained open, as Louis Simond noted in 1811 during his tour of the British Isles:

'English travellers, shut out of their accustomed track, have been obliged to shift their ground, and the shores of the Mediterranean are come into fashion. There is not a classical nook unexplored by these restless wanderers: they dispute with each other for the remains of Greece and Egypt, purchase antique marbles for their weight in gold, pack up and ship home a Grecian temple as other people would a set of china. We have just visited one of the learned cargoes, recently landed from Athens, no less than the spoils of the Parthenon, brought by Lord Elgin, late ambassador to the Porte.'[21]

This was a reference to the Elgin Marbles, which were being assembled in London between 1806 and 1812 before their removal to the British Museum in 1813.

It was an age when connoisseur-collectors aimed to display their carefully assembled treasures, and many of them arranged their houses accordingly. Horace Walpole had set an early precedent by opening Strawberry Hill to visitors with admission tickets and issuing a catalogue of the contents. This was a natural development when museums, in the modern connotation of the term, were practically unknown. The great mansion of Ickworth, Suffolk, one of the strangest houses in England, was planned in the mid-1790s as a collector's ideal 'temple of art'. The Earl Bishop of Bristol (the fourth Earl was also Bishop of Derry and, as one of Europe's greatest and best-known collectors, has given his name to Bristol Hotels throughout the world) intended to live here in the immense central rotunda, while the two vast wings stretching to east and west were to contain his pictures and statues.

Hope's large collection of antique sculpture and vases—he bought the surviving part of Sir William Hamilton's second collection of vases in 1801, the first having gone to the British Museum—his Italian and Dutch paintings, and the works of contemporary Neo-Classical sculpture were set out in two houses. One was in Duchess Street, London, a mansion

Mahogany cross-framed chair, reeded and fluted decoration, based on a design 'after the manner of the ancient curule chairs', Plate 20 (figure 3) in T. Hope's *Household Furniture*, 1807.

[47]

originally built by Robert Adam which Hope purchased in 1799 and completely remodelled by 1804.[22] Here approved members of the public were admitted to see the collections. Hope, who lived in smaller rooms above those open to visitors, also personally invited notabilities of all kinds, and the Duchess Street galleries became one of the show places of London. Hope's other house was The Deepdene, Surrey, which he bought in 1807 and remodelled, under the direction of the architect William Atkinson, between 1819 and 1826. Both houses have since been demolished, the London one in 1851 and The Deepdene in 1969. The contents of The Deepdene, which included some of the collections removed from Duchess Street, were auctioned by Christie's in 1917. *Household Furniture* refers specifically to the furniture which was made to Hope's design in the Duchess Street house, and does not refer, as was formerly supposed, to the contents of The Deepdene.

Hope was a fervent supporter of the Greek revival, which indeed may be said to have dated from 1804 when he published a pamphlet which was instrumental in having James Wyatt's proposed Roman plan for Downing College, Cambridge, changed in favour of William Wilkin's Neo-Greek. Hope's missionary zeal is clearly shown in his somewhat wordy introduction to *Household Furniture* with its carefully balanced sentences, its thoroughly classical composition, and its tone, as didactic as Pugin's writings a quarter of a century later. His views on furniture centre round his praise of classical pieces for:

'that breadth and repose of surface, that distinctness and contrast of outline, that opposition of plain and enriched parts, that harmony and significance of accessories, and that apt accord between the peculiar meaning of each imitative or significant detail, and the peculiar destination of the main object, to which these accessories belonged, which are calculated to afford to the eye and mind the most lively, most permanent and most unfading enjoyment'.

He then writes of furniture being 'capable of uniting to the most essential requisites of utility and comfort . . . a certain number of secondary attributes of elegance and beauty'. His own collection of antiquities, 'Grecian and others', has led him to apply these attributes to the design of furniture adapted to current usage 'towards forming the entire assemblage of ancient and of modern handicraft thus intermixed collectively into a more harmonious, more consistent and more instructive whole'. He confesses that he has had difficulty in finding craftsmen of sufficient skill to execute work for him, and indeed the justification for publishing his designs has been to prevent 'extravagant caricatures such as of late have begun to start up in every corner of this capital'. He rails against the debased taste of the upholder (i.e. upholsterer) who 'borrowed from the worst models of the degraded French school of the middle of the last century' and against furniture 'wrought by the most mechanical processes only', the insipidity of which has encouraged the search for novel forms. He notes that furniture makers 'are rarely initiated even in the simplest rudiments of design, whence it has happened that immense expense has been employed in producing furniture without character, beauty or appropriate meaning'. These three features, 'character, beauty and appropriate meaning', are the keynotes of Hope's conception of furniture design, 'appropriate meaning' being the most important of all in view of the narrative symbolism which distinguishes many of the Duchess Street pieces.

Hope's furniture was to be influential, but it was immediately and strongly criticized by devotees of the Romantic school. His book was attacked with bitter irony by Sydney Smith in the *Edinburgh Review* in July 1807. Smith derided the publication of a work dealing with 'paltry and fantastical luxuries' in the middle of the life-and-death struggle with Napoleon, and he took to task Hope's missionary zeal:

'If the salvation of Europe depended on Mr. Hope's eloquence, he could not have exercised it with more earnestness and animation; and we are convinced that neither the restorers of learning nor the reformers of religion, ever spoke of their subjects in terms half so magnificent, nor of their own abilities with such studied and graceful modesty, as this ingenious person has here done, in recommending to his countrymen a better form for their lamps, sideboards and cradles.'

Smith took his stand on the principle that 'the chief source of beauty will always be the visible sign of utility' and condemned Hope's furniture as 'too bulky, massive and ponderous'; his chairs, for example, being quite unsuitable for use until the time when 'aldermen wear armour and take their afternoon naps in Guildhall'.[23] But other reviewers were more favourable and one can note at this point that two decades after the publication of *Household Furniture* Hope's widespread influence was still being acknowledged.

The extraordinary depth of Hope's scholarship is confirmed by the list of sources at the end of the book which had been of most use to him. He had clearly tapped the best results of research of his age, French, German, Italian and British, the latter including Robert Adam's *Ruins of Spalatro*, Stuart and Revett's *Antiquities of Athens*, Wood's *Ruins of Palmyra* and *Ruins of Balbec* and Chandler's *Ionian Antiquities*. John Flaxman's *Compositions* from Aeschylus and Homer had been of great influence. Hope also paid tribute to his friendship with Percier, the creator with Fontaine of the French Empire style. To these acknowledged sources, of which the above is a brief selection, Hope could, of course, add the fruits of his own researches.

Hope re-arranged the first floor of the Duchess Street house to display his furniture in a manner which accords very much with present-day museum practice. His pieces were set against appropriate backgrounds, the arrangement which is found today in the Victoria and Albert, the Geffrye Museum and the Castle Museum, York, to name but a few. *Household Furniture* is, in effect, a guide book to the collection. It takes the reader on a tour round the house. The preliminary plates show complete galleries and rooms; the rest contain sketches of individual pieces. It is a tragedy that the contents have been scattered, but a fair number, including tables, chairs, stools, couches, a bookcase, a clock, firescreens, wall-lights, *torchères* and wine coolers have been identified and traced through Christie's Sale Catalogue at The Deepdene auction of 1917. These prove that the plates were meticulously accurate. A description of the interior of Hope's house, confirming again the accuracy of the plates, appears in C. M. Westmacott's *British Galleries of Painting and Sculpture*, published in 1824.[24] Hope's book, as a record of a collection of furniture actually executed from the author's designs, thus radically differs from the traditional pattern books of the Georgian era in that these present mainly unexecuted drawings, however much they may have been influenced by executed examples.

The plates of the main rooms illustrate the catholicity of Hope's taste. The Picture Gallery, devised as an austere Greek interior in the form of a temple, includes four thrones with sides formed of winged sphinxes, tables with lion monopodia supports, pedestals, chairs of *klismos* form and an organ designed as a small Ionic temple. Greek furniture is also shown in two of the Vase Rooms—chairs of *klismos* form, other chairs with padded backs, a circular table with supports of winged lion monopodia on a pedestal base and benches with ends in the form of headless winged lions. Some of these pieces were based on Pompeian models. The Indian or Blue Room, the chief drawing-room in the house, took its name from its pictures of Indian views and from the colour of its walls. It is described as decorated 'in the most costly style of Oriental splendour'[25] —obviously the result of Hope's travels in the Near East—with Persian carpets and a ceiling copied from Turkish models. Saracenic or Moorish taste had a particular appeal to Hope. His full-length portrait in Turkish dress, painted by Sir William Beechey in 1798, hung in the staircase hall and was one of the first things seen by visitors. It is worth noting in this context that there is an elaborate Turkish border framing the title-page of *Household Furniture*. The plate shows that this room contained two rows of cross-framed stools, two massive thrones with their solid sides decorated with winged lions, a table with four Egyptian term supports, benches with sculptured winged lions at their ends, firescreens composed of shields supported on javelins and pendant wall-lights of carved and gilt wood, which are now in the Royal Pavilion, Brighton.

The Flaxman or Star Room (which was partly reconstructed with

Rosewood circular library table, carved and gilt monopodia supports and gilt brass mounts; similar to a table in Plate 2 in T. Hope's *Household Furniture*, 1807.

some of its original contents at The Age of Neo-Classicism Exhibition at the Victoria and Albert Museum in 1972) was named after Flaxman's statue of Cephalus and Aurora, which was commissioned by Hope in 1790 and dominated one end of the room. The special arrangement of this room, so disposed as to make a kind of narrative background to the subjects of the statue, make it one of the most significant in the house, and Hope's own description is well worth recording:

'The whole surrounding decoration has been rendered, in some degree, analogous to these personages, and to the face of nature at the moment when the first of the two, the goddess of the morn, is supposed to announce approaching day. Round the bottom of the room still reign the emblems of night. In the rail of a black marble table are introduced medallions of the god of sleep and of the goddess of night. The bird consecrated to the latter deity perches on the pillars of a black marble chimney-piece, whose broad frieze is studded with golden stars.

The Drawing-Room, Plate 6 in Thomas Hope's *Household Furniture and Interior Decoration,* 1807.

The sides of the room display, in satin curtains, draped in ample folds over pannels of looking-glass, and edged with black velvet, the fiery hue which fringes the clouds just before sunrise: and in a ceiling of cooler sky blue are sown, amidst a few still unextinguished luminaries of the night, the roses which the harbinger of day, in her course, spreads on every side around her. The pedestal of the group offers the torches, the garlands, the wreaths, and the other insignia belonging to the mistress of Cephalus, disposed around the fatal dart of which she made her lover a present. The broad band which girds the top of the room, contains medallions of the ruddy goddess and of the Phrygian youth, intermixed with the instruments and the emblems of the chace, his favourite amusement. Figures of the youthful hours, adorned with wreaths of foliage adorn part of the furniture, which is chiefly gilt, in order to give more relief to the azure, the black, and the orange compartments of the hangings.'[26]

No other room in the house carries Hope's profuse symbolism so far. The furniture–cross-framed armchairs, a pier table supported by four caryatids set in pairs, an Egyptian clock and, at each side of the statue, a side table with lion monopodia supports and an elaborate glass case on top–help to continue Hope's theme. He notes, with reference to the pier table and clock, 'Front of a table, in the room dedicated to Aurora. Females, emblematic of the four *horae* or parts of the day, support its rail, the frieze of which contains medallions of the deities of night and sleep. On the table stands a clock, carried by a figure of Isis, or the moon, adorned with her crescent.'[27] Both this pier table (on which the *horae* were goddesses of the seasons, not, as Hope states, parts of the day) and the clock (which Isis, now minus her crescent, holds in front of her) have survived, and their significance is that they are examples, like so many other pieces in the house, of that narrative and anecdotal symbolism which is so often considered a particular contribution of the Victorian era. Yet here it is displayed and explained with full approval by the champion of English Neo-Classical furniture, to set off statuary by the outstanding English Neo-Classical sculptor, just thirty years before Victoria's accession to the throne and almost half a century before the Great Exhibition of 1851.

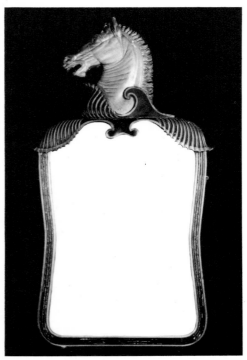

This narrative theme is repeated on other pieces of furniture in the house. The Dining-Room, one of the most soberly decorated rooms in the house, has a chimney-piece on which stands Flaxman's bust of Hope's brother, Henry Philip Hope. This is flanked by two antique horses' heads, an allusion to the name Philip which means 'lover of horses'. The jambs of this chimney-piece have Bacchanalian masks.[28] The sideboard is 'adorned with emblems of Bacchus and of Ceres' while its cellaret, appropriately enough, is 'ornamented with amphorae and with figures, allusive to the liquid element'.[29] Hope's Plate 44 shows an 'end view of a cradle in mahogany, ornamented in gilt bronze, with emblems of sleep, of dreams, and of hope'. His Plate 30 illustrates a chandelier of bronze and gold, ornamented with a crown of stars over a wreath of nightshade. Figure 3 in his Plate 29 is a bedstead of mahogany and bronze, 'the pilasters ornamented with figures of night, rising on her crescent, and spreading her poppies'. Figure 4 in the same plate, a toilet stand for ewer and basin, has 'sea monsters and other aquatic emblems round the frieze'.

Hope's eclecticism and meticulous attention to the background decoration of his collections are confirmed by the remaining rooms in the house. In the Egyptian Room, the furniture of which is described in detail in Chapter 2, the frieze is decorated with figures inspired by those of papyrus scrolls, the ceiling painted in a pattern taken from that on mummy cases, and the general colour scheme, applying also to the furniture, is of pale yellow and bluish green, 'which hold so conspicuous a rank among the Egyptian pigments'.[30]

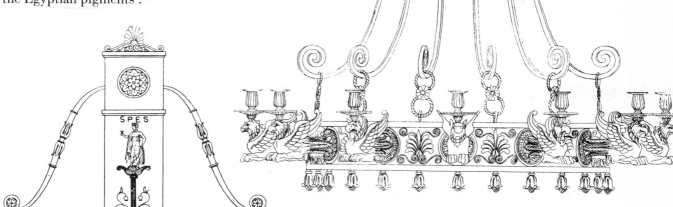

Above 'Chandelier of bronze and gold; ornamented with a crown of stars over a wreath of night-shade.' Plate 30 in T. Hope's *Household Furniture*, 1807.

Left 'End view of a cradle in mahogany, ornamented in gilt bronze, with emblems of night, of sleep, of dreams and of hope.' Plate 44 in T. Hope's *Household Furniture*, 1807.

Opposite
Top Mantel clock in bronze, ormolu and 'rosso antico' in the Egyptian taste, made for the Flaxman Room in Duchess Street and illustrated in Plate 7 of T. Hope's *Household Furniture*, 1807.
Bottom Mirror, painted black and parcel gilt, surmounted by a horse's head similar to that on a mantelpiece in Plate 50 of T. Hope's *Household Furniture*, 1807.

[53]

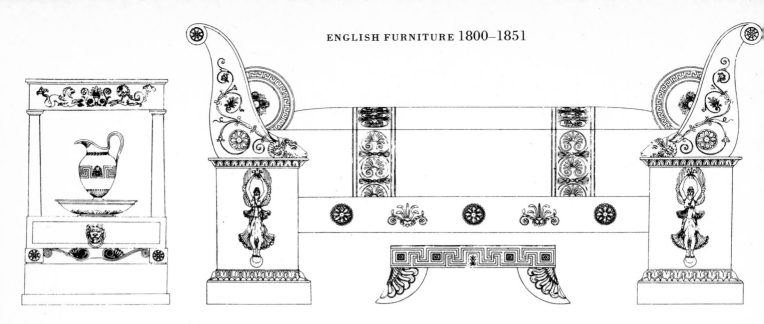

Bedstead of mahogany and bronze, and toilet stand, illustrated in Plate 29 in T. Hope's *Household Furniture*, 1807.

But the strangest room of all in the house was undoubtedly the Lararium, described as a 'closet or boudoir fitted up for the reception of a few Egyptian, Hindoo and Chinese idols and curiosities'. This room, as illustrated in Plate 10 of *Household Furniture*, has a ceiling of bamboo laths. The exhibits are even more widely ranging in their cultural and historical themes than those named in the text, for these include a small Italian bronze of the early seventeenth century of the equestrian statue of Marcus Aurelius, a large crucifix, described by Westmacott but not appearing in Hope's plate, and within a semicircular niche small busts of Dante (by Flaxman) and of Napoleon. A settee from this room (figure 5 in Hope's Plate 18) has survived, though it is without its former frieze of small 'figures of the twelve great gods of the Greeks and Romans'.

The narrative symbolism of so much of Hope's furniture was, of course, too good a target for Sydney Smith to miss in the *Edinburgh Review*. As a whole-hearted devotee of the Romantic movement in English poetry he complained that 'after having banished the heathen gods

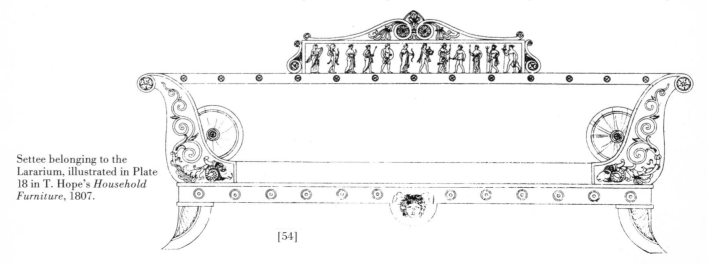

Settee belonging to the Lararium, illustrated in Plate 18 in T. Hope's *Household Furniture*, 1807.

[54]

and their attributes pretty well from our poetry, we are to introduce them habitually into our eating-rooms, nurseries and staircases'. His parting shots were reserved for Hope's chimney-piece, which 'brought two horses to his parlour fireside', for the attempted pun in ornamenting the chandelier with nightshade, and for the cradle with its emblems of 'Dreams, Night, and–*Hope*'. Indeed in Smith's view the equine chimney-piece alone was sufficient to discredit Hope's whole collection, along with the system and taste of its author.

In addition to the literary and artistic sources which Hope quotes at the end of *Household Furniture*, he frequently makes reference in the text to antique fragments in foreign museums and private collections which had inspired his designs. The armchairs, for instance, which are shown in the Indian Room (Hope's Plate 6 and, in more detail, in his Plate 18), have on their sides large winged lions which 'were copied from a sarcophagus in the collection of Prince Braschi at Rome'.[31] In Hope's Plate 26 a box or coffer is imitated from one in a small mosque in Constantinople, while the settee in the same plate has its ends 'copied from a fine antique chimaera of marble in the studio of Cavaceppi at Rome'. A table illustrated in Hope's Plate 12 (the actual table is now in the Ashmolean Museum, Oxford) was based on part of a red marble throne in the Vatican and had already been imitated by others, Percier and Fontaine, for instance, before 1801. Tatham in 1799 had a similar design from a chapel in Rome.[32] In his Plate 24 Hope illustrates a pedestal belonging to

End and front view of a table, illustrated in Plate 12 in T. Hope's *Household Furniture*, 1807.

Left Table now in the Ashmolean Museum, Oxford, illustrated in Plate 12, figure 6, of T. Hope's *Household Furniture*, 1807.

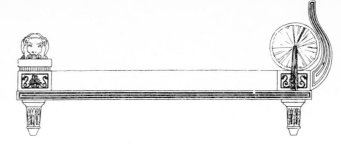

Side and end view of a couch, illustrated in
Plate 28 in T. Hope's *Household Furniture*, 1807.

a sideboard; this as he explains on page 35 of his text, was 'imitated from an Etruscan altar in the Villa Borghese'. And to take a final example (of many) of Hope's eclecticism, his Plate 28 shows a couch with a watching greyhound lying at the end, 'after the manner of similar animals on Gothic sarcophagi'.

The outline technique which Hope employed for his drawings—the 'mere outlines'[33] and 'lineal engraving'—was derived from Flaxman, who was one of the first artists to use it and whose *Compositions* from Homer and Aeschylus produced, in Hope's words, 'the finest imitations I know of the elegance and beauty of the ancient Greek attire and furniture, armour and utensils'.[34] *The Gentleman's Magazine*, in its review of *Household Furniture* (Vol. LXXVII, Part ii, July 1808), welcomed the 'excellent engravings though they are only outlines'. Flaxman based the drawings of furniture in his *Compositions* on published engravings of vase paintings. His *Odyssey* contained many more drawings of furniture than either the *Iliad* or the *Aeschylus* and included a throne, chairs—usually of the *klismos* type, but with some straight-back examples—tripod stands, a bed, lamp stands, a couch, tripod table and a four-legged table. His *Phemius singing to the Suitors*, for instance, showed three chairs of *klismos* type and a tripod stand which was very similar to figure 5 in Hope's Plate 17.[35]

This outline technique has undoubtedly done much to heighten the impression, a misleading one of course, of the somewhat austere, even cold, precision which many associate with Hope's furniture. It entirely omits the interplay of light and shade to which Hope, as quoted above, refers in his introduction, and the rich colours which distinguish his pieces and the decoration of his rooms. But as he himself confesses, to have introduced these elements into his drawings would have made his book too expensive for general use.[36]

The form, construction and decoration of Hope's furniture can be fully and accurately gauged from the plates in *Household Furniture*, from the surviving examples of his work and from his own observations in the text. As his aims and sources of information and of inspiration are also revealed, and can be related to his achievements, it follows that far more is known about him in these respects than about any other furniture designer of the Georgian period. It is clear that taking his pick of the evidence of antiquity, with added influences from the Near East, he

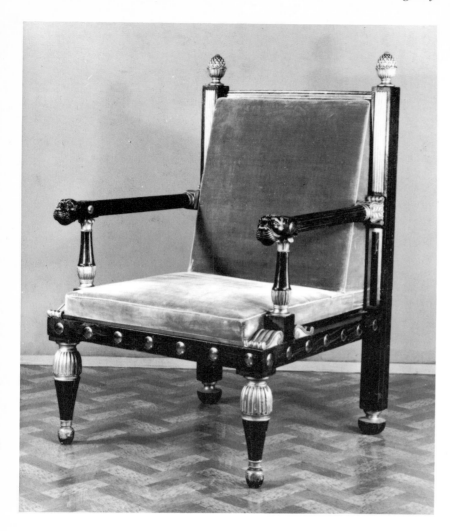

Above Painted beech arc-back chair in 'Grecian' taste, in the style of Thomas Hope, *c.* 1807.

Left Beechwood armchair, *c.* 1810, based on a design, Plate 22, (figures 5 and 6) in T. Hope's *Household Furniture*, 1807. Carved, grained and parcel-gilt decoration.

Below 'Trafalgar' chair, early 19th century, painted beech, cane seat and rope cresting.

subjected all to a distinct and strongly personal interpretation. His was an individual style, his was the creative mind behind this last phase of English Neo-Classical furniture, concurrent with, but never a close version of, the French Empire style.

Hope's influence on furniture mainly stamped itself on the Classical forms, of the type which gained the current name of 'Grecian', fashionable for some two decades after 1805. Chairs were of various kinds: cross-framed types (cross-framed stools were also fashionable); armchairs with winged supports, with winged chimerae forming the front legs and arm supports or, in smaller versions, arm supports only; chairs with arc-backs; and the celebrated 'Trafalgar' type, related to the *klismos*, with concave 'sabre' or 'scimitar' front legs, rounded knees and scrolled uprights and cresting.

[57]

Left Armchair, carved mahogany, with original leopard skin upholstery. Two other chairs from the same suite (now in the Metropolitan Museum, New York) are dated 1811 and 1820.

Above Mahogany armchair, *c.* 1820, in Classical taste, shoulder board decorated with studs.

Left Mahogany chair, the top rail veneered with an ebonized panel inlaid with brass anthemion, the rectangular ebonized splat inlaid with a brass lyre; inlaid Greek key pattern on the seat rails, and inlaid anthemion on the apron and legs. Similar to a design in Plate 24 (figure 2) in T. Hope's *Household Furniture*, 1807.

Regency mahogany library chairs, *c.* 1820, in the manner of Thomas Hope; U-shaped backs on panelled supports headed by leaf-carved brackets; sabre legs headed by acanthus leaves.

Some tables of rectangular form had caryatid supports arranged in pairs. There were also circular tables, of common Regency type, with triple chimera monopodia supports, or with a single pedestal base. An example of this last-named type is perhaps Hope's best-known piece, rescued from The Deepdene and now in the Victoria and Albert Museum –the monopodium on a tripod base with lion's-paw feet, made of mahogany and inlaid with Classical ornament in ebony and silver, illustrated in two drawings in Hope's Plate 39. Other tables had lyre-shaped supports; Hope's example of this kind was intended for a music room. Tripod stands, serving as *torchères* or as supports for vases, were very popular. The classical couch, with scrolled ends and outward-curving short feet, became one of the most characteristic of Regency pieces.

Hope's designs gave clear and accurate precision to the long-familiar repertoire of classical ornament such as the anthemion, palmette, acanthus and fir-cone. The lotus was a more recent introduction. Hope was fond of the French-inspired attractive device of a double lotus meeting in the centre of a member such as a table leg, or at the intersection of the cross-framing of a chair. Another ornament of novel character, also probably French in origin, was the metal bolt head, round or star-shaped, which was used by Hope in running sequence, along a couch rail for instance. This device is also found inlaid on the top of his circular monopodium. The star was to become a particularly familiar Regency feature. A general display of Hope's ornaments appears in Plate 41 of *Household Furniture*.

Above Plate 39 in T. Hope's *Household Furniture*, 1807, 'top and elevation of a round monopodium, in mahogany, inlaid in ebony and silver'. This table, now in the Victoria and Albert Museum, is illustrated below.

Table in the style of Thomas Hope, large double lotus-leaf supports.

[59]

Regency rosewood library table, *c.* 1810, supported on standards; drawer fronts decorated with brass bolts.

Sofa table, *c.* 1810, in finely marked rosewood; brass star and urn ornament on drawer fronts; brass Classical leaf ornament and lion's paw feet on trestle supports.

Scrolled consoles, formulated by Hope, appear at the junction of a flat base and vertical member, as on the standards of a table or the uprights of a dressing (cheval) glass. For larger pieces of furniture Hope confirms the fashion for flat surfaces of veneers of dark woods set off by metal decoration. This metalwork was, of course, as much prompted by the restrictions of the war years, which severely cut down the expensive methods of carving, marquetry and curvature of forms, as by the requirements of antique Classical ornament. Hope had a great fondness for mahogany, which he described as 'so much in use in this country'.[37] For ornamentation he advocated inlay in metal on a ground of ebony or dyed wood, which he stressed as particularly useful on chairs, more so than raised ornaments which collected dust and dirt. But he also devoted a long paragraph in *Household Furniture* to ornaments in cast bronze, advocating that the metal be 'left simply to exhibit its own green patina'.[38] These cast ornaments could be reproduced cheaply, applied to many varieties of materials, be removed, if necessary, and applied to other pieces of furniture, and be gilded if threatened by damp, though they were normally well able to stand the effects of weathering or dirt. Hope intended his furniture to be durable, like its Classical prototypes. In his introduction to *Household Furniture* he is very critical of much fashionable furniture for 'the insipidity of the outline and the unmeaningness of the embellishments'.[39]

There was undoubtedly some, but not a preponderant, French influence on Hope's designs. The interrelationship between English and French styles, already examined in the instance of Henry Holland, was not entirely disrupted by the war. The short-lived Peace of Amiens in 1802 between England and France gave English connoisseurs the oppor-

Details of Classical ornament,
  Plate 41 in T. Hope's *Household
Furniture*, 1807.

tunity of visiting Paris again. Hope himself was there in May 1803 after a visit to Italy, and the resumption of war in May caused him to leave hurriedly. Hope always paid tribute to his friend Percier, who had been appointed with Fontaine in 1799 to refurnish the former French royal palaces pillaged during the early Revolution. The designs of Percier and Fontaine, the basis of the Empire style, appear in their celebrated *Receuil de Décorations Intérieures*, which was not published in complete form until 1812, although some of their designs were available from 1801. A comparison between their designs and those of Hope demonstrates the strong independent spirit of the latter.

The interior decoration and furniture of Percier and Fontaine can be criticized as marking the triumph of the upholsterer (or 'decorator'), who over-stressed ornament and thus destroyed the intimate connection between furniture and its surroundings. One must compare the innovations of these two French designers with the masterly control exercised by English furniture designers of the Hepplewhite-Sheraton era—control over the proportions of furniture, its decoration and the relationship between furniture and its surrounding space. With their 'devaluation of symbols' Percier and Fontaine also 'annihilated' space with their massive pieces and luxurious upholstery,[40] whereas Hope's designs were in full accord with English traditions of stressing simple proportions in surroundings that were on the whole less sumptuous. These are the fundamental differences between English Neo-Classical furniture at this stage and the Empire style, which was to become a European fashion after the establishment of Napoleon's military and political hegemony on the Continent.

Hope's influence on furniture design was widely acknowledged by discerning contemporaries for two decades after the publication of *Household Furniture*, quite apart from the trade pattern books which were obviously influenced by his work. In 1827 John Britton, whose publications were to do so much to sponsor the Gothic revival, praises Hope in his *The Union of Architecture, Sculpture and Painting* 'for the classical and appropriate style which now generally characterises our furniture and ornamental utensils'. After reference to former caricatures of Hope's style, he continues: '*Household Furniture and Interior Decoration* has not only improved the taste of cabinet-makers and upholsterers, but also that of their employers'.[41] In similar vein J. T. Smith (*Nollekens and his Times*, 1828) refers to 'the beautifully classic change brought in by Thomas Hope, Esq.'. He also hints at the return to fashion of the 'unmeaning scroll and shell-work' of Louis XV's reign, thus echoing Hope's strictures in his introduction to *Household Furniture* upon the 'wretched ideas and trivial conceits borrowed from the worst models of the degraded French school of the middle of last century'.[42]

Also in 1828 the *Quarterly Review*, in complete contrast to Sydney

Smith's early criticism of the 'too bulky, massive and ponderous character of Hope's furniture, comes out wholeheartedly in favour of the 'richness, variety and solidity' of contemporary taste:

> '*An ordinary chair, in the most ordinary parlour, has now something of an antique cast–something of Grecian massiveness, at once, and elegance in its forms. That of twenty or thirty years since was mounted on four tapering and tottering legs, resembling four tobacco pipes; the present supporters of our stools have a curule air, curve outwards behind and give a comfortable idea of stability to the weighty aristocrat or ponderous burgess who is about to occupy one of them.*'[43]

So much for Sydney Smith's aldermen in armour!

From its first issue for many years Ackermann's *Repository of Arts* frequently illustrates pieces in the full Classical style of Hope in its monthly presentations of 'Fashionable Furniture'. References to the 'classical elegance of Greece and Rome', to the 'Grecian school' and to the recent revolution in furniture design 'effected principally by the study of the antique' are to be found in the May and August numbers of 1809. Hope is quoted in October 1813 as pointing out the lack of furniture-makers with ideas–a deficiency which the *Repository* no doubt felt able to remedy itself through its illustrations. Over a decade later, in June 1824, a drawing-room table, chairs and footstools in full Hopeian taste are illustrated with the note that 'the furniture executed by the late Mr. Bullock was of this character and style and is continued with much taste by the chief upholsterers of the day'. Bullock, as will be seen, was a designer of versatility, but his Grecian pieces continued to be made in full Classical vein.

GEORGE SMITH AND THE PATTERN BOOKS

All the Georgian furniture styles after 1750 were popularized by cabinet-makers' pattern books. This task was performed for Hope's Classical version by George Smith's *A Collection of Designs for Household Furniture and Interior Decoration*, 1808.[44] This translated into general terms for 'the extensive mansion or a social villa', with particular reference to the trade and middle-class homes, a style originally conceived and developed for a wealthy milieu. The 158 coloured plates in the book are dated 1804–7, and the designs may very well have been among those to which Hope was making reference in the introduction to *Household Furniture* when he spoke of cabinet-makers who were attempting to exhibit 'not only a general approximation to the style for which I wished to introduce a taste, but frequently a direct imitation of the individual objects, of which I had planned the designs for my own exclusive use'.[45]

Smith himself remains, like so many other Georgian cabinet-makers,

Sideboard cupboard, rosewood, with four lion monopodia in simulated patinated bronze, the feet and heads water gilt; wire trellis doors. Monopodia resembling illustrations in T. Hope's *Household Furniture*, 1807, Plate 32, and in George Smith's *A Collection of Designs for Household Furniture and Interior Decoration*, 1808, Plates 83 and 87.

a somewhat shadowy figure. His claim to be 'Upholder Extraordinary to H.R.H. the Prince of Wales' (like his later claim, in the introduction dated April 1826 to his *Guide* of 1828,[46] to be 'Upholsterer and Furniture Draughtsman to His Majesty') is not corroborated by any evidence in either the Lord Chamberlain's accounts or in the Windsor Castle archives. Smith's publication of 1808, its title echoing that of Hope's of the previous year, lacks Hope's scholarly touches. It includes designs in Gothic and Chinese taste, which will be discussed in Chapters 2 and 3 and thus represents the popular version of the Regency style in its widest sense.

Smith paid considerable attention to window cornices and curtains – evidence, repeated in many later pattern books, some of which were devoted entirely to the subject, of the growing nineteenth-century preoccupation with upholstery, and a sign also, with increasing eclecticism, of the desire for conformity between the style of the curtains and that of the decoration and furniture of the room. Smith's plates of 'continued drapery' festooned the windows with additional hangings to the curtains.

Animal monopodia, single or paired, are a feature of Smith's designs and appear on his chairs, sofas, sofa tables, sideboards and library tables. They are also used, sometimes winged, as front chair legs. The chair designs stress on the whole rectilinear forms. Where monopodia are not used, straight legs or winged female supports, and, in the case of armchairs, horizontal arms supported on posts or sometimes on winged sphinxes, emphasize this angular appearance, giving chairs, and seats in general, a certain stiffness and rigidity. This, no doubt, was Smith's attempted formulation of the Classical principle of the straight line, with the result that in spite of illustrating some chairs with curved or rounded backs, he failed to develop the attractive Trafalgar type of chair with its theme of contrasted curves. He popularized the use of the winged claw foot on tables and cabinets and also used effectively the typical Regency feature of the structural member with a central double lotus leaf ornament, and that of bolt heads and stars taken from Hope's designs. Another characteristic feature which he favoured was the console support which, as has been noted, was taken by Hope from Tatham's marble seat in a chapel near Rome. A mahogany dressing table, now in the Victoria and Albert Museum, is very similar to a design (Plate 72) in Smith's book. The drawer fronts are decorated with stars inlaid in ebony. The console support ends, inlaid with scrolls like those on the console itself, are similar to the ends of a table by Hope from The Deepdene and now in the Ashmolean Museum, Oxford. On Hope's table the anthemion is carved on the console (as is shown on Plate 12 of Hope's *Household Furniture*); Smith also adopts this console support for library and hall seats.

Footstool, early 19th century, decorated with black painted panels and gilt gesso female busts on lion's paw feet.

Rosewood occasional table, *c.* 1810–15, the galleried top supported on a reeded parcel gilt column based on a triangular concave plinth.

Mahogany dressing-table inlaid with ebony stars and stringing lines, closely resembling Plate 72 in George Smith's *Household Furniture*, 1808.

Smith's designs, while failing to match the elegance and precision conveyed by Hope's, and displaying a fondness for ornate decoration, nevertheless are marked by a certain vigorous and robust quality. Beyond doubt his and Hope's published works gave a fresh and, as it proved, a final lease of life to Neo-Classical furniture. In 1812 Smith published *A Collection of Ornamental Designs after the Manner of the Antique*, in which he speaks of the 'generally diffused knowledge of the classic designs of Grecian workmanship'. This work was not primarily intended for furniture-makers and in fact had only one page of furniture drawings, consisting of four designs for sideboard supports. But it closely succeeded another edition (1810) of Tatham's *Examples of Ancient Ornamental Architecture*, to which it seems to have owed a great deal, and both books appear to have inspired the continuation of Classical forms and decoration in furniture of high quality. Certainly under their inspiration, and that of course of Hope, a number of furniture pattern books of George IV's reign fought a rearguard action for Classicism. Of course, the whole theme of the archaeological version of Classicism can be, and often has been, criticized for its assumption that the arts and crafts of the remote past were superior to those of the present, and for its imposition, as some would maintain, of a tyranny that could stifle a designer's spontaneity and divorce his creative impulses from the realities of a rapidly changing world. But there is equally no question of the attractiveness of the best Regency furniture, even when it followed Classical precedents most closely. It was to be another matter when scholarly precision was absent, or was misunderstood, as it was by some of Hope's successors. It is also clear that Hope's Classicism was competing with his eclecticism and that the latter was to become more and more extensive in its scope and in its opportunities for indiscipline.

Particular significance is attached to the first pattern book of furniture to follow, after an interval of twelve years, Smith's *Household Furniture* of 1808. This was Richard Brown's *Rudiments of Drawing Cabinet and Upholstery Furniture*, 1820, with twenty-five plates almost all in colour. There was a second and improved edition in 1822. Brown, 'an architect and professor of perspective', had published *Principles of Practical Perspective* in 1815, and was an exhibitor at the Royal Academy from 1804 until 1828.[47] The great importance of his work of 1820 lies in the fact that while rooted in Classicism, his designs also incorporate those elements in furniture which are considered to be typically Victorian—symbolical and narrative ornament, rounded forms and the desiderata of ease and comfort—presented at the end of George III's reign. In this sense his may well be considered the first furniture pattern book to herald unmistakably the 'Victorian' style.

Brown freely acknowledges his main source of inspiration. After criticizing cabinet-makers for their 'unvarying sameness' before they became acquainted with the works of the Greek school, he continues:

'But within these few years their productions have assumed a new character, bold in outline, rich and chaste in the ornaments, and durable from the rejection of little parts. This style, although in too many instances resembling the Grecian tombs, has evidently arisen in a great measure from Mr. Hope's mythological work on Household Furniture, Mr. Smith's excellent book of Unique Designs, and Percier's splendid French work on Interior Decoration.'[48]

Brown's great preoccupation is with what he calls 'purity of ornament'. This, as he explains by quoting the words used by Hope in the introduction to *Household Furniture* (1807), 'once gave to every piece of Grecian and Roman furniture so much grace, variety, movement, expression and physiognomy'. Also under the obvious inspiration of Hope, Brown advocates that in large houses rooms should be decorated in a uniform style 'wholly Grecian or Roman, Egyptian or Etruscan, Gothic or Moresque'. He particularly urges that cabinet-makers should be skilful in 'harmonising metals with woods, so as not to overload the articles with buhl, bronze or or-molu which is too frequently to be seen'.

Brown carried symbolic and narrative ornament further than any previous designer, employing traditional Classical decorative motifs and figures and a wide range of flowers, trees and plants. This symbolism was no doubt prompted by a search for novelty, for Brown complains more than once that the production of new forms was a baffling task. As befitted an architect and professor of perspective he followed the Georgian tradition of including sections on geometry and perspective and finished with drawings of Classical ornaments and of the origin of the Corinthian capital, the ornate decoration of which suited the general mood of the late Regency. For flowers and plants Brown recommends the works of Dr R. J. Thornton (*c.* 1768–1837), the author of many books on botany, and suggested that the designer should follow the advice that Dr Johnson gave to the poet: 'he should range mountains and deserts for images, and picture upon his mind every tree of the forest and flower of the valley'. Brown's symbolism went to whimsical, not to say absurd, lengths. Sofa ornaments, he suggested, should relate to 'ease and composure' and should include the *gramen caninum* or – a nice play upon words – the couch flower and the garden heartsease or 'honeysuckles, eglantine or Turkish ornaments'. A cheval glass could have the figure of Narcissus 'to show our folly in being too much in love with our own persons', while a dressing table could be decorated with 'foliage and flowers producing perfumes, as bergamot, jasmines, roses, lilies of the valley, etc.; and running fig-leaves, to denote the dress of our first parents'. The symbolism of the fig-leaves can surely vie with anything the Victorians were to produce. As can be seen, Brown was a great advocate of the use of English flowers and plants as ornaments and he pays tribute to George Bullock for using them as well as native woods.

The proportions of the furniture illustrated in the designs in the *Rudiments* are becoming noticeably heavier as much of the severe geometrical outline of the Grecian style tends to be lost. A great deal more turned work, often of clumsy appearance, is evident. Chair legs are straight and turned and no longer of 'sabre' form. A dining table with hinged oval top (*Rudiments*, Plate XI) is supported on four turned legs and a thick central pillar which stands on a square platform with round, protruding feet at its corners. A sofa (*Rudiments*, Plate XII) has stumpy turned feet. The turned colonnettes of a lady's bookcase and cabinet (*Rudiments*, Plate XVIII) now stand well clear of the cabinet. The elaborate end-supports of a sofa writing table (*Rudiments*, Plate IX) have their boldly curved edges decorated with deep grooving instead of reeding, and a dressing table (*Rudiments*, Plate XIV) has outward scrolling end-supports of three members meeting centrally in a circular boss to which the turned stretcher is attached. Dining-room and drawing-room chairs illustrated in the *Rudiments* have curved backboards of yoke shape ending in spiral volutes.

A furniture pattern book in which the Grecian taste in 'chaste' form was strongly affirmed was *The Practical Cabinet Maker, Upholsterer and Complete Decorator*, published by Peter and Michael Angelo Nicholson in 1826–7.[49] Peter Nicholson (1765–1844), architect and mathematician, was born at Prestonkirk, East Lothian, of humble parentage. He was trained as a cabinet-maker in Scotland and worked at

Drawing-Room commode in Grecian taste from P. and M. A. Nicholson's *The Practical Cabinet-Maker*, 1826, Plate 74.

the craft for a time in London; later he practised as an architect of some standing in England and Scotland, and became well known for his studies of scientific methods in building construction, for which he was awarded the gold medal of the Society of Arts in 1814. He was the author of numerous publications on mathematics, architecture, building, carpentry and joinery. The *Practical Cabinet Maker* was 'illustrated by upwards of 100 coloured and plain drawings', most of the plates being the work of Peter's son, Michael Angelo Nicholson (*c.* 1796–1842), an accomplished architectural draughtsman and probably the designer of many of the pieces in the book. The work was issued with descriptive text in eight parts at 5s. each. It was dedicated to George IV. Both the decorative title-page and the introduction (signed by Peter Nicholson) are dated 1 May 1826. Some of the plates are dated 1827. On the reverse of the title-page of the fourth part, dated June 1826, appears a recommendation of the work to the furniture trade by eight prominent cabinet-makers in London, including Wilkinson and Sons, Thomas and George Seddon, and the royal craftsmen, Edward Bailey and John Bywater. A later edition, with some illustrations re-engraved and dated 1835, was issued without text. Indeed the work was reissued as late as 1846 (at least); the conservative element which is emphasized clearly appealed to the taste of many prospective purchasers.

The pretentious wording of the dedication, which spoke of 'this elegant, unique and superb work', is echoed in parts of the introduction, which claims to give cabinet-makers rules that will ensure 'order, harmony, symmetry and beauty' for, though fashions are fickle, 'yet the scientific principles, upon which alone these fashions are built, are imperishable and eternal'.[50] It is laid down that a careful and attentive study of the works of the ancients is most eminently useful, and compared with other contemporary pattern books, which all paid tribute to the Classical tradition, the Nicholsons' work shows a distinctly closer adherence to the Classical style as interpreted in the earlier part of the century and does this in a competent and highly individual manner. The designs are mainly in the Grecian taste, but some of the last examples of the Egyptian style are included in Greek and Roman detail. There are also some Gothic designs. Some of the plates (e.g. those illustrating sofas and a bookcase) are strongly reminiscent of the style of Hope. A design for an escritoire, with outward-pointing feet and curved apron piece, even preceded Hope in that it was of the type associated with Hepplewhite's *Guide* of 1788.[51] Some concessions to current fashions appear in the extended Classical scroll incorporating honeysuckle and acanthus motifs, which is found on the backs of sofas, on the backboards of sideboards and on the pediments of cabinets, bookcases, wardrobes and similar pieces. Occasionally profuse leaf decoration and carved ornament are found, especially on the feet and legs of chairs.

[69]

A number of chair designs show yokes ending in spiral volutes. The distinctive, later Regency drawing-room tables of circular and octagonal form are also illustrated. Some unsigned plates at the end of the work, of interior draughtsmanship and apparently by another hand, illustrate massive furniture more appropriate to the style of the mid-century. But the general character of the Nicholsons' designs, coinciding with the fourth edition (1826) of Tatham's *Etchings*, strongly suggests a sustained interest in the archaeological version of Classical forms. It is very probable that their work effectively prolonged the best features of Regency furniture and helped to postpone debased elements evident in the 1820s.

John Taylor, upholsterer and furniture designer, who had been at one time in the employ of the firm of Oakley and later had his own upholsterer's business in Bedford Court, Covent Garden, and who had contributed several designs between 1821 and 1824 to Ackermann's *Repository of Arts*, published about 1825 two small volumes of furniture and drapery designs, without text, entitled *The Upholsterer's and Cabinet Maker's Pocket Assistant*. These designs, of no particular merit, reflect the growing popular interest in mixed styles, including furniture both in the Classical taste, obviously derived from Hope and Tatham, and in the French style. Some features, such as the heavy foliate cresting on sideboards and sofas, and the heavily turned peg-top and bun feet on cabinets and tables, herald early Victorian fashions.

Henry Whitaker, whose pattern books were to be more representative than those of any other designer of the changes in taste in the second quarter of the century, published *Designs of Cabinet and Upholstery Furniture in the Most Modern Style* in 1825.[52] Here again the tendency towards more florid ornamentation is apparent. Somewhat coarsely carved, foliate scroll work, for instance, is seen on chairs, on the central crest of the top rail and on the top of the turned front legs. Yet in 1827 Whitaker published *Five Etchings from the Antique*, which, though not applicable to furniture, strongly reaffirmed the Classical tradition in the spirit of C. H. Tatham, with drawings of objects of antique origin owned by C. C. Western MP, and 'brought to England in the year 1826'.

George Smith's *Cabinet-Maker's and Upholsterer's Guide, Drawing Book and Repository* is the last furniture pattern book of the Georgian period. The furniture plates are dated from 1826 (which is the date commonly given to its publication), but the book cannot have been published before 1828 as that is the date of its designs of interior decoration. It has 150 plates, thirty-seven in colour. At the time of the *Guide* Smith admits to forty years' experience in the trade and to having received 'the most flattering testimonies from Mr. Thomas Hope'. He still proclaims, but not very convincingly as it turns out, the superiority of the Classical tradition–'the perfection of Grecian architecture and ornament'. He has to confess that his *Household Furniture* of 1808 has 'become wholly obsolete and inapplicable to its intended purpose, by the change of taste and rapid improvement which a period of twenty years has introduced'.

There is almost a note of apology in Smith's text, a grudging acceptance that disintegration has set in. He echoes the complaint of contemporary designers of the difficulty of finding new forms in furniture. For this he blames the 'necessity of economy urged by many at the present day'—this was a passing reference to the economic ills and social distress that plagued the post-war years—with the result, he maintains, of a monotony of character and lack of inspiration in design. He is critical of the rising tide of eclecticism—'a *mélange* or mixture of all the different styles associated together'—but, although his designs continue to be chiefly Grecian in character, he also submits others in Egyptian, Etruscan, Roman, Gothic and French styles. In consequence his designs lack the authority, accomplishment and individuality of those of the Nicholsons. Smith is clearly much readier than the Nicholsons to make concessions to changes in fashionable taste while extolling the primacy of the past.[53]

Smith's essays in the Gothic had been evident in his *Household Furniture*. He must also have been well aware of the growing interest in the Elizabethan style, while he notes, with some disapproval, the Louis Quatorze revival in the *Guide*. His designs exemplify the dilemma which now faced well-established architects and craftsmen in George IV's reign, for they had been trained in their profession or trade in the full Classical tradition, taught by teachers who had known no other. Now, confronted with the ideas of a younger generation reared in a changing world, they were forced to modify cherished principles.

Smith's chair designs illustrate the growing heaviness of form. In general he favours straight turned front legs; the yoke rail or shoulder board develops spiral volutes at the ends into *paterae* or scrolls. One chair design is an example of the French revival, with lavish carved decoration of shells and C-scrolls, in the Rococo taste which distinguished so many pieces in the so-called 'Louis Quatorze' style. Many of the larger of Smith's pieces—writing tables, cabinets, washstands, dressing tables and the like—are mounted on platform bases, heavy in appearance, with rounded corners and short, stumpy, often bun-shaped feet. Such bases were to become one of the commonest features of Victorian furniture. Another development was the ornamental pediment or scrolled cresting on mirrors and wardrobes, often centring in an anthemion or palmette. A lady's screen writing table, for example (Plate LXXXIII in the *Guide*), shows a desk with two detached forward column supports at the front on a thick recessed base; its movable firescreen at the back has a carved scrolled decoration at the top.

CHAPTER 2

THE GRECIAN, EGYPTIAN AND CHINESE TASTES

THE GRECIAN TASTE

The situation in the 1830s was summarized by Loudon in his *Encyclopaedia* (1833) as follows:

'*The principal Styles of Design in Furniture, as at present executed, in Britain, may be reduced to four; viz., the Grecian or modern style, which is by far the most prevalent; the Gothic or perpendicular, which imitates the lines and angles of the Tudor Gothic Architecture; the Elizabethan style, which combines the Gothic with the Roman or Italian manner; and the style of the age of Louis XIV, or the florid Italian, which is characterised by curved lines and excess of curvilinear ornaments. The first or modern style is by far the most general, and the second has been more of less the fashion in Gothic houses from the commencement of the present century; since which period the third and fourth are occasionally to be met with, and the demand for them is rather on the increase than otherwise.*'[1]

Circular satinwood centre table, *c.* 1833, triangular support decorated with gilt scrolls; gilt paw feet.

Mahogany break-front bookcase, *c.* 1830, in
traditional Classical taste; carved Ionic capitals
to pilasters at base.

Chair, early 19th century, cane seat and back, legs of sabre form; framework painted black with gilt paterae and Greek key pattern.

Armchair, c. 1805, painted black with gilt decoration; scrolled arm supports with lion's paw feet; fan-shaped canework back.

Above Beech armchair, c. 1810, carved and gilded and japanned dark green; female terminal figures in Grecian taste. Similar design for drawing-room chairs in Plate 55 in G. Smith's *Household Furniture*, 1808.

Right Mahogany dining-chair, c. 1825–50, broad shoulder board with anthemion mouldings; turned and reeded legs.

Table, *c.* 1830, in Grecian taste, veneered with burr walnut and maple; the top has boulle decoration. This type of table continued as a fashionable piece into the Victorian period.

Mahogany stools, *c.* 1850, upholstered in Berlin woolwork.

'Grecian' became the accepted term for the furniture based on Regency patterns which was produced in the last phase of the Classical tradition. To describe some of its later examples, designed when purity of form and decoration were being lost, the term 'sub-classical' has been coined by Peter Floud. It would, however, be altogether misleading to apply this term in a pejorative sense to all post-1830 furniture. Classicism died hard, and much sound and attractive Grecian furniture continued to be made. At its best it retained a sober solidity and good taste and

Mahogany dining-room side table, *c.* 1810, with peach-coloured marble top, the frieze inlaid with brass and ebony, similar decoration on the supports which are headed by parcel gilt bronze female masks; inlaid brass arcading on the plinth.

Detail of inscription from the side table illustrated opposite.

remained in fashion until the mid-1850s. It was particularly fashionable for dining-rooms, and was also in demand for the new clubs. The architect, Philip Hardwick, designed some of the best pieces in this Grecian style in 1834 for Goldsmiths' Hall, London. His designs were executed by W. and C. Wilkinson, and were intended for rooms devoted exclusively to men's use. His dining-room chairs had leather seats and back rests, cresting boards (or yoke rails) with carved palmette decoration, and front legs of sabre form. This late version of one of the most typical of Regency types has a dignified and handsome appearance.

The established Regency forms continued well into the 1830s. In 1835 the rapidly growing London firm of Taprell and Holland supplied a Colonel Robbins with 'a handsome rosewood Grecian Scroll Couch, the frame highly polished' for £14 16s., and with '2 solid rosewood grecian cross window seats with carved pateras on centre' for £6 16s. These window seats were of the cross-framed variety in fashion in the early years of the century.[2]

Above Dining-chair of carved mahogany designed by Philip Hardwick and made by W. and C. Wilkinson for Goldsmiths' Hall in 1834. This sober and handsome version of the Regency klismos chair is a perfect example of the 'Grecian' taste.

Above Mahogany games table, 1825–50, carved anthemion ornament.

Left William IV side table with top of black marble veined in yellow and white; frieze carved and pierced with vine decoration; eagle monopodia supports; mirror at back. The back boldly signed Del Vecchio, Westmorland St, 5 February, 1831.

[77]

The photographs on these pages illustrate the development of the rounded chair backs during the second quarter of the 19th century.

Above left Mid-century mahogany chair, moulded fan back.

Above centre Dining-room chair, *c.* 1845, rosewood, balloon-back, spiral-turned front legs in the Elizabethan style.

Above right Mid-century mahogany drawing-room chair with oval padded back in the French taste.

Far left Mid-century mahogany chair; the back retains faint traces of Regency Classical forms.

Left A graceful mid-century drawing-room chair in 'Old French Style'. Cabriole legs were normal on drawing-room chairs, straight legs on dining-room chairs.

Another version of the mid-century balloon-back in mahogany for the dining-room.

An excellent example of a mid-century drawing-room balloon-back chair in mahogany, with serpentine seat rail and leaf carving on the back.

Child's chair, mahogany, c. 1850. The child could sit, with chair lowered, at its own table, or, with chair as illustrated, at the adults' table.

Mahogany balloon-back chair, c. 1845–50, bearing printed label of J. Nutter, Upholsterer, Bradford.

Walnut mid-century chair with porcelain plaque in the back.

Octagonal table, carved mahogany with inlaid maple top, designed by Henry Whitaker for the Conservative Club, 1844.

In 1844 Henry Whitaker designed Grecian furniture for the Conservative Club which represented the later stages of the style.[3] The Victoria and Albert Museum has a carved octagonal mahogany table which formed part of his suite. It has a maple top, inlaid, edged with a foliate Classical decoration; the four feet of the table's pedestal support end in claws, with carved acanthus ornament. Grecian tables, in fact, showed less change than other pieces, but this example of Whitaker's design illustrates the increasing tendency towards heaviness. In other pieces of furniture the straight lines which were essential features of Regency design came under competition from the growing fondness for rounded forms dictated by the search for comfort. Chairs, for instance, which had long adhered to the broad cresting, extending well beyond the uprights, gradually began to acquire rounded top rails. This development, and the increasingly curved backs which contemporary drawing-room chairs in Louis Quatorze style assumed, led ultimately to the emergence of that Victorian innovation, the balloon-back.

Rosewood stool, second quarter of the 19th century, gilt acanthus ornament on arms, cross pieces also gilt with double lotus leaf in centre; gilt lotus-leaf ornament on feet.

Two drawing-room chairs 'with sweep back', Plate 16, T. King's *Original Designs for Chairs and Sofas*, c. 1840.

Grecian sideboard from Plate 44 of T. King's
Modern Style of Cabinet Work, 1835.

A wardrobe in Grecian taste from Plate 58 of T. King's *Modern Style of Cabinet Work*, 1835.

Mahogany dining-room chair, 1825–50, with spiral-reeded front legs and carved leaf ornament on cresting rail.

Sofas in 1830 almost always kept to the Classical rectangular plan, with straight back, front rails and ends. One end in elevation was curved – the 'scroll couch' in Taprell and Holland's bill. The decoration, such as a carved or inlaid anthemion on the front rail, was kept to a minimum. During the 1830s rounded backs and scrolled forms and ornament, of Baroque or Rococo inspiration, signalled the influence of the Louis Quatorze. Sideboards and chiffoniers, however, showed the greatest changes by 1850. Sideboards preserved pedestal form throughout the early Victorian period and were strictly rectangular in plan as late as 1840, even though, by that date, their backs had increased in height as they acquired mirrors, usually three in number – a large central one flanked by two smaller ones – following the tripartite division of the base. By 1850 the backs, now higher, were of semicircular form in the centre, and gradually the whole took on this form, while the corners of the base were rounded. Chiffoniers followed very much the same course. In 1830 these had two cupboard doors with brass trellis fronts and a small shelf supported by balusters or trusses attached to a backboard above. Later a mirror replaced the backboard, the trellis doors were replaced by wood or glass, and the whole piece took on a semicircular plan.

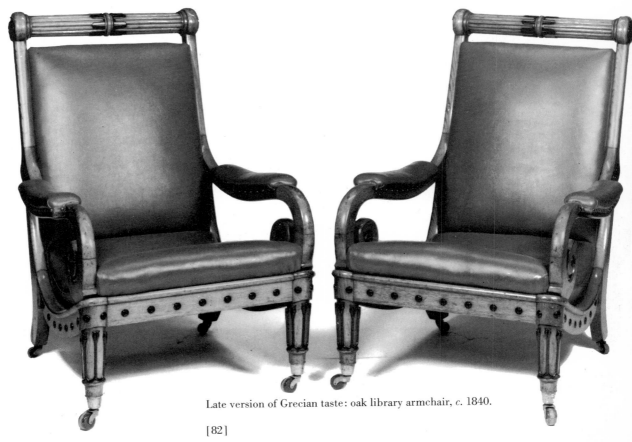

Late version of Grecian taste: oak library armchair, c. 1840.

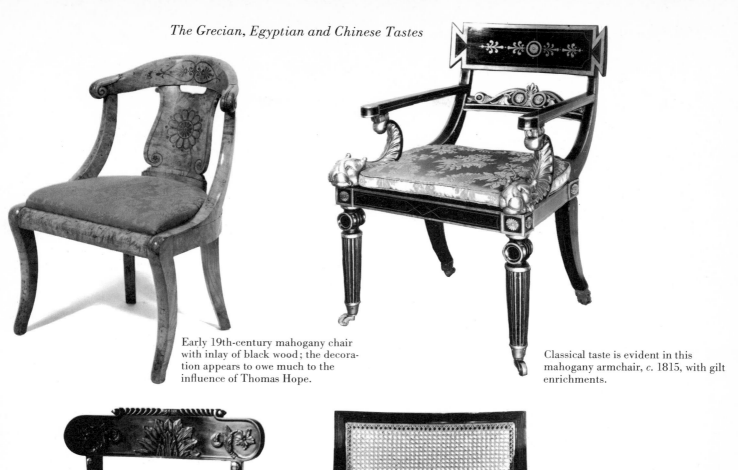

Early 19th-century mahogany chair with inlay of black wood; the decoration appears to owe much to the influence of Thomas Hope.

Classical taste is evident in this mahogany armchair, *c.* 1815, with gilt enrichments.

A good example of dining-room chair design *c.* 1830; spiral-reeded and carved foliate designs on the broad cresting.

Mahogany cross-frame chair, *c.* 1825, cane seat and back, reeded decoration on frame and front legs.

[83]

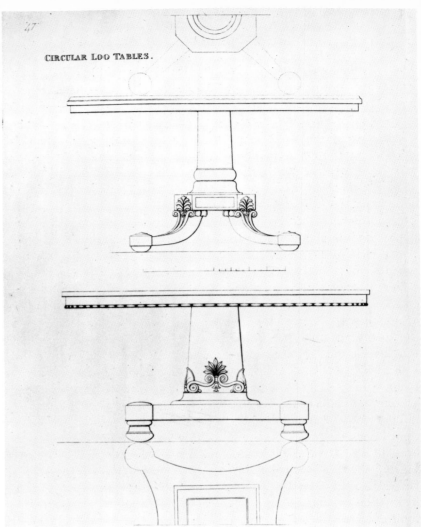

'Tea Poys' from Plates 3 and 4 of T. King's *Modern Style of Cabinet Work*, 1835.

Above 'Circular Loo Tables' in Grecian taste from Plate 47 of T. King's *Modern Style of Cabinet Work*, 1835.

Left 'Writing Desks' (Davenports) from Plate 5 of T. King's *Supplementary Plates to the Modern Style of Cabinet Work*, c. 1840.

THE EGYPTIAN TASTE

The Egyptian revival of the Regency, which occurred principally after Napoleon's expedition to Egypt in 1798, contained two main, and in many ways conflicting, elements. One sprang from the archaeological study of antiquities, the movement which, as has been seen, occupied a select circle of men of taste throughout western Europe in their scholarly search for 'pure' Classical design; the other was the popular craze for Egyptian motifs which swept over England after Nelson's victory at the Nile in 1798.[4]

As in other manifestations of Regency taste the Egyptian vogue had its roots deep in the eighteenth century. Interest in Egyptian antiquities had long preceded Napoleon. Some Egyptian designs, incorporated within the general framework of Classical decoration, had been used during the Renaissance and were familiar in the form of the palmette, anthemion, sphinx, pyramid and obelisk. Until the late eighteenth century, however, there was little detailed knowledge of ancient Egypt. Egypt itself, under nominal Turkish rule, was an unfriendly country for European travellers, difficult to reach and explore. To most Europeans its past was a dim image created by the Bible and the inventiveness of playwrights and poets. It remained a realm of fantasy, a source of inspiration for imaginative creation, similar to, but never as potent as, the 'vision of Cathay'.

The growing archaeological interest in Egyptian antiquities was centred at first in Italy, following the discoveries of Egyptian relics brought there under the Roman Empire. In 1748 the Capitoline Museum in Rome opened a gallery of the Egyptian remains excavated at Hadrian's villa at Tivoli, the fruits of the Emperor's campaign in Egypt in the early second century AD. French scholars showed increasing interest in the subject and the publication, between 1752 and 1767, of seven volumes on Classical antiquities by the Comte de Caylus (a source book used by Thomas Hope in his *Household Furniture* of 1807) spread information throughout Europe about the Egyptian remains in the chief national and private collections of that time.

So far Egyptian motifs had been confined in England to architecture, represented by the obelisks, pyramids and sphinxes used in landscape gardening in the early eighteenth century, especially by Vanbrugh, and in the employment of the sphinx by Kent and Adam. Piranesi is credited with the first important use of designs of Egyptian character in interior decoration in the 1760s—in Italy once again—in his Egyptian Room at the English Coffee House in the Piazza di Spagna, Rome, and through the publication of these designs and others in his *Diversi Manieri d'Adornare i Cammini* in 1769. As the Coffee House was familiar to many Englishmen making their grand tour or studying in

Satinwood chiffonier, *c.* 1810, the superstructure with a mirror back; the cupboard doors flanked by Egyptian masks, the frieze decorated with anthemion.

Rosewood side table, *c.* 1810; scagliola top depicting a port scene within a guilloche border; double supports headed by Egyptian masks; shelf stretcher also of scagliola.

Early 19th-century secretaire illustrating the contemporary love for dark, glossy and striped woods; mahogany veneered with zebra wood and crossbanded with satinwood; decorated with Egyptian heads.

The Egyptian Room, Plate 8 in T. Hope's
Household Furniture, 1807.

Rome, and as Piranesi's folio was available in England, Egyptian designs must have become well known to English dilettanti. It was in France, however, in the last years of the *ancien régime*, that this archaeological trend was first seen in furniture, in which Egyptian motifs were mixed with Greek, Etruscan, Pompeian and others.

In England Egyptian designs of archaeological character were being employed in interior decoration shortly before 1800. The drawings which C. H. Tatham sent Henry Holland from Rome included Egyptian antiquities, and at Southill Holland, from 1796 used Egyptian elements in his interior work. No doubt he designed the exquisite pair of side tables, with pedestals of lotus form (one of the most widely employed Egyptian motifs), which flank the Egyptian fireplace in the drawing-room.

Napoleon's expedition to Egypt gave particular impetus to the Egyptian revival because it was fully equipped for serious study as well as for conquest. Napoleon was accompanied by a large team of savants, ('from astronomers to washerwomen' as Lord Collingwood irreverently described them), including archaeologists, the most famous of whom, Dominique-Vivant Denon, later director-general of French museums, published the result of his researches in 1802 in his *Voyages dans la Basse et la Haute Egypte*. An English translation by F. Blagdon appeared in the same year and aroused the enthusiasm of English scholars.

Right Lararium, 'closet or boudoir fitted up for the reception of a few Egyptian, Hindoo and Chinese idols and curiosities'. Plate 10 in T. Hope's *Household Furniture*, 1807.

Above Egyptian chair, now at Buscot Park, Berkshire, illustrated in Plate 17 of T. Hope's *Household Furniture*, 1807.

In England Nelson's dramatic victory over the French fleet at the Nile on 1 August 1798, with its thrilling details of the night action, the brilliant seamanship of the British and the destruction of the French ships, coming as it did after lean years of war and the temporary loss of naval supremacy in the Mediterranean, and leading to the defeat and surrender of the French army in 1801, caused an immense sensation. Popular imagination had no truck with scholarship. Gillray's famous cartoon showed Nelson destroying the revolutionary crocodiles of the Nile, and henceforth crocodiles and Nelson were firmly connected.

The first English publication to illustrate the Egyptian taste in furniture was Sheraton's *Encyclopaedia*, 1804–6, which, unlike his previous pattern books, tried to absorb the prevailing archaeological trends but without proper understanding. In 1804–5 the younger Chippendale supplied two mahogany writing-tables to Sir Richard Colt Hoare at Stourhead with carved 'Egyptian heads', one of the early examples of the new taste. The scholarly study of Egyptian furniture

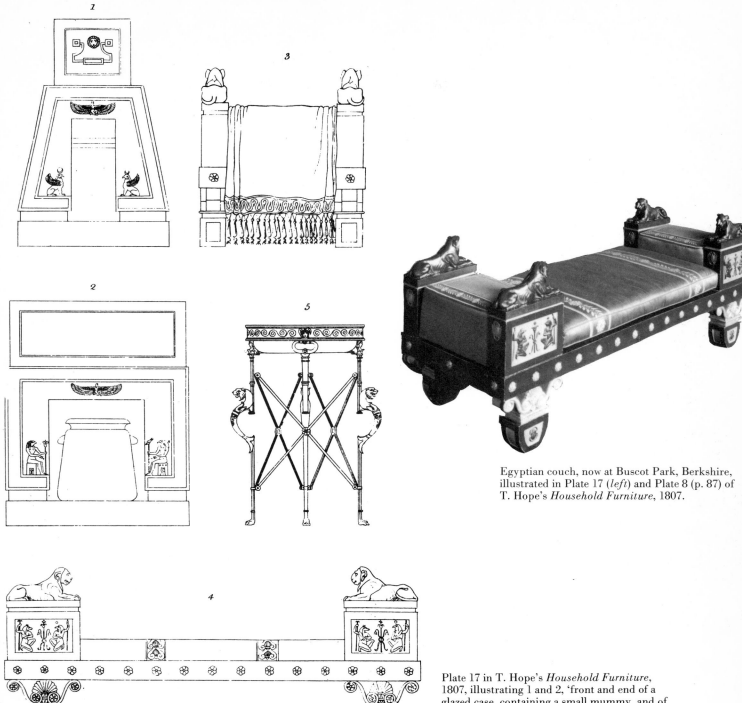

Egyptian couch, now at Buscot Park, Berkshire, illustrated in Plate 17 (*left*) and Plate 8 (p. 87) of T. Hope's *Household Furniture*, 1807.

Plate 17 in T. Hope's *Household Furniture*, 1807, illustrating 1 and 2, 'front and end of a glazed case, containing a small mummy, and of the sloping or pyramidic pedestal which supports this case'; and 3 and 4, 'front and end of settees belonging to the Egyptian room'.

and decoration reached its peak in England in Hope's *Household Furniture*, which includes (in Plate 8) a drawing of his famous Egyptian or Black Room, designed and furnished for his collection of Egyptian antiquities. Plate 10 illustrates the Lararium, or closet, which contained Egyptian curiosities among others. The Egyptian Room contained two couches and four matching armchairs, painted black and gold, of which one couch and two chairs survive at Buscot Park, Berkshire. They rank as the most important pieces of English furniture in Egyptian taste owing to the archaeological accuracy of their decoration. The throne-like chairs, with unusually deep shoulder boards, which are surmounted by a pair of bronze canopic vases, have a bronze winged disc of the sun god Ra on their front seat rail, and seated figures of Egyptian priests for arm supports. Double inverted lotus plants form the front legs. A small central panel in the back of each chair is decorated with a cow, sacred to the goddess Hathor. The long low couch terminates in blocks which are surmounted by couchant lions, and is decorated, in panels at the sides, with bronze figures of two gods, the hawk-headed Horus and the jackal-headed Anubis. The scarab, the sacred beetle of Egypt, appears, also in bronze, in panels on the stump feet. Gilt rosettes are painted all round the rail. Hope's Egyptian furniture in general displays the trend towards simplicity of outline, and emphasis on unbroken surfaces marked by straight lines, which distinguishes the best Regency furniture. Well-established motifs, like the palmette and anthemion, were given a fresh clarity.

Plate 13 in T. Hope's *Household Furniture*, 1807. *Above*, end and front of a table in the Lararium; *right*, front of a table, the clock showing the figure of Isis.

Opposite Regency cabinet, rosewood, super-structure with top of 'verde antico' marble and mirror back; cupboard doors with brass grilles backed with satin flanked by gilt columns with lotus-leaf ornament.

The popularization of the Egyptian style was largely due to George Smith's *Household Furniture* of 1808, 'studied from the best examples of Egyptian, Greek and Roman styles', the pattern book which, while lacking Hope's scholarship, though clearly owing much to him, was of a practical nature and of great influence to the trade. Furniture in the Egyptian taste now varied from Hope's purism to popular imaginative interpretation. Lion supports became common. Egyptian heads and feet were used as terminations of pilasters on bookcases, commodes and cupboards, and as table legs. Sphinx-headed figures were much in evidence in library furniture. Writing tables sometimes had pylon supports, with sides sloping inwards towards the top, in the manner of the ornamental doorways to Egyptian temples. Other motifs included the griffin (a fabulous creature with eagle's head and wings and lion's body), the canopic (viscera) vase, hieroglyphics, the winged disc of the sun, serpents, the uraeus (serpents as the head-dress of Egyptian deities and kings) and crocodiles. The lotus flower and bud – 'the water-lily of the Nile' – were widely used for the feet of sofas, as a double ornament centrally dividing a column, and as the capital and base of a column. Cross-framed stools often had the lotus attractively placed at the crossing of the supports.

Popular taste used Egyptian designs indiscriminately, but often boldly and vigorously, and if Classical details were as much the subject of confusion as the anatomy of fabulous creatures, the results were not without a degree of charm and fantasy. The standard of craftmanship

In full Regency Egyptian taste, this painted, bronzed and gilt armchair (*above*), with caned seat and sides, was probably made in 1806 from a design dated 1804 in George Smith's *Household Furniture*, 1808, Plate 56 (figure 110), illustrated below.

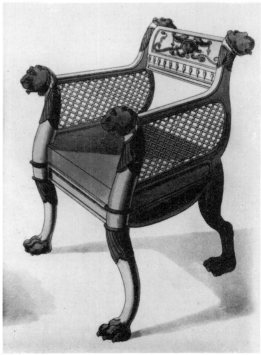

Couch, c. 1806–10, in the form of an Egyptian river boat, on crocodile feet; green painted wood, with carved and gilt enrichments of dolphins, scallop shells, serpents and reeds.

was still high. Miss Mitford poked fun at the more extravagant manifestations of the style; she found the Egyptian library at Rosedale Cottage in *Our Village* (written originally in 1819 and published in separate parts between 1824 and 1832) 'all covered with hieroglyphics, and swarming with furniture crocodiles and sphinxes. Only think of a crocodile couch and sphinx sofa!'[5] The Egyptian vogue probably reached its height about 1810. As we have seen, the Franco-American Louis Simond, visiting England in 1810 and 1811, noted how the English passion for archaeological research sought outlet in the Mediterranean since the re-opening of the war with France had closed the customary grand-tour routes, and he saw among the Elgin marbles 'some Egyptian specimens, such as a colossal beetle of green porphyry'.[6]

The divergence between the scholarly and popular conceptions of Egyptian decoration explains the constant criticism levelled by architects and designers against abuses of the style. As early as 1808 the architect C. A. Busby condemned the Egyptian style as the most absurd vanity 'that a sickly fashion has produced'.[7] Ackermann's *Repository*, in August 1809, stated that 'the barbarous Egyptian style, which a few years since prevailed, is succeeded by the classic elegance'. Yet the style lingered on owing to its obvious general appeal, and the *Repository* later illustrated (May 1812) a library table 'now in use for a nobleman's and gentleman's library' with sphinx monopodia supports, and (July 1814), a couch with Egyptian terminals. Even later some cabinet-makers who produced pattern books made use of Egyptian elements while joining in the chorus of criticism against them. Richard Brown in 1820 described the productions of the Egyptians as 'more appropriate to monumental purposes than to furniture for apartments', yet advocating that rooms should be fitted up each wholly in one style, he included the Egyptian among the other fashionable styles, and 'this should likewise be observed in the cabinet-furniture, upholstery, etc'. In 1828 George Smith included in his *Cabinet-Maker's and Upholsterer's Guide* a single plate of an Egyptian interior, while commenting that the style had 'been anathematized as barbarous, arising from the very unjudicious manner in which it had been adopted'. At the same time the Nicholsons also included the Egyptian among the fashionable styles of the day, but this was clearly the final phase of this Regency attempt to apply Egyptian forms and symbols to English interior decoration and furniture.

THE CHINESE TASTE

Furniture and decoration in Chinese taste had a long history in England, stretching back to late Stuart times with the beginning of the import of lacquered cabinets and other pieces by the East India Company, and the subsequent introduction of English japanning in an attempt to imitate oriental lacquer. This was evidence of the magnetic influence of the arts and crafts of the Far East upon European craftsmen. The 'vision of Cathay' provided an escape route into a world of fantasy and imagination wherein creative energies could turn almost with relief from the discipline of Classical rules.[8] It was no coincidence that the most famous period of English furniture in Chinese taste was that of Chippendale, the heyday of the English version of the Rococo, itself a declared revolt against the tyranny of Classicism. Much of the so-called 'Chinese Chippendale' furniture blended easily with the contemporary Rococo pieces, notably in the gilt mirrors whose asymmetrical frames were decorated with the whole range of accepted Chinese motifs—tiny mandarins and other Chinese figures, pagodas, icicles, bullrushes, long-necked birds, temples, bells and others. Of a different character, but an established part of decorative schemes, was the geometrical lattice work, the repeated fretwork, of the kind which appeared as 'Chinese railings' in Chippendale's *Director* of 1754.

With the advent of Neo-Classicism in the 1760s the zenith of English chinoiserie may be considered to have passed, but the taste was too deep-rooted to disappear altogether. It persisted to some extent in architecture and interior decoration, in which one can observe the influence of Sir William Chambers's *Designs of Chinese Buildings, Furniture, Dresses, etc.*, published in 1757. The pagoda in the gardens of Kew Palace was erected in 1761–2 to Chambers's design for the Dowager Princess of Wales. During the period of Robert Adam's ascendency some attention was paid to the fashion. Chinoiserie decoration was used on furniture which otherwise conformed to the new Classical outline. Bedroom furniture was particularly regarded as suitable for this kind of ornamentation. The furniture with green-painted Chinese decoration which Chippendale made, with other pieces, for the Chinese Bedroom at Nostell Priory in 1771 ranks among the most attractive of his creations. The well-known suite of bedroom furniture which was made for David Garrick about 1770 for his villa at Hampton, Middlesex (it is now in the Victoria and Albert Museum) is probably by Chippendale. The case furniture combines Neo-Classical forms with green-painted chinoiserie panels. This suite includes chairs of beech painted to simulate bamboo.

The Prince of Wales's name will always be connected with two major manifestations of interest in Chinese art—the Chinese Room at Carlton House and the interior of Brighton Pavilion.[9] Both examples have been quoted as the starting points of a revival of Chinese taste in the late Georgian period, yet neither seems to have exerted a wide influence, or to have altered the generally accepted forms of chinoiserie as they had developed in the last part of eighteenth century. Indeed, it has been maintained that the decoration of the Pavilion intensified the personal unpopularity of the Prince Regent and alienated interest in chinoiserie through its novelty and exaggeration. The Chinese Room at Carlton House—part of the Prince's rebuildings schemes about 1790—has disappeared, but it lives on in two drawings in the second edition (1794) of Sheraton's *Drawing Book*, which also gives a description of the contents. Most of the furniture in the room was taken to the Brighton Pavilion in 1802, and some of the pieces were subsequently removed to Buckingham Palace, where they still remain. The fine pier tables in the Chinese Room at Carlton House, two of its outstanding features, have already been described. They are the pair which are in French Louis Seize taste and can be credited to Weisweiler. The walls of the room, in Sheraton's description, were divided by 'Chinese columns' and had their panels painted with 'Chinese views and little scenes'.

The Prince's excursions into the Chinese taste at Brighton Pavilion

began in 1802 with the enlargement of the elegant Neo-Classical villa which Henry Holland had built in 1787. The Prince added a long gallery, inspired, it is said, by a gift of Chinese wallpapers, and stocked it with imported Chinese furniture and numerous curiosities supplied through the firm of Crace and Sons, later to be so intimately associated with A. W. N. Pugin. Chinese decoration was gradually extended to the whole interior, and important pieces of furniture were supplied by Elward, Marsh and Tatham, of Mount Street, London, the Prince's cabinet-makers. These pieces, of very fine quality, were made in the Chinese taste by English craftsmen. They include simulated bamboo chairs and a small commode of beech painted to imitate bamboo, with doors of Japanese lacquer panels.

One of a pair of cabinets, beech simulating bamboo in Chinese taste; scagliola top and brass gallery; made 1802 for the Royal Pavilion corridor, probably by Elward, Marsh and Tatham.

[95]

Chairs in beech simulating bamboo in Chinese taste, from two sets made for the Royal Pavilion in 1802; one example has pierced Gothic quatrefoils in the cresting. Made by Elward, Marsh and Tatham.

Regency chinoiserie side table, c. 1810, with marble top; supports of griffins with outstretched wings on monopodia resting on platform base: mirror back; painted dark green with gilt enrichments.

Opposite
Top The Crimson Drawing-Room, Carlton House, from Pyne's *Royal Residences*, 1816. Carlton House was the prime source of inspiration for Regency furniture and interior decoration.
Bottom The Circular Room, Carlton House, from Pyne.

Right Table, *c.* 1802, in beech simulating bamboo in the current interpretation of Chinese taste; probably part of the original furniture of the Royal Pavilion, Brighton.
Below Jardinière of japanned metal with painted decoration, early 19th century; the lambrequin ornament at the base is in Louis Quatorze style while the sphinx supports are in Egyptian taste.

Above Armchair, *c.* 1830, in Chinese taste, bamboo with ivory decoration.

Left Armchair, *c.* 1800, in Chinese taste; bamboo and pine.

Right Bamboo chair, *c.* 1830–40, in Chinese taste, from suite of bamboo furniture.

This furniture of simulated bamboo, intended particularly for bedrooms, remained very much in favour, a testimony to the general steadiness of English taste in its avoidance of excessive decoration. Light bedroom chairs with cane seats, the structural members turned, carved and painted to imitate bamboo, are a pleasant legacy of the time. Their stretchers are straight, or curved, or are sometimes replaced by curved struts or brackets at the junctions of legs and seat rails. The lightness was retained well after the tendency towards heavier padded furniture became apparent. Though by 1850 there were inevitable changes in the form of such chairs, part at least of their structure was often made to look like bamboo, as is shown in examples in Loudon's *Encyclopaedia* in its 1833 and subsequent editions.[10]

[99]

Chaise-longue, upholstered removable three-quarter back on simulated bamboo feet; stamped VR BP No. 100 1866, an indication of the persistence of Chinese taste.

Circular table, c. 1830, decorated with Chinese scenes and ornaments.

Lacquered or japanned panels continued to be the usual media for decorating case furniture in Chinese taste. There was a fashionable preference for black and gold, rather than the green and red (in each case also with gold) favoured in the later eighteenth century. The only innovations of any importance among current forms of case furniture were the small cabinets and commodes which were obviously influenced by Louis Seize models and were decorated with these lacquered or japanned panels, simulated bamboo supports and canework ornament.

This early nineteenth-century chinoiserie furniture, no more in most examples than fanciful oriental trimmings on standard pieces, complied with the prevailing conceptions of Romanticism and the association of ideas. Archibald Alison, whose theories of Classical furniture have been noted, explained the success of Chinese taste as an instance of 'accidental associations', for 'however fantastic and uncouth the forms in reality were, they were yet universally admired, because they brought to mind those images of Eastern magnificence and splendour, of which we have heard so much'.[11] But Alison, writing in 1790, had already noted that the Gothic had supplanted the Chinese and, as the nineteenth century progressed and the true China was exposed to view, her vision faded. The sober, not to say drab, reality thus revealed, defeated attempts at serious resuscitation in spite of lingering traces. There was no chinoiserie revival to coincide with the Rococo revival of the late 1820s. But the new Romanticism was many-sided, and if the oriental route to imaginative fantasy was gradually closing, other ways were now opening. Much of the fanciful approach in furniture design, occasioned by the romantic idealization of the past which is apparent in the medieval and other historical revivals of the second quarter of the century may very well have been intensified by the growing disillusionment with China.

Chair, 1830–40, beech simulating bamboo, the back in Gothic taste.

Chair in Chinese taste, framework of simulated bamboo painted with knottings and gilt scaling on a vermilion ground; cresting decorated with split cane panels; legs with ebonized chinoiserie brackets.

CHAPTER 3

THE HISTORIC REVIVALS

THE ELIZABETHAN TASTE

The Elizabethan and Jacobean revival had long been prepared for in architecture and interior decoration, for its roots went surprisingly deep down into Classical soil. It is apparent in the work of Sir John Vanbrugh (1664–1726), the exponent of the early eighteenth-century English version of the Baroque, who had a highly personal style with a strong feeling for the Picturesque. Seaton Delaval, Northumberland, the Classical house which he built between 1720 and 1729, has, with complete disregard for the established rules, a Jacobean plan and octagonal corner towers in Tudor style. The house has been described by Nikolaus Pevsner as 'the earliest instance on record of a conscious Elizabethan or Jacobean Revival or rather of an understanding of what the Elizabethan and Jacobean style was about'. In 1732 William Kent (1685–1748), the celebrated arch-apostle of formal Palladianism, rebuilt the east range of the Clock Court at Hampton Court Palace in Tudor Gothic style, and rooms on the first floor within the gateway were given elaborate imitation Jacobean plaster ceilings. Belhus, Essex, now demolished, was partly redecorated in Georgian 'Gothick' by Sanderson Miller from 1745 onwards. The staircase and an elaborate fireplace on the upper floor were done in Jacobean style, the fireplace being described by Horace Walpole in 1754 as 'good King James the First Gothic'.[1]

But it was not until the 1790s, when a much more precise meaning was given to the Picturesque through the works of Knight, Price and Repton, that an intimate relationship was established between their landscape and the Elizabethan style. This link is visually expressed in Knight's plea for the Picturesque, *The Landscape, a Didactic Poem in Three Books*, published in 1794 with a second edition in 1795. Two engravings of landscapes by Thomas Hearne are used in the poem to contrast the work of Capability Brown and his followers with Knight's own version of an ideal landscape. The typical Brown landscape has a Palladian mansion in its background, 'midst shaven lawns that far around it creep'. A smooth stream within neat banks meanders towards the foreground, crossed by two bridges, one, 'the thin fragile bridge of the Chinese', distinguished by its geometrical railings. The other engraving shows the same scene as a wildly overgrown landscape of dramatic quality, devoid, apparently, of any improvement. In the fore-

The cult of the Picturesque; two views of the same scene by Thomas Hearne from R. P. Knight's poem *The Landscape*, 1794.
Top The Palladian mansion 'midst shaven lawns'.
Bottom In contrast, the scene as nature intended, the stream flowing in its natural banks and, in the background, an Elizabethan mansion.

[103]

'Fashionable Chairs', 'from the repository of Mr. G. Bullock' as illustrated in Ackermann's *Repository of Arts*, September 1817, showing, from left, Gothic, Classical and Elizabethan taste. This is probably the first published example of an 'Elizabethan' piece.

ground, the stream flows more rapidly, crossed this time by a single sturdy rustic bridge. To complete the contrast, the house in the background is clearly and significantly Elizabethan.[2]

The Elizabethan could now be an accepted element in the Picturesque. It could, equally well, fit in with current literary trends. Moreover its undeniably English origins appealed strongly to the nationalist sentiment nurtured by the war years.

The Gothic and Elizabethan styles of the early nineteenth century were closely related. In September 1817 Ackermann's *Repository of Arts* illustrated three fashionable chairs 'from the repository of Mr. G. Bullock', which were in the Gothic, Classical and Elizabethan taste; the last-named indicating a tall chair with spiral-turned uprights, a semi-circular cresting containing a shield, deep upholstery round the seat rails and ball-turned legs. As this example shows, the term 'Elizabethan' was loosely and widely used at the time to include not only late Tudor and Jacobean furniture, but also that of the later Stuart period. In 1828 George Smith (*Cabinet-Maker's and Upholsterer's Guide, Drawing Book and Repository*) described 'the light spiral columns in the backs of chairs and the spiral twisted columns in the legs of their tables' as among the chief features of the furniture of the Elizabethans.[3]

Many aspects of this Elizabethan phase, however, had their roots in serious antiquarian research. Rare instances of documented suites of furniture in this style are those designed by Anthony Salvin (1799–1881) at Mamhead, Devon, built for Sir R. W. Newman 1827–33; and at Scotney Castle, Kent, built for Sir Edward Hussey 1835–43.[4] Salvin, architect, furniture designer and antiquarian, had been trained under John Nash and during a long career of some sixty years established a

Oak library table in Jacobean style, mid-19th century.

wide reputation as an authority on medieval and Tudor architecture. He restored or enlarged many castles, including Windsor, Alnwick and the Tower of London. He had artistic gifts and exhibited eight architectural subjects at the Royal Academy between 1823 and 1836. He competed unsuccessfully for the new House of Commons with designs of Tudor character.

Two Elizabethan chairs of *c.* 1845 illustrating the incorporation of late Stuart features into what was supposed to be a Tudor style.

Opposite
Top The Library, Scotney Castle,
Kent, designed by Anthony Salvin,
1835–43, in Elizabethan style.
Bottom Elizabethan furniture
designed by Anthony Salvin for the
Dining-Room, Scotney Castle, Kent.

Right Queen Adelaide's Bedroom,
Mamhead, Devon, with a complete
suite of furniture in Elizabethan
style.

Below The Library, Mamhead,
Devon, designed by Anthony Salvin
1827–33; an early example of the
Elizabethan revival.

Salvin's Elizabethan furniture is consistently designed and avoids the extravagance of many contemporary pieces following the same style; it nevertheless conforms with the interpretation of the time in freely incorporating Jacobean and late Stuart features. At Mamhead the furniture made to his designs includes a sideboard, several library tables (for which local ilex wood was used) and a complete oak suite in Queen Adelaide's Bedroom with incised surface decoration of interlaced, curvilinear, strapwork pattern. This suite, which was intended for the use of Queen Adelaide (wife of William IV), who was a frequent visitor to the house, comprises a half-tester bedstead, a long stool, couch, wardrobe, chairs and washstand. The decorative turned balusters with swell tops found on the bed and stool, the diagonal stretchers on the couch and the spiral-turned legs on the washstand are all of seventeenth-century inspiration and indicate once again the wide interpretation given to the style even by scholars.

At Scotney Castle Salvin's furniture includes two long stools with scrolled legs and spiral-turned stretchers, and two tables with turned baluster legs united by curved stretchers centring on a small platform with a finial. These pieces are reproductions and stand against walls lined with seventeenth-century Flemish wainscot. Other reproductions are high-backed chairs in Charles II style and a large cupboard–made up from seventeenth-century Flemish panels obtained from Hall of Wardour Street and executed, with skilled additions, to Salvin's design. This is the method of reconstructing furniture from genuine antique fragments to which Loudon refers in his *Encyclopaedia* of 1833. For the Dining-Room at Scotney Castle Salvin designed a joined dining table, ten chairs with turned legs and padded backs free of the seat rails, two sideboard tables, window stools, pier tables and a dresser. The dresser was carved and made up by Edward Wyatt at a cost of £97, after its commission had been declined by J. M. Willcox of Warwick, who was later responsible for the Charlecote sideboard. Salvin's furniture in the Library includes bookcases and two oak tables, one circular, the other square, each with a shaped pedestal base supported on boldly carved struts. An upholstered armchair has its back framework and its filling of four uprights decorated with knob turning. There is also a cheval firescreen with a spiral-turned framework. There survives, at Scotney Castle, a drawing by Salvin for an oak four-poster bedstead. The executed version in the house shows some modification of the design. The footboard has a baluster railing, reminiscent of that on the half-tester bed in Queen Adelaide's Bedroom at Mamhead.

In 1830 a scholarly study of Tudor furniture was published by the architect T. F. Hunt (*c*.1791–1831) in *Exemplars of Tudor Architecture adapted to Modern Habitations, with Illustrative Details selected from Ancient Edifices; and Observations on the Furniture of the Tudor*

Oak bedstead in Elizabethan style designed by
Anthony Salvin for Scotney Castle, Kent. On the
right is his sketch. Compare also the footboard of
this bed with that of the bed on p. 44.

Period, reissued in 1841.[5] The last section of the book described furniture in Tudor houses, with four plates (dated 1829) of examples at Penshurst, Cotehele and Conishead Priory. Hunt quoted a number of contemporary inventories and other sources, which can still be profitably used, and his descriptions are free from any attempt to romanticize the period. The publication of *Specimens of Ancient Furniture drawn from Existing Authorities by Henry Shaw, F.S.A., with Descriptions by Sir Samuel Meyrick* in 1836 gave further stimulus to these antiquarian styles. Shaw's aim, declared in his prospectus, was to establish 'a standard authority for all articles used for domestic purposes from the earliest period of which specimens exist to the reign of Queen Anne'. The plates, which are dated from 1832 to 1835, show in accurate detail, often with their measurements and sometimes in colour–Shaw was a pioneer in colour printing–furniture, silver and other metalwork and decorative objects in cathedrals, churches, colleges and in private collections. There are occasional lapses, which modern research has cleared up, such as the fanciful description of a late sixteenth-century folding chair in Plate IX of the book as belonging to the last Abbot of Glastonbury and dating from the early part of Henry VIII's reign–an error that probably explains the origin of the term 'Glastonbury', which has been used since the nineteenth century for this type of chair. But the illustrations of genuine Elizabethan and Stuart furniture made Shaw's *Specimens* a valuable source book for the Elizabethan revival. Most of the plates were done by Shaw himself. The book was reissued, unaltered, as late as 1866. The works of both Hunt and Shaw are referred to by Loudon in his *Encyclopaedia* of 1833, in which the Elizabethan style is said to be 'rather on the increase than otherwise'.[6]

As the Elizabethan furniture revival developed it aroused sharply different reactions. In an article entitled 'Old English Domestic Architecture' in the *Quarterly Review* in July 1831 the writer, reviewing Hunt's *Exemplars* of 1830 and A. Cunningham's *Lives of the British*

Another historical revival: The Ebony Room at Penrhyn Castle, North Wales, rebuilt in 'Norman' style, second quarter of the 19th century.

Architects of 1831, was wholeheartedly favourable.[7] As he paid particular attention to the problem of Elizabethan furniture, his words are worth quoting in some detail. He was heavily sarcastic over the 'tasteful upholsterers' who produced 'imaginary representations' of early Gothic furniture without having any surviving examples to guide them, and continued:

'—yet in the age of Elizabeth and her immediate successors, we meet with a highly rich and elegant style of moveables, capable of easy adaptation to all the luxurious wants of our most fastidious Sybarites. The couches and settees of carved and twisted ebony, the velvet and damask cushions, piled upon one another like our Ottomans, the canopied hangings, the ebony and ivory, or inlaid cabinets, cypress or cedar coffers, elaborately carved oaken buffets, tables spread with velvet, or damask, or "Turkie work" [Persian carpets], fringed with gold, the great folding screen covered with figured cloths, or stamped leather, or needlework, and the embossed andirons—these are all admissible in the present day; and the elegance of no modern boudoir would be disparaged, or its comforts diminished, by their introduction.'

Such furniture, it was argued, was infinitely more appropriate for surviving medieval buildings than the products of modern upholsterers, and comparison was made with what went for current fashions:

'What a disagreeable rebuff have our highly-wrought feelings sometimes experienced, when, on entering the arched porch of Gothic abbey or embattled castle, and penetrating its vaulted galleries, we have found ourselves in a room fitted up in all the flimsy frippery of a Brighton or Cheltenham lodging-house, with marble chimney-pieces from Leghorn, spindle-shanked rosewood chairs from Oxford Street, Grecian sofas, Italian cornices and French chiffoniers!'

The author expressed his satisfaction with the growing 'predilection for the rich and elegant designs of the Elizabethan age' which he described thus:

'Already there is a great and constant demand for its carved cabinets, scrolled chairs, tapestried hangings and figured velvet cushions; and France and Germany are ransacked for these articles in order to restore to our ancient manor-houses and Tudor mansions their appropriate internal fashion of attire. Our upholsterers (or, rather, we beg their pardon, "decorators") are already imitating the festooned canopies of Queen Bess; and many a carver is employed in framing seats after the model of the "great Turkey leather elbow-chair, with the tapestried cushions," which accommodated the person of "his most sacred majesty" at the castle of Tillietudlem. In short,

The prie-dieu chair, with tall back and arm-rest crest, and low seat with dwarf cabriole legs, as it had developed by *c.* 1850.

Carved and turned mahogany chair in full Elizabethan taste of *c.* 1845.

[111]

though the wisdom *of our ancestors is rapidly going out of fashion, it is some consolation that we are becoming daily more and more alive to the correctness of their* taste.'

But in 1836 'the present rage for Elizabethan' was severely criticized by the architect C. R. Cockerell (1788–1863), appearing before the Select Committee on Arts and Manufactures, as 'an imperfect and incongruous imitation of both Grecian and Gothic styles'.[8] Cockerell, architect to the Bank of England from 1834, had made a detailed archaeological study of Classical remains in the eastern Mediterranean, and was distinguished as a scientifically accurate scholar. He was, nevertheless, open-minded and designed (although reluctantly) at times in the Gothic style. His college, St David's, Lampeter, proclaimed him as well versed in 'Tudor Collegiate'. Yet nothing alleviated his condemnation of Elizabethan; he described it to the Select Committee as 'spurious and bastard; it is an adaptation of the Italian and Grecian architecture on the old English mode of building, and the only recommendation of it is, that it reminds us of our aristocratic prejudices'. Cockerell's strictures were aimed primarily, of course, at architecture, but by implication decoration and furnishings in their widest sense were included.

Furniture in Elizabethan taste continued to be commercially popular in the 1830s. The first pattern book to demonstrate this popularity was

Opposite Another example of the Norman revival: The Dining-Room, Penrhyn Castle.

'Elizabethan Chair', Plate 41 in R. Bridgens's *Furniture with Candelabra*, 1838.

'Elizabethan Table and Chair' from Plate 39 in R. Bridgens's *Furniture with Candelabra*, 1838.

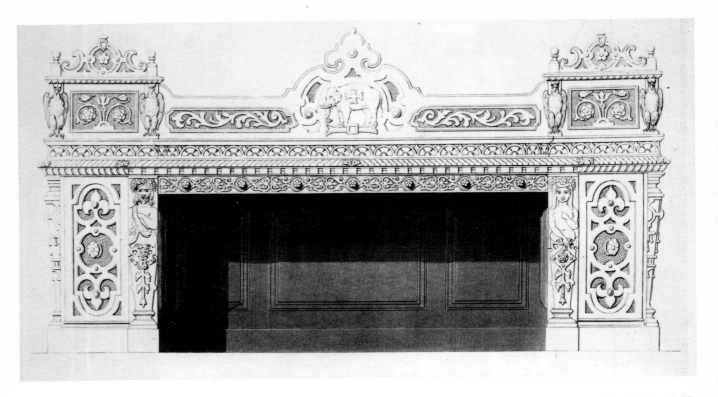

Above 'Sideboard at Aston Hall, Warwickshire', Plate 28 in R. Bridgens's *Furniture with Candelabra*, 1838. The pedestal sides and elephant emblem show that this is not an original piece, but is an example of applied 'Elizabethan' strapwork and other ornament to a standard sideboard of *c.* 1830.

Opposite Design (dated 1807) of a Gothic State Bed in George Smith's *Household Furniture* (1808), an example of adding an 'abundant variety of ornaments' (Smith) to standard forms.

Furniture with Candelabra and Interior Decoration by Richard H. Bridgens, published in 1838. Of the fifty-nine plates of designs in the book twenty-seven were devoted to the Elizabethan style, twenty-four to the Grecian and eight to the Gothic. Many of the 'modern' Elizabethan designs incorporated a great deal of strapwork ornament, the decorative form which was the most prominent feature of the style after 1830. Interspersed with these were engravings of old furniture at Aston Hall, Birmingham (where Bridgens was employed in restoring the Banqueting Hall and other rooms), Penshurst Place, Kent, Christ Church Cathedral, Oxford, Battle Abbey, Sussex, and of fire dogs, etc. 'of the time of Queen Elizabeth' at Haddon Hall, Derbyshire. A number of the Elizabethan designs were intended for James Watt, the owner of Aston Hall. Some examples of this furniture were made and survived until recent times in the possession of Watt's collateral descendants.[9]

Bridgens's pattern book is without text, so that there is no clue to the thinking behind his designs and certainly no information about his relationship with Henry Shaw over the production of the plates, which are all coloured. One is tempted to suggest that Shaw prompted Bridgens to include drawings of actual sixteenth- and seventeenth-century pieces, and he must in any case have been responsible for superintending the colouring of the plates in view of his own experiments

State Bed.

London, Published Jan.ry 1st. 1807, by J.Taylor. 59. High Holborn.

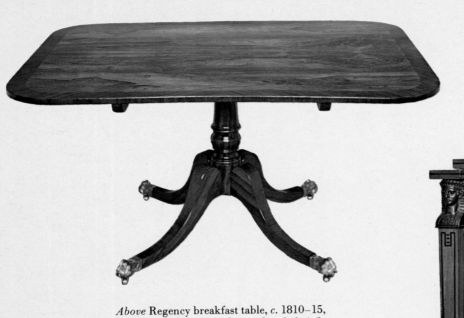

Above Regency breakfast table, *c.* 1810–15, veneered with rosewood, crossbanded. A fine example of late Georgian craftmanship.
Right Regency pedestal cupboard, *c.* 1810, mahogany inlaid with ebonized stringing and decorated in Egyptian taste with carved masks and feet, and a crocodile.

with colour printing.[10] Bridgens's attempted 'modern' designs include a chest of drawers, cellaret, bookcase, print cabinet, window seat, sideboard and occasional table. Elizabethan window curtains are shown draped from a pole beneath a bold strapwork cornice flanked by narrow upright supports also decorated with strapwork on a smaller scale. Typical features of a number of Elizabethan chairs of diverse forms are the tall backs, turned legs, spirally turned uprights and the incorporation of heavy strapwork carving.

The colour and richness of Elizabethan furniture was the theme of a paper read in February 1844 by George Fildes to the Decorative Art Society and entitled *On the Style of Furniture in Use in the Reigns of Elizabeth and James I, and its Applicability to Modern Purposes*. After speaking of the 'great prevalence of the Elizabethan style, both in the exterior and interior decorations of the present day', quoting extensively from Hunt's *Exemplars*, and maintaining that the style 'reached its utmost point of perfection at the commencement of James I's reign', he advocated the good effect that could be achieved by the use of open strapwork, 'knobs and bosses and imitative jewels', and the 'introduction of emblazoned letters and armorial bearings'. Concerning strapwork, he said:

'There is another feature of the Elizabethan style, that is, the introduction of elaborate open work in panels, friezes, etc., which modern improvement in mechanics renders easy of adoption, thereby affording a handsome and characteristic mode of decoration at a comparatively small expense. When the more prominent parts are slightly relieved with carving, the effect is greatly enhanced.'[11]

Nationalist sentiment was a strong point with Fildes. He was equally severe on careless use of strapwork – 'there is no style, not even the Louis Quatorze, that affords a more fatal facility than the Elizabethan for the exercise of bad taste' – and on the 'immense quantities of rubbish imported of late years from the Continent' to be made up into wretched combinations, under the name of Elizabethan, for the profit of mercenary speculators. The appeal of historical and romantic associations easily enabled Fildes to brush aside the condemnation of Elizabethan as 'redundant and unmeaning ornament' in Joseph Gwilt's recently published *Encyclopaedia of Architecture* (1842), and to quote with approval the novels and poems of Sir Walter Scott and Joseph Nash's *Mansions of England in the Olden Time* (1838–49), in which almost all of the fifty-three houses which were finally described were Tudor or Jacobean.[12]

Scott's influence was certainly a powerful one. As has been noted, in 1868 G. A. Sala (*Notes and Sketches of the Paris Exhibition*) attributed the revival in medieval and Renaissance art, not to Pugin and Ruskin

Above Elizabethan firescreen of papier mâché painted in various colours, by Jennens and Bettridge, *c.* 1850.

but to Scott's novels and the library at Abbotsford.[13] At the time of Fildes's address a type of high-backed upholstered chair resembling late Stuart examples (and then, of course, considered Elizabethan), became known as the 'Scott' or 'Abbotsford' chair. One appears among the illustrations of the furniture in a room in a garden pavilion at Buckingham Palace, which was decorated in 1844 in fresco with subjects from Scott's works. The frescoes of this charming little summer-house, which was demolished in 1928, were carried out at Queen Victoria's request under the superintendence of Ludwig Gruner, who published an illustrated account of the project in 1846 (*The Decorations of the Garden-Pavilion in the Grounds of Buckingham Palace*).[14] The legs, uprights and stretchers of the 'Scott' chair are spiral-turned, the back has openwork carving and the deep seat upholstery is heavily fringed.

The stamp of fashionable respectability was given to the style with the publication in 1840 of the *House Decorator and Painter's Guide* by the firm of H. W. and A. Arrowsmith of New Bond Street, 'Decorators to Her Majesty'. Though this publication was concerned with the usual multiplicity of styles (nine were named), a number of Elizabethan interiors were illustrated as appropriate for 'antique carved furniture'. One of these, suited for a library with walls decorated with Jacobean panelling, carried the note that 'of all the modes of decoration, none are in themselves more picturesque or so well suited to the manners and customs of the English people . . . it may, with propriety, be termed a native English style'.[15] Versions of the typical Elizabethan chair, with tall back and seat of padded upholstery or of cane, were illustrated in Thomas King's *Original Designs for Chairs and Sofas* (*c*.1840), a work which, like the same author's *Modern Style of Cabinet Work Exemplified* of 1829 (improved edition 1835), is preoccupied with the 'Old French Style'.[16] Henry Whitaker's *Treasury of Designs* (1847) devoted nearly one-third of its total designs in 108 parts to the Elizabethan taste, including a four-poster bed for the Marquis of Exeter, and drawing-room window curtains for Lord Crewe. The use of oak or walnut was strongly advocated, 'mahogany not being, at any time, at all suitable for Elizabethan furniture'. With reference to the design of a sideboard heavily decorated with strapwork, Whitaker explained that 'this design is, perhaps, richer than a work of general utility would justify, were it not for the carving companies who very much now facilitate the bosting [*sic*] of carvings, and with whose assistance a design of the present description might be got up at a comparatively modest expense'.[17] 'Boasting' (or 'boosting') was the carvers' term, defined by Sheraton in his *Cabinet Dictionary* of 1803, for shaping the rough outline of the wood before the details of ornament, etc., were completed.

Elizabethan furniture of the hack commercial designer of the mid-

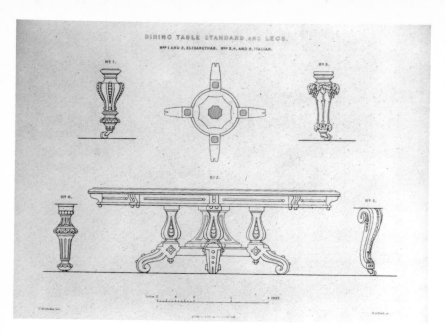

DINING TABLE STANDARD AND LEGS.
Nos 1 AND 2, ELIZABETHAN. Nos 3, 4, AND 5, ITALIAN.

23

RISING SIDE TABLES.
No 1, FRONT VIEW OF No 3, ELIZABETHAN STYLE. No 2, ITALIAN STYLE.

GLASS FRAME IN THE ELIZABETHAN STYLE.

SECTION IN THE CENTRE.

PETER JACKSON, LONDON & PARIS.

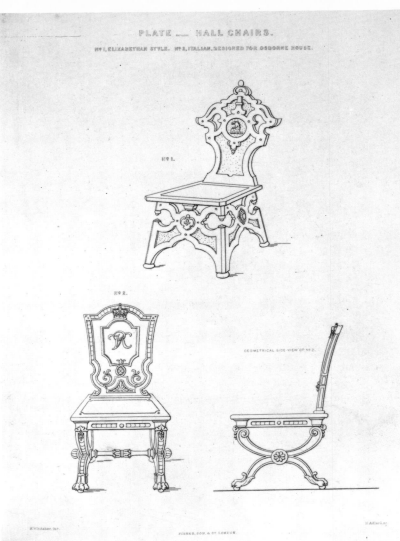

Nº 1.

Nº 2.

GEOMETRICAL SIDE VIEW OF Nº 2.

FISHER, SON, & CO. LONDON.

1840s is represented in the series of pattern books published by Henry Wood, described as a 'decorative draughtsman' of 24 Percy Street, London. Wood's main interest was to provide subjects for the ubiquitous use of Berlin woolwork for all types of upholstery in all the prevailing styles. In one of his publications, *A Useful and Modern Work on Chairs* (*c*.1845), published by Ackermann, with twelve plates containing forty-two coloured designs (but no text), there are a number of tall Elizabethan chairs with fully upholstered backs, some with spiral uprights. Wood's designs can be taken as examples of the average taste of the 1840s, which made the tall Elizabethan type the typical early Victorian drawing-room chair.[18]

An example of the common method of assembling Elizabethan furniture from old fragments is found in a bill of 1834 from the firm of Robert Trappes of Clitheroe, Lancashire, who supplied antique oak pieces (a bed head, ambry, three chairs, two chests and flowered ornaments) at a total cost of £28 to furnish an Elizabethan bedroom at Broughton Hall, Yorkshire, for the Tempest family. Most of these pieces, some with additional decoration, can still be identified.[19]

The records of the firm of Gillow provide examples of original designs of a very elaborately carved oak Elizabethan suite, which was made in 1841 for T. R. G. Bradyll of Conishead Priory, Lancashire. The suite included seats, which were given special names in the fashion of the time—an Arthur's chair, Anglesea chair, Lucan chair and a Medleycott seat (a composite piece of two inward-facing seats with a chess table in the centre). These seats are decorated with spiral turning, except for the Arthur's chair, which has carved bulbous front legs and arm supports in the form of fluted Ionic columns. Bulbous legs with Ionic capitals are also found on a writing table with heavy strapwork carving on the frieze. An octagonal loo table has its columnar support carved with acanthus leaves, fluting and gadrooning. A small 'fly' table has a slender spirally turned pillar on a triangular base. The bookcase in the suite, 8 ft long, has raised wings and recessed centre. The wings have grotesquely carved terminal figures at their angled corners and strapwork of pronounced Jacobean character on the frieze.[20]

An excellent example of an Elizabethan suite supplied at the beginning of Victoria's reign is that in the Dining-Room at Charlecote Park, Warwickshire, the home of the Lucy family. This room forms part of the western annexe, which was built between 1829 and 1834 and decorated shortly afterwards in the latest fashion. A bill dated 8 December 1837 among the Lucy papers records the purchase of twenty-two 'antique' oak chairs and two matching elbow chairs for the Dining-Room from Thomas Bott of 28 Margaret Street, Cavendish Square, London, for the sum of £158. 13s. 6d., including package. These chairs, upholstered in tomato-coloured Genoa velvet, have spiral-turned

Opposite

Top left 'Glass Frame in the Elizabethan Style.' Part 19 in H. Whitaker's *Treasury of Designs*, 1847. Elizabethan strapwork at its most exuberant.

Top right 'Hall Chairs; No. 1 Elizabethan Style; No. 2 Italian, designed for Osborne House.' Part 4 in H. Whitaker's *Treasury of Designs*, 1847. The chair (No. 2) actually made for Osborne House differs slightly from the design (*see* p. 188).

Bottom The development of the Elizabethan chair by about 1850; three examples in H. Wood's *A Useful and Modern Work on Chairs*, *c*. 1845.

The Dining-Room, Charlecote Park, Warwick-shire. Elizabethan chairs purchased in 1837. The heavily carved sideboard, by J. M. Willcox of Warwick, is later.

uprights, legs and, in the case of the armchairs, arm supports; the stretchers are bobbin turned. Their backs have a pronounced backward rake and narrow, slightly curved cresting boards. The firescreen, also with spiral-turned uprights and a panel of Berlin woolwork surmounted by a strapwork cresting, is of about the same date. The pair of side tables in the room, in carved light oak, are also in Elizabethan taste. The sideboard is a later addition. It was carved by J. M. Willcox of Warwick and was bought by the Lucy family for £1,600 after the Queen had declined it, when it was offered to her as a gift by the county of Warwick.[21]

The Great Exhibition, 1851, 'Elizabethan New Patent Grand Oblique Pianoforte', exhibited by P. O. Erard, who was awarded the Council Medal for 'his peculiar mechanical actions applied to pianofortes'.

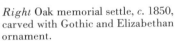

Right Oak memorial settle, *c.* 1850, carved with Gothic and Elizabethan ornament.

Far right This chair in Elizabethan style of *c.* 1840 has two unmistakable Victorian features: its prie-dieu form with tall back and low seat, and its material, papier mâché, decorated with painted ornament and mother-of-pearl.

THE GOTHIC TASTE

Gothic is the style which is associated more than any other with the Victorian period and with some of the most interesting and progressive designers of the nineteenth century. Of the historical revivals in fashion between 1800 and 1850 Gothic was above all the one which embodied at the same time the prevailing concepts of the Picturesque, the Romantic and the patriotic. While the Grecian represented the dying phase of a centuries-old tradition, and the Elizabethan and Louis Quatorze were newcomers, little understood at first and faced, particularly the last-named, with hostile criticism, Gothic was welcomed because it could claim, through its links with the past, to be the true national style. There were also important religious influences which sprang from the great programme of church building at the end of the Napoleonic Wars, from the Roman Catholics, who achieved emancipation in 1829, and from the Oxford Movement, which sought to demonstrate the close connections between Anglicanism and the medieval church. All these served to increase interest in the Middle Ages and promote antiquarian research.

The continuity with the past that was claimed for the Gothic style had been very tenuous at times and subject to various interpretations. But it had been a force for much of the eighteenth century. All Georgian architects were expected on occasions to produce designs in medieval fashion. Gothic was employed by Vanbrugh, Hawksmoor and Kent in the Baroque period, and by Horace Walpole at Strawberry Hill during the Rococo phase. 'Strawberry Hill Gothic', fashionable for a time though later much derided, was the inspiration behind the Gothic furniture designs which played a part, admittedly a subordinate one, in Chippendale's *Director* of 1754. Towards the end of the century the picturesque qualities of medieval architecture were exploited to the full by James Wyatt, and the great house, Fonthill Abbey, Wiltshire, which he built for the eccentric millionaire, William Beckford, in the late 1790s, has always been regarded as the epitome of the romantic possibilities of the style. Wyatt's work can be accepted as bridging the gap between Strawberry Hill Gothic and the scholarly medievalism of the early nineteenth century.[22]

Antiquarian research, discounting both the Strawberry Hill and Fonthill versions, took its stand on the national origins of the style. This attitude was greatly strengthened by the patriotic fervour aroused during the Napoleonic Wars, which also helped to postpone the inevitable discovery that the pointed arch was in use on the Continent before it reached England. Already from about 1780 the influential *Gentleman's Magazine* had become an enthusiastic supporter of the archaeological study of Gothic, and after 1800 its monthly issues always contained illustrations of Gothic buildings. A writer in the *Magazine* in June 1802, stressing

The Great Hall, Penrhyn Castle, North Wales:
furniture of Gothic, Elizabethan and Louis
Quatorze tastes against a 'Norman' background.

the growing distaste for the term 'Gothic' and pointing out the 'peculiar
propriety' of using 'English' instead, was confident 'that no English
Antiquary will be offended at the substitution of an accurate and honourable name in the place of one which is both contemptuous and inappro-
priate'. Against this general background it is not surprising that Gothic
became the dominant fashion for English country houses during the
Regency, under the direction of, among others, James Wyatt, William
Atkinson, Jeffry Wyatt and Anthony Salvin (whose work in the Tudor

One of a pair of oak Gothic throne chairs, c. 1850. The Gothic carving is skilfully elaborated, with pinnacles, linenfold panelling, crockets and tracery.

and Elizabethan styles has already been noted). It is noteworthy too that much of this building took place before 1820, the date when it is generally accepted that the medieval romanticism of Sir Walter Scott's novels began to exert its influence. After 1820 Gothic was increasingly used for churches. Serious archaeological study did not, of course, imply accurate information; that took a long time to establish. According to a writer in the *Gentleman's Magazine* in November 1800, 'English Gothic was first established in the reign of Henry III; perfected in those of the three Edwards in the fourteenth century, and rendered flourishing in the two succeeding centuries', and it was on the basis of this chronological sequence that judgements were passed. Clearly there were to be long arguments concerning which version of the Gothic was the 'correct' one.[23]

Gothic designs had retired well into the background in the furniture pattern books of the late eighteenth century, the heyday of Adam's Neo-Classicism. There are none, for instance, in Sheraton's *Drawing Book* of 1791–4. Some Gothic elements, however, appear in the *Cabinet-Makers' London Book of Prices* of 1788, where two designs of bureau-bookcases by Thomas Shearer show graceful glazing bars of Gothic character, four different patterns being presented. A number of surviving pieces of furniture made c. 1785–1800, including bookcases, china cabinets and bureau-bookcases have glazing bars of this kind and occasional carved ornament on their cornices. Shortly after 1800 Gothic designs in trade manuals become more evident, tentatively at first, then in increasing numbers. Sheraton's *Cabinet Dictionary* of 1803 has a Gothic bookcase and a buffet canopy, while his final work, the unfinished *Encyclopaedia* of 1804–6, includes Gothic designs for a bed, two pier tables, a candelabra (or 'light', on a curiously heavy Classical base) and a bookcase.

The first furniture pattern book of the nineteenth century to illustrate a comprehensive range of Gothic designs is George Smith's *Household Furniture* of 1808. The range is comprehensive indeed, unmatched in scope for twenty years in a trade publication, and including chairs of various kinds (for hall, parlour, i.e. dining-parlour and drawing-room), a sofa, lady's dressing table, quartetto tables, canterburies, a sofa table, dumb waiters, cellaret and wine cisterns, cylinder desks and bookcases, bookcases, chiffoniers, a cradle, bed cornices, a state bed and a general view of one side of a Gothic drawing-room. The state bed is a grandiose affair; the bed itself, complete with pinnacled posts and carved headboard, stands free beneath an elaborately carved tester surmounted by ogee arches and supported on four columns, which have niches and statues. Smith's own comments on the state bed claim that the use of Gothic admits 'of a more abundant variety of ornaments and forms than can possibly be obtained in any other style: and as many mansions of our Nobility and Gentry are at this time furnished in a similar taste, this

Early 19th-century Gothic: a rosewood wardrobe in Regency interpretation of the style, *c.* 1810.

Design may not be deemed inacceptable'. This 'abundant variety of ornaments and forms' was not, of course, of strict accuracy as far as Smith's own Gothic designs were concerned. The forms remained obstinately those of furniture in current use, and to these were added the pinnacles, crockets, pointed arches, pierced quatrefoils (a favourite carved motif of Smith's) and other ornaments culled from archaeological drawings. Many of the pieces are certainly not without some charm, derived, as in so many similar instances, mainly from the quality of quaintness which time has given them.

In addition to the 'mansions of our Nobility and Gentry' mentioned by Smith in connection with Gothic furnishings, the Gothic cottages and villas, which were to become so fashionable in the first three decades of the nineteenth century, stimulated demand for furniture of this kind. Both 'cottage' and 'villa' were now acquiring a distinct change of meaning. While the cottage rose in esteem to become in fashionable terms a small country house affecting a rustic appearance according to the tenets

Far left In contrast to Pugin's reformist Gothic, this Gothic chair of carved and gilded wood and velvet upholstery of *c.* 1830 is a chair of standard design with Gothic trimmings (which could easily have been changed to Elizabethan).

Left Mahogany 'Gothick' chair made *c.* 1823 for Eaton Hall, Cheshire; another standard type with Gothic trimmings. Probably designed by William Porden.

Oak hall chair in Gothic taste, mid-19th century.

Chair, *c.* 1830–40, in ebonized wood with Gothic arcading in the back; the front legs and rear uprights show turning of Elizabethan character.

of the Picturesque, the villa, on the other hand, lost its original Palladian connotation and became a less grand but more compact building. Both types were principally intended for the new rising class, increasing in social importance, of merchants, industrialists, bankers and professional men who no longer invested in large estates but preferred to live on a smaller though still substantial scale within easy carriage drive of their places of business. London was ringed with residences of this kind which were built in a wide variety of styles with Gothic one of the most favoured. A Gothic chair illustrated in the *Repository of Arts* in September 1813 is described as 'composed after the designs which prevailed in the six-teenth century, when the national taste was yet unsettled, and the fancy adopted forms and embellishments not in unison with the refined and classic taste of modern times: the very circumstances probably make this design analogous to the purpose of a *cottage orné*'. This type of fur-niture is also described as 'lately introduced as furniture for buildings of a castellated character'.

The library became the *locus classicus* of Gothic furniture, which could readily conjure up the quiet and studious atmosphere of the monastic scriptorium. As early as June 1810 the *Repository* illustrates a Gothic sofa, table, chair and footstool for the library, with the cautionary note that 'articles in this style must fit the general appearance of the house'. In a lyrical passage a writer in the *Repository* in March 1827 thus expresses his feelings concerning Gothic furniture and the library: 'No style can be better adapted for its decoration than that of the middle ages, which possesses a sedate and grave character, that invites the mind to study and reflection. The rays passing through its variegated case-ments cast a religious light upon the valuable tomes on either side, the beautiful arrangement of its parts combining to produce an impressive grandeur in the whole design.'

The late 1820s marked an important stage in the development of Gothic furniture. The group of pattern books of the decade 1820–30 which followed Smith's introduction of Gothic furniture designs–Brown's *Rudiments*, 1820, Taylor's *Pocket Assistant*, c. 1825, Whitaker's *Most Modern Style*, 1825, the Nicholsons' *Practical Cabinet-Maker*, 1826, and Smith's own final work, his *Guide* 1828–all made a strong final stand for Classicism and represent the mature phase of the Regency style, a late interpretation of the designs of Holland, Tatham and Hope, with evidence of French Empire influence and some concessions to the Louis Quatorze revival. Brown's decorative symbol-ism and advocation of English plants as subjects for ornamentation did indeed introduce new elements into furniture design and forecast future trends, but the general effect of these publications, especially that of the Nicholsons, was to maintain traditional standards of Classical design. In complete contrast, the *Repository*, like the *Gentleman's Magazine*,

Oak chair, *c.* 1840, Gothic tracery on a standard type, in the Great Hall of Penrhyn Castle, North Wales, a house built in 'Norman' style.

Oak Gothic dining-chair, 1825–50, columnar legs, crenellated carved back.

Regency cabinet, *c.* 1815, rosewood with parcel gilt decoration in Gothic taste; the marbled top with cusped gallery later. Good example of Gothic ornament on essentially late Georgian piece.

Above Card table, 1825–50, of finely figured walnut, legs in Gothic style.

Right Dining-table, *c.* 1830, ebony with ivory mounts in Gothic taste; octagonal marble top

Centre table, *c.* 1840, oak with slate top, carved Gothic ornament mixed with early Renaissance ornament.

took up the Gothic cause with great enthusiasm at this time. The trickle of Gothic furniture designs in its pages—including the three chairs by Bullock in 1817, with the Grecian and Gothic standing with the newly introduced Elizabethan—now became a flood. Beyond doubt the stimulus came from the growing fashion for cottages and villas in old-time style, illustrated for instance in J. B. Papworth's *Designs for Rural Residences*, 1818, and, more particularly, in P. F. Robinson's *Designs for Ornamental Villas*, 1827.[24] Robinson, so typical of his time, began as Henry Holland's pupil and eventually became perhaps the most eclectic of all the architects of the period. His publication of 1827 offered villas in eleven styles, of which seven were medieval or Tudor. (The fact that he built London's Swiss Cottage in 1829–32 underlines his versatility.) It was now that the largest group of continuous designs ever to appear in the *Repository* can be found, and all are in the Gothic style. They begin with two plates in June and August 1825 and then run on without interruption from October 1825 to October 1827, ending with an interior incorporating the pieces previously illustrated, under the title of 'Pugin's Gothic Furniture'. The text adds that 'the Gothic style, which we have shown to be so well adapted to domestic arrangements and decorations, is becoming much more general than it was a few years since'. These twenty-seven designs were published separately by Ackermann in 1827 as *Gothic Furniture*. The commercial aspects, rarely far away when stylistic considerations were involved, were noted in the *Repository* in August 1827, thus: 'we have now so many skilful workers in Gothic, that very elaborate pieces of furniture may be made at a moderate price, compared with what it was a few years ago'—and the use of 'very elaborate' is worth special record.

Until recently it has been assumed that the 'Pugin' of *Gothic Furniture* was Augustus Charles Pugin (1762–1832), a refugee from Revolutionary France who worked as an architectural draughtsman for John Nash, first in Wales and later (from 1796) in London, specializing in making perspectives in watercolour for his employer's clients. He exhibited at the Royal Academy, established business contacts with publishers, including Ackermann, and published two illustrated works on Gothic architecture, having developed an interest in medieval architecture, and assisted Nash in the latter's work in the Gothic style. The Gothic furniture of the *Repository* shows some accuracy in its incorporation of fourteenth- and sixteenth-century ornament, although this is still superimposed on current pieces.[25]

But it is now largely believed that the author of *Gothic Furniture* was A. C. Pugin's son, Augustus Welby Northmore Pugin (1812–52), architect, designer, writer and medievalist, who, in the course of his short and frantically busy life, can justifiably claim to be the first important furniture reformer of the post-1830 period.[26] In 1827, aged fifteen, he was already at work in the Gothic style, producing designs in silver for Rundell and Bridges, the royal silversmiths, and in furniture for Morel and Seddon, royal cabinet-makers, at Windsor Castle. In 1826 Nicholas Morel of Great Marlborough Street was appointed by George IV to furnish the royal apartments at Windsor. This furnishing was carried out by Morel in partnership with George Seddon—the partnership seems to have been solely for this commission—using Seddon's well-known workshops in Aldersgate Street for the manufacture of the furniture under A. W. N. Pugin's supervision. In notes of an unfinished autobiography, which are now in the Library of the Victoria and Albert Museum, Pugin writes that on 26 June 1827 he 'went to design and make working drawings for the gothic furniture at Windsor Castle at £1. 1s. per

Two of a set of Gothic dining-room chairs, rosewood in part gilded with gilt bronze enrichments, probably designed by A. W. N. Pugin and made by Morel and Seddon for the Dining-Room at Windsor Castle, 1827.

Settee, parcel gilt, stamped 'Windsor Castle Catalogue 1909'. In Gothic taste associated with A. W. N. Pugin, *c.* 1820–30.

day for the following rooms. The long gallery, the coffee rooms, the
vestibule ante-room, halls, grand staircase, octagon room in the Brunswick tower, and Great Dining-Room'.[27] This Gothic furniture reveals
the catholicity of George IV's taste, for it was supplied in addition to
furniture of the Louis XVI and Empire periods, and to pieces in the new
Louis Quatorze (in this instance Louis Quinze) revival. It is very probable
that the King showed his personal interest in the Gothic by ordering
special canopied superstructures for the Dining-Room sideboards, and
a matching canopy for the mirror above the fireplace. In a scholarly and
fully documented study of the King's furnishing of Windsor Castle,
related to some seventy drawings of the private apartments dating from
about 1827 (auctioned at Sotheby's on 9 April 1970) and accompanied
by photographs of surviving Gothic furniture in the Castle identified
from the drawings, Geoffrey de Bellaigue and Patricia Kirkham leave

Two sideboards and canopy in Gothic taste,
rosewood part gilded, with gilt bronze enrichments, probably designed by Pugin for the
Dining-Room, Windsor Castle, 1827. Made by
Morel and Seddon.

Above One of a pair of tables, rosewood, part gilded with gilt bronze enrichments, probably designed by Pugin, 1827. Made by Morel and Seddon for Windsor Castle.

Right One of a pair of tables, rosewood, part gilded, probably designed by Pugin, 1827. Made by Morel and Seddon for the Dining-Room, Windsor Castle.

little reasonable doubt that these pieces were made from Pugin's designs.[28]

This surviving furniture provides an excellent example of fashionable Gothic at the conclusion of the Georgian period. Some pieces are of oak with carved ornament and sometimes panels of burr walnut. Three occasional tables in this group all have cluster column legs, in one instance also with a buttress, but the ornament of each table takes a different form—a cusped pendant in the angle between legs and frieze, or a trefoil arcading running beneath the top, or two pairs of arches, one flattened pair below the length of the table, the other pair, ogees, across the width.

A suite of dining-room furniture at Windsor—a large sideboard, two smaller sideboards, chairs and two pairs of side tables—is of rosewood partly gilt, with gilt bronze enrichments. The chairs of this suite are particularly well known. The gilding picks out the Gothic columns and tracery at the rear of their backs (the fronts are upholstered), the quatrefoil ornament at the junction of uprights and seat rails, and the floral decoration on the seat rails themselves. According to the firm's estimates in the royal archives at Windsor, Morel and Seddon made forty-eight of these chairs altogether. H. Clifford Smith records in 1931 that twenty-four of the chairs were then in the Throne Room at Buckingham Palace, having been brought there from Windsor for the furnishing of the Throne Room in 1834.[29]

Pugin's own views on Gothic furniture in general and the Windsor furniture in particular, delivered in the course of two lectures at Oscott College and published in 1841 in *The True Principles of Pointed or Christian Architecture*, are naturally of considerable interest to us in this context:

'. . . *upholsterers seem to think that nothing can be Gothic unless it is found in some church. Hence your modern man designs a sofa or occasional table from details culled out of Britton's* Cathedrals, *and all the ordinary articles of furniture, which require to be simple and convenient, are made not only very expensive but very uneasy. We find diminutive flying buttresses about an armchair; everything is crocketed with angular projections, innumerable mitres, sharp ornaments and turreted extremities. A man who remains for any length of time in a modern Gothic room, and escapes without being wounded by some of its minutiae, may consider himself extremely fortunate. There are often as many pinnacles and gablets about a pier-glass frame as are to be found in an ordinary church, and not unfrequently the whole canopy of a tomb has been transferred for the purpose, as at Strawberry Hill. I have perpetrated many of these enormities in the furniture I designed some years ago for Windsor Castle. At that time I had not the least idea of the principles I am now explaining.*'[30]

About his designs he added that 'although the parts were correct and exceedingly well executed, collectively they appeared a complete burlesque of pointed design'.

After a period on the staff of Covent Garden Theatre, working on stage design and machinery, Pugin set up on his own to produce Gothic furniture in 1830. A series of ten letters and twenty-one sheets of designs (in the Department of Prints and Drawings, Victoria and Albert Museum), dated between June 1830 and September 1831, reveal that Pugin then had a furniture-making business, and his final letter refers to his decision to close it as unprofitable and to resume his 'original profession of an architect and designer'. The designs of furniture in this collection, intended for Perry Hall, Birmingham, are undistinguished versions in Gothic, Tudor and particularly Elizabethan styles.[31]

The significant change is evident from 1835, the date of Pugin's conversion to Roman Catholicism, the most momentous decision of his life. After that date he devoted himself with extraordinary energy to building numerous Roman Catholic churches, writing books and pamphlets, and designing furniture, textiles, wallpaper, jewelry and (mainly ecclesiastical) metalwork and stained glass. His zealous attachment to the medieval period changed the whole character of the Gothic revival. 'Gothic was fortified with principles stricter and more comprehensive than those on which classical buildings were based; and architects had come to look on Gothic not as a style but as a religion.'[32] Thus Gothic was the first of the furniture revivals to follow grammatical forms instead of relying on empirical adaptations.

Pugin was the first furniture designer of the nineteenth century to study the fundamental principles of medieval art, and he applied to

Stools

Pubᵈ April 1ᵗ 1835 by Ackermann & Cᵒ London.

Two stools in A. W. N. Pugin's *Gothic Furniture of the Fifteenth Century*, 1835.

furniture the two great rules of design which he laid down in *True Principles*: '1st, that there should be no features about a building which are not necessary for convenience, construction and propriety; 2nd, that all ornament should consist of enrichment of the essential construction'.[33] Through his understanding of the technique of medieval joinery he emphasized rational structure, in contrast to his contemporaries, who borrowed Gothic ornament (as he himself had done in 1827) to apply to their furniture. In his *Gothic Furniture in the Style of the Fifteenth Century*, 1835, in a small collection of pen drawings dated 1838 (in the Victoria and Albert Museum), apparently intended for publication but never completed, and in the furniture designs among his architectural drawings, he often reveals the structural framework.[34]

This open display of constructional features was quite contrary to established cabinet-making practice, in which considerable skill was expended on concealing construction. Pugin's drawings often marked with dots the pegs which secured the mortise and tenon joints in framed panels. The beholder could delight in seeing how attractive furniture was put together and of course honest work, thus fully revealed, was assured. To Pugin the eternal truths, the ideal in art and civilization, which so many preceding generations had sought in Classical antiquity, were to be found in the religious message of the Middle Ages. Art, crafts and morals were in association; with truth and simplicity in mind, he aimed to reproduce the essential elements of medieval furniture, not merely its ornament. The designs in his work of 1835 display a richness of decoration which is absent in the later furniture designed for clients. The fifteenth-century versions that he shows make much use of linenfold panels, crockets, ogee arches, carved columns and medallioned heads, and the intricate tracery of the Decorated Gothic period. His inventive powers appear in a cheval screen, sideboard, cabinets and a bookcase. This rich profusion reflects the early fervour of the convert, a counterpart to the splendour and colour of Catholic worship. Moreover, Pugin's Gothic ornament was derived from natural forms, as he subsequently proved in his *Floriated Ornament* of 1849. This was based on an old botanical work of 1590, which identified the original plants from which some Gothic ornaments were taken. In following nature Pugin anticipated Ruskin, while his emphasis on honest construction openly displayed was a dominant note in the work of later progressive furniture designers, among them Talbert, Burges, Seddon, Webb and Godwin.

The publication of *Gothic Furniture* in 1835 and Pugin's many attempts to propagate a true understanding of Gothic principles did not have any marked immediate effect on furniture design. His book had no explanatory text, and his prolific designs of sound Gothic furniture for private clients were not published. He may have met a certain amount of Protestant prejudice, and he himself is said to have refused for a long

time to work for Protestants. For the trade the source books for the Elizabethan revival–Shaw's *Specimens*, for instance–served also for Gothic reproductions, which were so often made up, as Loudon points out, from old fragments. The architect Lewis Nockalls Cottingham (1787–1847) employed this method for the Gothic furniture which he designed for Snelston Hall, Derbyshire, from 1828 for John Harrison. Eleven sheets of designs in the Victoria and Albert Museum, signed and dated 1842–3, show an interesting series of carved and painted Gothic pieces, including chairs, stool, sideboard and a 'conversation chair' or sofa, which were made up from 'ancient material' purchased while the house was being built.[35] On the other hand Pugin's designs may well have served as a useful guide for connoisseurs. In November 1836 Coleman Isaac, the antique dealer with numerous influential clients, wrote from Venice to his wife that he had 'ordered one of those large Gothic Arm Chairs out of Pugin's Book, it is to cost £2. 7s'. The reference is most probably to the 1835 publication, in which one of the chairs must have inspired Isaac's search for medieval antiquities. 'A. Welby Pugin' appears among Isaac's clients.[36]

The development of reformist Gothic; a room by B. Talbert in *Gothic Forms Applied to Furniture*, 1867.

Oak armchair designed by A. W. N. Pugin for Oscott Seminary, *c.* 1838.

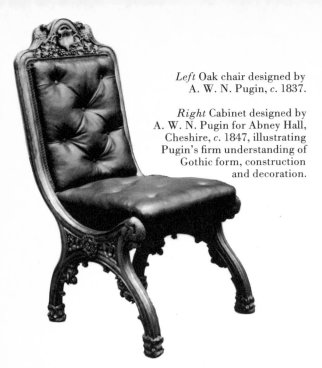

Left Oak chair designed by A. W. N. Pugin, *c.* 1837.

Right Cabinet designed by A. W. N. Pugin for Abney Hall, Cheshire, *c.* 1847, illustrating Pugin's firm understanding of Gothic form, construction and decoration.

Below Oak armchair with imitation leather designed by A. W. N. Pugin, and made by J. G. Crace for Scarisbrick Hall, Lancashire, *c.* 1837. A fine example of 'reformist' Gothic of the early Victorian period, illustrating Pugin's clear grasp of Gothic principles.

The chairs, designed by Pugin and made by J. G. Crace for Scarisbrick
Hall, Lancashire, about 1840, are among the best known of Pugin's
simpler pieces. They are of oak, upholstered with leather, with cross-
frame construction, their carved ornament completely subordinated to
the general design. They typify the vigour of reformed Gothic. Furniture for Abney Hall, Cheshire, also made by Crace to Pugin's design
about 1847, include a library table, a walnut cabinet bookcase (both of
which remain in the house), a cabinet (now in the Salford Museum) and
a celebrated walnut octagonal table with its top decorated with marquetry. The base of the table is somewhat clumsy, but the marquetry of
the top makes brilliant use of formalized natural patterns and is a
triumph of craftsmanship. This table and the Scarisbrick chairs are in
the Victoria and Albert Museum; so is the most famous piece of the
Pugin-Crace association – the carved and painted oak cabinet with
wrought-brass panels and fittings which was exhibited at the Great Exhibition, 1851. The Exhibition won acclaim for the Gothic style through
the Medieval Court, which Pugin was commissioned to arrange.

Right Marquetry top of the
table shown opposite, in various
coloured woods in formalized
natural decoration.

Left Table, carved walnut with
marquetry decoration, designed
by A. W. N. Pugin for Abney
Hall, Cheshire, *c.* 1847.

The celebrated cabinet of carved oak with brass panels and mounts designed by A. W. N. Pugin and made by J. G. Crace for the Great Exhibition of 1851. The masterly use of 15th-century Gothic forms in this piece singles it out from its Exhibition competitors (*see* pp. 288–9).

Above The standard House of Commons chair, oak decorated with dome-headed nails on the seat rails, designed by A. W. N. Pugin *c.* 1845 for the rebuilt Houses of Parliament.

Right Octagonal table, oak, 1847, designed by A. W. N. Pugin and made by John Webb, Bond Street. Prince's Chamber, House of Lords.

Left The most elaborate of the large bookcases in the rebuilt House of Lords; oak, with linenfold panelling on the cupboard doors and carving of high quality on the drawer fronts; fine brass drawer mounts. Designed by A. W. N. Pugin, probably late 1840s.

Below Small portable oak writing table with flaps, designed by A. W. N. Pugin for general use as well as at the front benches of the House of Lords.

Librarian's desk, House of Lords, oak, linenfold decoration on the cupboard doors, wrought-iron tinned handles and plates by Hardman of Birmingham. Designed by A. W. N. Pugin, (design in Lords Record Office). The first of such desks was recorded as being made in March 1849.

The finest of the small oak carved standing desks in the House of Lords, designed by A. W. N. Pugin. Original and elegant example of Pugin's Gothic.

From 1836 Pugin worked with Charles Barry on the new Houses of Parliament and was responsible for the designs of interior decoration, fittings of all kinds and the furniture.[37] Although the latter is outside the province of domestic furniture, it also influenced the production of Gothic furniture by the firm of Gillow. Designs in this style, known as 'New Palace Westminster' or 'N.P.W.', were to be found in the firm's order books until the 1880s. The use of carved monograms and of roundels incorporating a Tudor rose or thistle was a feature of furniture of this kind.

Pugin designed furniture for a number of great houses including Eastnor Castle, Herefordshire (where there is a chandelier copied by him from one in Nuremberg Cathedral, and made by John Hardman and Co., at a cost of £100), Leadenham House, Lincolnshire, Alton Towers,

'Library Fittings', Plate 64 in Thomas King's *The Modern Style of Cabinet Work*, 1835. The two central designs are described as 'Gothic patterns'.

Staffordshire, and Lismore Castle, Co. Waterford, Ireland.[38] In the last-named, where the decoration was undertaken by Crace, there is a good deal of furniture in Pugin's style, though only a few designs survive. The dining-room chairs are similar to a design made by Pugin for Crace in 1846 (numbered E1575–1912 in the Department of Prints and Drawings, Victoria and Albert Museum), and there is a Pugin design dated 1849 for a small bookcase. Pugin is also almost certainly responsible for the design of the dining-room sideboard.

The furniture pattern books published between Smith's *Guide* 1828 and the Great Exhibition are primarily concerned with the fashionable eclecticism of the day and make no reference to Pugin. Bridgens (*Furniture with Candelabra*, 1838) is far more concerned with the Elizabethan, which he divides almost equally with the Grecian, than with the Gothic, which has only eight plates at the end. Whitaker (*Treasury of Designs*, 1847), the most versatile designer of them all, is preoccupied with the Renaissance and Italian styles, which, to his evident satisfaction, he claims to be superseding the Louis Quatorze, and the Gothic is of only minor importance. Pugin's impact on furniture design seems to have been felt only after his death, through the carved pieces made by the firm of Crace. It is possible, however, that further research may reveal more extensive influence of his simpler designs on commercial production than has hitherto been realized. It is, moreover, clear that discerning contemporaries were alive to the implications of Pugin's pioneer work. In 1856 Matthew Digby Wyatt, in his report on the furniture at the Paris Exhibition of 1855, thus describes Pugin's achievements:

'. . . *there can be no doubt that this groping after the past revealed to that great man, whose loss the world as well as his friends must deplore, the late A. W. Pugin, those sensible principles of structure and*

Oak table, octagonal top decorated with parquetry; Gothic taste showing influence of Pugin. Stamped 'Howard and Sons, Berners Street', c. 1850.

Carved oak table in Gothic taste; *below*, carved figure of St George and the Dragon. Probably from a design by A. W. N. Pugin, c. 1850.

ornament which, as applied to furniture, have given to some of our leading cabinet-makers, such as Mr. Crace, the power to revive the best characteristics of the middle ages without demanding any servility in reproduction'.[39]

And about the same time, soon after Pugin's death, J. G. Crace, in a paper 'On Furniture, its History and Manufacture', read to a meeting of the Royal Institute of British Architects in the session 1856–7, stressed Pugin's contribution to design: '. . . that the construction be evident; carving, etc. should be by decorating that construction itself, not by overloading it and disguising it'.[40]

THE LOUIS QUATORZE TASTE

The so-called Louis Quatorze revival was merely one more aspect of French influence, that constant element in English furniture design. Ever ready to take their cue from the latest developments in France, English designers and craftsmen quickly took up the styles that the restored French monarchy had reintroduced in France after the overthrow of Napoleon. They were encouraged by the interest shown in the revival from the mid-1820s by influential members of the English aristocracy and by George IV in part of his refurnishing of Windsor Castle. It was natural enough that the Bourbons should restore to fashion the style of the greatest monarch of the *ancien régime*; this fully accorded with nationalist as well as with royalist sentiment in post-war France. Anglo-French cultural ties were strong enough to survive over twenty years of warfare. Copies of Percier and Fontaine's *Recueil de Décorations Intérieures*, the great pattern book of Napoleon's Empire style, first published in 1812, were soon available in England, and in 1814, after the restoration of Louis XVIII, the Paris shops were open to the many English visitors. In 1812 Ackermann's *Repository of Arts* illustrated French furniture in four successive numbers from June to September. In 1815, four months before the battle of Waterloo, the *Repository* remarked that:

'the interchange of feeling between this country and France, as it relates to matters of taste, has not been wholly superseded in the long and awful conflicts which have so greatly abridged the intercourse of the two nations, and as usual the taste of both has been improved'.

The Louis Quatorze taste differed from other contemporary revivals in two respects. It was the only one which was based on a style of the eighteenth century, the period that was otherwise studiously ignored at the time; it was also the only one which affected the actual structure of furniture and did not merely add decorative trimmings to current forms.

But it shared with all other contemporary revivals the confusion that arose from the prevailing lack of precise knowledge of historical styles, for much of what passed for Louis Quatorze was in effect Louis Quinze (which was the name often given to the revival), and the style was also known variously as Rococo, Old French and, in Loudon's words, 'the florid Italian' ('characterized by curved lines and excess of curvilinear ornament').

Some Louis Quatorze influence can already be detected in the bold supports of double scroll form on a circular table supplied to Samuel Whitbread at Southill between 1812 and 1815, and on a similar table of octagonal form supplied at about the same time to Whitbread's friend, William Lee Antonie of Colworth. In addition to the boulle decoration found on contemporary English pieces in the early nineteenth century – a matter to be examined in more detail later – the structural forms of the Louis Quatorze period came into use, including large dwarf commodes on plinths or on ball or bun feet. Console supports also, in some cases, replaced animal monopodia or columns. But these features had, of course, to compete for some time with English interest in the more recent Empire furniture, examples of which were to be found in many large houses. In April 1822 the *Repository of Arts*, ever francophil, illustrated a secretaire-bookcase, which it described as 'after the style so exquisitely perfected by M. Persée [i.e. Percier], the French architect to Buonaparte', and a French sofa bed in the November issue of the same year was accompanied by the statement that 'the taste for French furniture is carried to such an extent that most elegantly furnished mansions, particularly the sleeping-rooms, are fitted up in the French style'.

But as Louis XVIII (1814–24) and Charles X (1824–30) showed increasing preference for the *ancien régime* styles, regarding the immediate pre- and post-Revolutionary taste as associated with Jacobinism, it is not surprising that the revived French styles begin to take root in England. Among early instances are the opulent chairs and settees introduced in the 1820s in the Drawing-Room at Tatton Park, Cheshire, where Lewis Wyatt (1777–1853), the nephew of James Wyatt (1746–1813), had been working for the Egerton family since 1807.[41] Other members of the Wyatt family introduced decorative schemes entirely in the revived French idiom. During the rebuilding of Belvoir Castle, Leicestershire, Benjamin Dean Wyatt (1775–c.1850) and Matthew Cotes Wyatt (1777–1862), eldest and second sons of James, decorated the principal rooms about 1825 in the Louis Quatorze style. This was at the request of the fifth Duchess of Rutland after whom was named the celebrated Elizabeth Saloon, which had panelling said to have come from a château belonging to Madame de Maintenon, the wife of Louis XIV. A great deal of French furniture at Belvoir, in the Duchess's bedroom and in the King's bedroom, dressing-room and sitting-room (used by

Drawing-Room, Tatton Park, Cheshire, furnished in the Louis Quatorze style introduced by Lewis Wyatt in the 1820s.

George IV), was probably bought in France by the Duke and Duchess on the occasion of their visit there in 1814. Benjamin Dean Wyatt and his youngest brother, Philip (d. 1836) decorated four buildings in the Louis Quatorze style: York House (afterwards Stafford, now Lancaster House), 1825–6; Londonderry House, 1825–8; Crockford's Club, 1827; and Apsley House for the Duke of Wellington, 1828. A design for a 'Louis Quatorze Room', said to be based on the interior of Crockford's Club, the famous gaming house, appears in George Smith's *Guide* of 1828, which also presents a chair in extravagant Rococo style with the following criticism of the new trend: 'as this mansion is solely appreciated to nightly purposes of pleasure, perhaps such a taste may be in unison with the wasteful transfer of property made in such establishments'.

This statement was formerly taken to denote that the decoration of Crockford's marked the precise date for the introduction of so-called Louis Quatorze or Rococo taste into England, but, as has been shown, this building was only one, and not the first, of the series to be decorated and furnished in the new style in which the Wyatt family, and in particular Benjamin Dean Wyatt, may justly claim to be the pioneers.[42]

Another member of the Wyatt family, Jeffry–later Sir Jeffry Wyattville (1766–1840), the nephew of James Wyatt–carried out alterations for George IV at Windsor Castle, for which he was knighted in 1828. In 1826, as has already been shown, the King commissioned Nicholas Morel to furnish the royal apartments at Windsor, a commission which he executed in partnership with George Seddon in 1827. This Windsor furniture showed that the King was still faithful to Louis XVI and Empire styles, but it was typical of the diversity of his taste that he had the Ball Room, now the Grand Reception Room, decorated in Louis Quinze style. Significantly, too, he had rooms furnished in Gothic style, for which A. W. N. Pugin produced the designs. Morel was sent to France in 1826 to bring back patterns and drawings and thus keep the King abreast of the latest developments.[43]

As the style still generally known as Louis Quatorze gained popularity in England the Baroque forms of the Louis XIV period became more and more confused with the Rococo of Louis XV, and increasing use was made of elaborately carved and gilt scrolls, swirls, shells and feathers. Commercial productions of this kind were strongly criticized by the architects J. B. Papworth and C. R. Cockerell in their evidence before the Select Committee on Arts and Manufactures, 1835, Papworth declaring that the style was not Louis XIV's but 'the debased manner of the reign of his successor, in which grotesque varieties are substituted for design'.[44] Some competent designers avoided confusing the styles. H. W. and A. Arrowsmith, the New Bond Street firm styled 'House Decorators to the Queen', made a clear distinction in their *House Decorator and Painter's Guide* of 1840 between the 'ponderous and massive elegance' of the Louis Quatorze and the 'lightness, grace and variety' of ornaments of the Louis Quinze.[45] But most pattern-book authors made indiscriminate borrowings of profuse ornaments, which were particularly liable to debased interpretation. Critics could be moved equally by their insularity of outlook and dislike of easily repeated decoration. In 1845 John Pye, in his *Patronage of British Art*, supported Papworth's condemnation of 'the adoption of the designs of the era of Louis XV, commonly dignified with the name of Louis XIV, a style inferior in taste and easy of execution'.[46]

According to Loudon in 1833 the Louis Quatorze style was 'rather on the increase than otherwise'. This was borne out by the pattern book which first reflected wholeheartedly the demand for the new taste, Thomas King's *Modern Style of Cabinet Work Exemplified*, which was

Firescreen, *c.* 1840, carved and gilt wood in revived Rococo style, panel of Berlin woolwork.

'A Chair and a Flower Stand', Plate 25 in R. Bridgens's *Furniture with Candelabra*, 1838. Though these designs appear in the 'Grecian' section of the book (exemplified in the flower stand), the chair is in Louis Quatorze taste.

A CHAIR & FLOWER STAND.

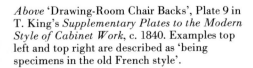

Above 'Drawing-Room Chair Backs', Plate 9 in T. King's *Supplementary Plates to the Modern Style of Cabinet Work*, c. 1840. Examples top left and top right are described as 'being specimens in the old French style'.

Right Two 'Work Tables' in (*left*) Grecian and (*right*) French taste in Plate 14 in T. King's *The Modern Style of Cabinet Work*, 1835.

published in 1829 and was followed by a second and improved edition in 1835. This book was intended to popularize the French styles, among others in fashion, for commercial production, the introduction announcing that 'as far as possible the English style is carefully blended with Parisian taste', adding that 'in the gilded parts, carving will only be required in the boldest scrolls or in the massive foliage, while composition ornament may be used for rosettes, enriched mouldings, ornamental borders and generally in the minute detail'. To encourage the cheap and rapid production of furniture was King's clearly stated aim, for he wrote, with reference to the seventy-two plates containing 227 designs in the 1835 edition of the *Modern Style*, that 'peculiar attention has been bestowed in an economical arrangement of material and labor which . . . is presumed will render the collection of the greatest utility to the Cabinet Manufacturer'. King, who was described in his *Upholsterer's Accelerator* of 1833 as 'an upholsterer of forty-five years' experience', with an address at 17 Gate Street, Lincoln's Inn Fields, published a number of pattern books of furniture, upholstery and carving until about 1840, in which attention was paid to what was invariably called the Old French Style. The *Modern Style* was obviously in brisk demand. *Supplementary Plates to the Modern Style*, published about 1840, had twenty-eight plates with sixty-eight new designs. As already noted, the *Modern Style* was reissued unaltered as late as 1862. Another work published by King was *French Designs* (undated), in which the eighteen plates were advertised as 'displaying the French taste for lightness and elegance and shewing various descriptions of the present style in Paris'.

'Lightness and elegance' was clear enough reference to the Rococo, while the 'boldest scrolls' of the *Modern Style* were obviously Baroque —evidence of continued confusion. King's designs for drawing-room chairs have, in broad terms, either elaborately carved scrolls on the cresting rail or rounded backs with scrollwork on crest and splat. The plinths or 'blocks' of teapoys, card and loo tables, washstands, etc., increasingly heavy and ornamented, come in for a great deal of attention, and a number of drawings in plan, of varied forms, are presented. The

'Supports for Sideboard Tables,' Plate 17 in T. King's *Supplementary Plates to Modern Style of Cabinet Work, c.* 1840. Number 5, right, is in the 'old French style'.

'A Sofa in the old French style', Plate 9 in T. King's *Original Designs for Chairs and Sofas, c.* 1840.

One of '6 satinwood and gold chairs, the seats stuffed in the best manner in fine linen . . . £7 3s. . . . £42 18s.' supplied by Holland and Sons to the Queen's Drawing-Room, Osborne, Isle of Wight, 1845. An exceptionally fine example of the early Victorian balloon-back chair in the French taste.

'Easy chairs with inclined seats' from Plate 27 of T. King's *Modern Style of Cabinet Work*, 1835.

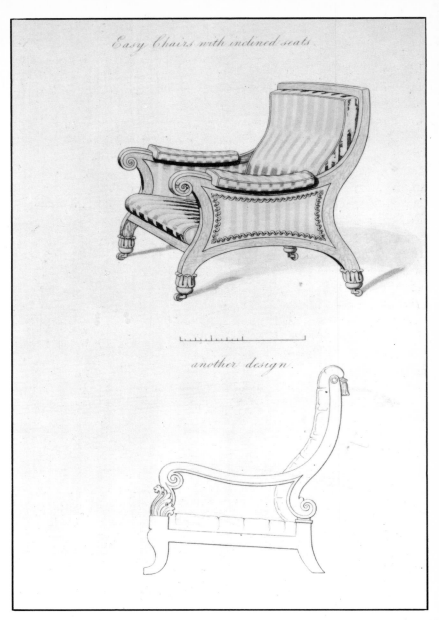

central cresting of acanthus and honeysuckle now appears commonly on sideboards, commodes and larger types of furniture. In the *Supplementary Plates*, which illustrate designs for many types of furniture (especially smaller pieces) not included in the *Modern Style*, there is much more reference to the Old French Style, which is marked by the free use of scrolled ornament on the 'stuffed backs' of drawing-room chairs, the feet of a 'fancy table', the base of a flower stand and of a firescreen, etc. 'Old French Style' is, in fact, the inevitable accompaniment of any design liable to show a great deal of scrollwork, often of interlaced curves.[47]

The designs in King's works show that swelling curves, emphasized by naturalistic carving and thick upholstery, reflected the growing fashion of the time for rotundity and comfort. But decoration was not all overloading and heaviness. The French taste was favoured for drawing-rooms and boudoirs and for the latter in particular much delicate and graceful furniture was made. In the drawing-room the slender 'fly' chair, with carved and curved cresting rail and cabriole legs, its framework painted white with the carved decoration picked out in gilding, is among one of the most charming products of the Victorian era. It has been pointed out that the furniture designed by the architect Philip Hardwick and made by W. and C. Wilkinson in 1834 for Goldsmiths' Hall can be divided into masculine and feminine categories typified by the timbers and styles employed—mahogany in Grecian style for the main rooms reserved exclusively for men, and painted and gilded furniture in Louis Quatorze style for the Court Drawing-Room to which ladies were admitted.

Henry Whitaker in his *Practical Cabinet-Maker and Upholsterer's Treasury of Designs*, 1847, wrote that 'the Louis Quatorze style is going out very fast'. But this was to dismiss the Old French Style altogether too soon. Whitaker may have been prompted in his opinion partly by his own preference for the newly fashionable Renaissance taste and partly by his interest in seeking English native material as a basis for ornamentation. French styles of the eighteenth century continued to exercise a formative influence on English designers for the rest of the century and indeed into Edward VII's reign. A year after the publication of Whitaker's *Treasury of Designs* political troubles in France (to be repeated in 1851 and 1871) supplied England with a stream of immigrant French craftsmen. French furniture at international exhibitions never failed to excite the admiration of English critics, and when it became fashionable for leading English firms to employ French designers, the links between France and England were as strong as they had ever been. The Old French Style gradually absorbed Louis Seize taste, which Matthew Digby Wyatt praised in 1855 for its 'technical excellencies',

'Fly' chair, beech carved, painted and gilded, designed by Philip Hardwick and made by Wilkinson for Goldsmiths' Hall, *c.* 1834.

This chaise-longue, *c.* 1845, has decided French influence in its shaped back, seat rails and cabriole legs.

Walnut marquetry card table, mid-19th century, an example of literal English copies of French furniture of the *ancien régime*.

Mahogany marquetry occasional table; mid-19th-century English copy of French furniture.

Centre table, burr walnut with marquetry decoration; another English example of the mid-19th century of French influence.

DRAWING ROOM IN THE LOUIS SEIZE STYLE. ⊹ JAMES SHOOLBRED & COMPY
TOTTENHAM HOUSE. TOTTENHAM COURT ROAD, W.

Whiteman & Bass *Photo-Litho'rs to the Queen* 236 Holborn

and English firms began to use the term 'Louis Style' for anything connected with French fashions of the eighteenth century.[48] It was even carried abroad, for in 1887 we find a wealthy English family furnishing a luxurious villa at Palermo, Sicily, in 'Belgrave Square style', which included both a Louis Quinze and a Louis Seize drawing-room.[49]

Louis Quatorze remained strongly current at the 1851 Exhibition. R. N. Wornum admitted that the Cinquecento Renaissance was the favourite style of the day, but immediately added that 'the Louis Quatorze varieties perhaps prevail in quantity, the Louis Quinze and the Rococo'. With special reference to carving on furniture he maintained that 'the Louis Quatorze can appropriate any curves, provided they have given them the characteristic roundness of members of this style'.[50]

'Drawing-Room in the Louis Seize Style', from the catalogue of James Shoolbred and Co., late 19th century, illustrating the continuity of French influence.

[153]

Firescreen, *c.* 1840, beech and Berlin woolwork, in 'Naturalistic' style.

Occasional table carved in 'Naturalistic' style, top of Copeland and Garrett porcelain (marked for 1833–47).

THE NATURALISTIC STYLE

In spite of the proliferation of historical styles and the all-embracing eclecticism of the second quarter of the century it is clear that a great deal of the commercial production of furniture in the fifteen years or so before 1850, and continuing into the 1850s, had an unmistakably original stamp about it. It was not designed in one of the styles of the past even though there was a certain amount of free borrowing from historical sources, and even though its designers appeared on occasion to imagine that they were faithfully interpreting a particular historical style. Its general commercial background must be stressed. Such furniture was to become very popular in the 1840s and 1850s and was very prominent at the Great Exhibition of 1851, but it does not appear in the better-known pattern books and is ignored in studies of architecture and interior decoration of the time.

The main characteristics of this 'nameless' style are rounded forms, abundant upholstery and considerable use of naturalistic carving. This last feature has given the modern name of 'Naturalistic Style' to the whole range. In many respects it had distinct affinities with the Rococo revival, replacing the opulent curves and scrolls of that style with naturalistic flowers, foliage and sinuous tendrils. This commercial innovation, difficult to define in exact terms, can rank as the first truly original Victorian style to emerge, marking an achievement of self-expression and the fulfilment of an independent approach to design at the time when rigid Classical rules were finally becoming outmoded. The emphasis on rotundity, accompanied often by a certain plasticity, produced pieces of novel form. The all-important element was comfort. It was this which made such an earnest appeal equally to the commercial producer and to the growing mass of the public, who rated comfort far above aesthetic considerations or adherence to approved historical styles.

The Naturalistic style remains largely anonymous; its designers and makers are almost all unknown. It is perhaps best represented in the pattern books of Henry Lawford, 'architectural designer and lithographer', who published a number of undistinguished designs beginning, as far as is known, about the mid-1840s and extending beyond 1850. His is a record of what can justifiably be described as the average taste of the late 1840s and 1850s. His earliest publication appears to be the *Chair and Sofa Manufacturers' Book of Designs* (*c.* 1845), to be followed in the 1850s by two very small volumes of chair designs. He presents commercial versions of seating furniture in historical styles, but his obvious taste for all-over upholstery, dictated by considerations of comfort, are examples of this new Victorian style.

Variety of interpretation was a strong feature of the Naturalistic style, well illustrated by all types of seats. The typical upholstered chair of the 1840s has a broad back of curvilinear outline and a low seat with squat front cabriole legs and rear legs splayed back at a pronounced angle. The well padded seat and back have buttoned upholstery or, very frequently, Berlin woolwork. All efforts at anything like attractive form are plainly sacrificed to the demands of comfort. Such chairs, which are also of course found with Louis Quatorze and other historical decorative details, provide one of the most commonly produced pieces in the Naturalistic style. Well-known examples of the development of the style, emerging for once from anonymity, can be seen in the chairs which were made by Henry Eyles of Bath about 1850 for the Great Exhibition and which are now in the Victoria and Albert Museum. Made of walnut, they have carved and pierced naturalistic ornament and marquetry decoration, and have a Worcester porcelain plaque set in the back. The single chair, which has its plaque of Queen Victoria framed in scroll-work, achieves with its graceful cabriole legs, a lightness and elegance appropriate to the subject of the plaque. But these elements have been lost in the corresponding armchair, which has a low seat, short thick cabriole legs and a much heavier framework of naturalistic carving for the plaque of Prince Albert on the back.

Henry Eyles also designed for the Great Exhibition the oak 'Star of Brunswick' table, which takes its name from the white Worcester porcelain star, painted and gilt, and set in the centre of the top. In this case the rich naturalistic carving of the base, which is made up of four dolphins, and of the deep frieze of the serpentine top, on which there is a continuous linked chain, illustrates another aspect of the Naturalistic style—its tendency to massive decoration of Baroque quality. In the hands of less accomplished makers and carvers such pieces could degenerate into ostentatious vulgarity.

Chair, armchair and 'Star of Brunswick' table, made by Henry Eyles of Bath for the Great Exhibition, 1851.

Right Late essays of 'Naturalistic' design; two 'Drawing-Room Couches' in Lorenzo Booth's *Original Design Book for Decorative Furniture*, 1864. A good example of the opulent curves favoured by the style.

Opposite top Sofa, *c.* 1850, papier mâché with mother-of-pearl and painted decoration in 'Naturalistic' style.

Below Mid-19th-century rosewood chair with original *gros point* and *petit point* upholstery; basically in 'Naturalistic' style but with some Louis Quatorze detail.

Below right Library sofa, carved walnut, buttoned velvet upholstery, a typical 'Naturalistic' piece of *c.* 1840.

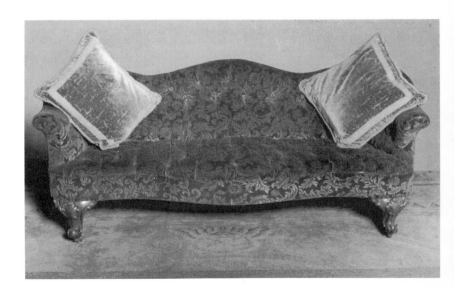

[156]

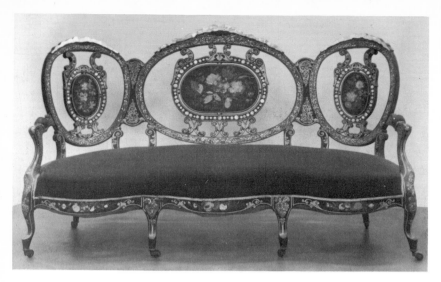

Papier mâché furniture lent itself to plastic forms and was often decorated with naturalistic details. In many ways this furniture illustrated both the limitations and the achievements of curvilinear plasticity, for while in numerous instances such forms showed little real understanding of the capabilities of the material, in others the moulded shapes were a triumph of inventiveness and heralded the various kinds of moulded furniture of the twentieth century. In examples of case furniture which assumed curved forms the decorative details frequently mixed naturalistic features with those of other styles. Naturalistic carving was often seen, for instance, on the frame of the mirror, of rounded form or D-shaped, which was commonly placed at the back of a sideboard, which itself had a rounded front flanked by convex shelves.

Whatnot, mid-19th century, papier mâché with painted and mother-of-pearl decoration; the 'mixed' character of the decoration suggests another example of the 'Naturalistic' style.

Dressing-table mirror (toilet glass), papier mâché, in 'Naturalistic' style of the mid-century; the relationship with Louis Quatorze taste is evident.

The touches of rotundity in the novel form of this papier mâché chair, c. 1840, inlaid on the back with a romantic cathedral scene, ranks it as a version of 'Naturalistic' style.

Mahogany armchair of the mid-century carved with current versions of Renaissance ornament.

'Glass Frame in the Renaissance Style', Part 22 in H. Whitaker's *Treasury of Designs*, 1847. Another example of Whitaker's interpretation of the style which he described as 'now the prevailing fashion in this country and in France'.

R. N. Wornum criticized the ornament of exhibits in 1851 for the use of 'imitations from nature as principals in the design, instead of mere accessory decorations', and summed up his impressions thus:

'This naturalist, or, as we may call it, horticultural school of ornament, has made rather inordinate progress of late, and unless at once contested by other styles, bids fair to constitute the characteristic mannerism of the Ornamental Art of the age; it seems alone to share the favour with Rococo in silver-work.'[51]

THE RENAISSANCE STYLE

The latest of the historical revivals at the time of the Great Exhibition was that of the Renaissance. Its advocates had youthful fervour on their side; the very term 'Renaissance', for the revival of art and letters in Italy under the influence of Classical models, became current only in the 1840s.[52] Whitaker's *Treasury of Designs* has a dozen illustrations of pieces of furniture in this style, made up of five items of seating (three chairs, a seat and a couch), three tables (writing, pier and console), two frames for glasses, a chiffonier and a window cornice.[53] These show no departure from the accepted principle of illustrating a fashionable style by adding, in this case, supposedly Renaissance decoration to standard forms. A glass frame, for instance (Part 22 in the *Treasury*), professes to be 'in the Renaissance style, now the prevailing fashion in this country and in France', by including a miscellany of foliage, flowers, birds, fruit, and a central mask in its cresting. Whitaker's Part 6, illustrating two

'Couch in the Renaissance Style', Part 8 in H. Whitaker's *Treasury of Designs*, 1847. Whitaker's version of the Renaissance relied mainly on exuberant use of foliage and floral decoration in concession to contemporary taste.

writing tables, one in the Elizabethan style, the other in the Renaissance, makes the situation even clearer. Both tables are identical in construction and shape, except that the Elizabethan example has a stretcher about half way up the standards (i.e. trestle end-supports), while the other is without a stretcher, unless, Whitaker writes, a low one is required 'to be stuffed as a foot-stool, as is sometimes done in this description of table'. The Renaissance 'style' is simply denoted by arches and pendants on the cornice and by scrolls incorporating lions' heads at the

Above left Whitaker was far more interested in the 'Italian Style' than in any other. His more formal approach to Classical models is clear in this 'Sideboard and Wine Cooler' designed for the Conservative Club in Part 18 of his *Treasury of Designs*, 1847.

Above 'Chair in the Italian Style', presented to the Rev. Mr Andrews by the parishioners of St James's, Westminster, in Part 10 of H. Whitaker's *Treasury of Designs*, 1847.

Left 'Wing Chiffonier in the Italian Style', Part 9 in H. Whitaker's *Treasury of Designs*, 1847. Similarity to the Elizabethan style is obvious.

base of the standards, here shaped like elongated pillars. The usual kind of strapwork decoration identifies the Elizabethan version.

Fortunately the definition of the Renaissance, in the terms in which it was understood by the early Victorians, is available to us in Wornum's prize essay, in which there was enthusiastic acceptance of the merits of Renaissance ornament in general and of the Cinquecento in particular. The dividing line between 'Renaissance' and 'Cinquecento' is put by Wornum as occurring about 1550. Before that date the Cinquecento, the 'real goal of the Renaissance', was 'the culminating style in Ornamental Art' with 'the most perfect forms and the most pleasing varieties'. The 'mixed Cinquecento or Renaissance' was the style that developed in Italy in the second half of the sixteenth century.[54]

Wornum's own classification of the chief phases of the Renaissance are named as the Trecento (the 'mixture of Venetian and Siculo-Norman, the Venetian being purely Byzantine in its origin'), Quattrocento, pure Cinquecento and mixed Cinquecento or Renaissance. These divisions, to us so arbitrary, were widely accepted at the time, even by Richard Redgrave, who wrote the *Supplementary Report on Design* of the Exhibition and who described the Renaissance or mixed Cinquecento as 'the best understood style' practised by 'the most able designers of Italy, France, Austria, Belgium and England'.[55]

Wornum gives us an analysis of what he considers typical Renaissance ornament:

'A design containing all the elements indiscriminately, can be designated only by the vague term Renaissance; and such a design may contain the classical orders and ornaments combined with conventional Byzantine scroll-work, Moorish tracery and interlacings, scrolled shields, fiddle-shapes, and strap-work, natural imitations of animal or vegetable forms of every description, and the grotesque arabesques. Such is the mixture we find in the works of Benvenuto Cellini, and also in the great majority of the foreign cabinet and silver-work in the Exhibition.'[56]

Wornum was naturally in the opposite camp to the Gothicists. He scoffed at Pugin's Medieval Court as 'strangely misnamed . . . as if the Gothic were the only medieval style or even the medieval style *par excellence*' (he maintained that the Romanesque, Byzantine, Saracenic and several Italian varieties were infinitely more extensive in their influence in the Middle Ages than the Gothic, which he limited mainly to the neighbourhood of the Rhine and bordering countries and which was comparatively short lived).[57] In his review of furniture in the Renaissance taste he cites a number of 1851 exhibits, most of which are illustrated in the *Art-Journal Illustrated Catalogue*. The style was certainly international, for among the examples were pieces by foreign

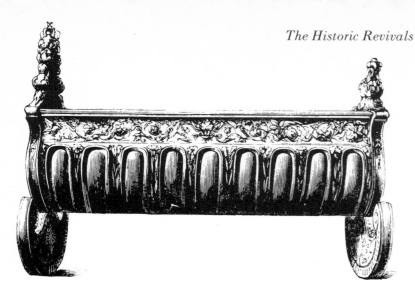

The celebrated boxwood cradle, executed for the Queen by W. G. Rogers and exhibited at the Great Exhibition, 1851; selected by R. N. Wornum as an example of 'the Cinquecento in its purity'.

firms: Barbetti of Florence (walnut cabinet), Fourdinois of Paris (sideboard), Leistler of Vienna (bedstead), and Wirth of Stuttgart (dressing table and wardrobe). But there is special interest for us in the English furniture which Wornum selects as 'admirable specimens of the Cinquecento in its purity'. These are the Queen's well-known cradle by Rogers, the bookcase by Holland and Sons and the three sideboards exhibited by Levien, Johnstone and Jeanes, and Hoyles.[58]

'The work of the greatest pretension in the collection', Holland and Sons' prize-winning chimney-piece and bookcase, in Cinquecento taste, exhibited at the Great Exhibition, 1851.

Rogers's cradle was obviously influenced by the carved decoration which was typical of Italian Cinquecento furniture, reminiscent, for example, of the repetitive gadrooning on fashionable cassoni of sarcophagus form. But pride of place for an English exhibit in what was described as full Cinquecento taste was given by Wornum to Holland and Sons's prize-winning chimney-piece and bookcase, 'the work of the greatest pretension in the collection'. But even here there were modifications of judgement:

'The ornamental details are in the Cinquecento taste, and are beautifully executed, but as a whole the design expresses much more the feeling of the ordinary Renaissance, notwithstanding the absence of the cartouches and strap-work; the somewhat Moorish feeling of the tracery of the doors supplies the place of the latter.'[59]

This monumental piece is one of the few furniture exhibits of 1851 that can claim the double distinction of having survived to the present day and of being fully documented in the makers' ledgers, for in 1852 it was sold to T. B. Hildyard of Eaton Square for £500. It remains in the possession of the purchaser's descendants and is now at Flintham Hall, Newark, Nottinghamshire. It was designed by the architect, T. R. Macquoid, who is otherwise wrapped in obscurity. Here is the description of the 'decoration for the side of a room' in Holland and Sons's accounts:

'. . . divided into 3 compartments, the centre part appropriated to a fire place united by a richly ornamented Entablature at 11 ft from the ground; the frieze diversified with bold carvings and inlays of marble, the cornice surmounted by niches, the centre one in each compartment raised higher than the others for the reception of works of art in marble or bronze.
The pillasters [sic] of the bookcases filled with the most elaborate and highly relieved carvings representing Birds and Boys disporting amid the foliage and fruit of the vine, lofty circular headed doors of perforated metal opens [sic] between the pillasters; the spandrils [sic] and imposts of arches inlaid with marbles beneath this an elaborate long panel in high relief filled with boys fighting with nondescripts amid the branches and leaves of the oak.
The pedestals immediately beneath the pilasters also richly carved and support shields brought forward to receive figures or armorial bearings. The doors of the lower portion are filled in with panels of the ivy leaf and berry in full relief very delicately sculptured; from the dados of the pedestals at the side of these project bosses of marble (Mona and lizard) the lower portion of the chimney piece is of red marble from Mona finely varied in color; a bold richly ornamented cornice of wood occupies the place of the usual marble slab and above this divided by

Mahogany sideboard, exhibited by Johnstone and Jeanes at the Great Exhibition, 1851; described by the *Art-Journal Illustrated Catalogue* as 'Italian of the best period'.

Walnut sideboard designed and made by H. Hoyle of Sheffield and exhibited at the Great Exhibition, 1851; another example in what was considered pure Cinquecento style.

small pillars full of carvings are three niches for vases or figures.
The style may be termed Cinque Cento but with a freer application of
natural forms; the principal feature of this elaborate work of art is that
the whole has been designed and executed by English people and all
articles employed both wood and marble are of English production.
£500.'[60]

The emphasis on the native contribution ('the principal feature') to an object inspired by the purest ideals of early sixteenth-century Italy is certainly worth special note.

GEORGE BULLOCK

George Bullock was probably the earliest of the pioneers in the Regency furniture world to experiment in new styles, materials and decorative media.[61] His influence was at its greatest during the Napoleonic Wars, when his work caught up the wave of patriotic enthusiasm that swept the country. To contemporaries his distinction was his employment of native woods and materials for fashionable furniture and his use of native plants and flowers for decoration. He also interpreted the mood of the times with his revival of national styles, in which Romanticism was combined with antiquarianism. It was not only the Gothic which concerned him, for he could also claim credit for the introduction of the Elizabethan taste. As has been noted, the plate of three fashionable chairs 'from the repository of Mr. Bullock', which appeared in Ackermann's *Repository of Arts* in September 1817, included the first-known publication of a chair in Elizabethan style, in the version that was to become current in the first half of the century. As a designer of fashionable furniture he was inevitably influenced by French fashions, but even here an anglicized rendering was apparent in his production of 'English buhl'. In addition to his activities as cabinet-maker and upholsterer he was a sculptor, marble mason and owner of an antiques depository. He had a national reputation, with commissions in Scotland as well as England. His well-known business in London, whence he came from Liverpool, was established for only five years, for his name first appears in the London *Post Office Directory* in 1813, as upholsterer, and he died in 1818, as recorded in the *Gentleman's Magazine* of May of that year: 'May 1st—Tenterden street Hanover-square, suddenly, Mr. Bullock, proprietor of the Mona Marble Works'. It is worth noting that Bullock's work in developing the fashions that were accepted features of the early Victorian scene was accomplished before the end of George III's reign. His special contributions to furniture were widely acknowledged at the time.

The most powerful medium for the transmission of Bullock's achieve-

Early 19th-century mahogany cabinet, cross-banded in kingwood and finely inlaid with brass and ebony borders in the manner of George Bullock.

ments was the *Repository of Arts*, which published six plates of his furniture and upholstery designs between February 1816 and September 1817, and a seventh, posthumous plate ('by the late Mr. G. Bullock') in June 1824. As early as February 1816 the *Repository* pays tribute to Bullock's enterprise in thus describing a cabinet by him:

'designed for execution in our native woods, relieved by inlaid metal ornaments; a style happily introduced both in respect of taste and true patriotism. There are no woods more beautiful, or better suited to the purpose of cabinet embellishment than those indigenous to our own country.'

But Bullock's production of 'English buhl' did not pass without criticism. Two years after his death Richard Brown, whose use of symbolic ornament has already been described, had this comment to make on Bullock's work in *Rudiments of Drawing Cabinet and Upholstery Furniture*, 1820:

'The late Mr. Bullock was the only person who ventured into a new path: though some of his designs were certainly too massy and ponderous, nevertheless grandeur cannot be obtained without it; such are the standards to his octagon tables. There was great novelty without absurdity, as well as happy relief, in his ornaments; yet many of his articles were considerably overcharged with buhl; sometimes the buhl-work was sunk in brass, and on other occasions the counterpart was of the same wood as the furniture itself, and the whole surface presented a brazen front.'

Brown, however, reiterates the *Repository's* praise of Bullock's use of native material for construction and decoration:

'Most of his ornaments were selected from British plants, and his woods were of English growth, which were admirably well polished. He has shewn that we need not roam to foreign climes for beautiful ornaments, but that we have abundance of plants and flowers equal to the Grecian, which, if adopted, would be found as pleasing as the antique.'[62]

Before he came to London, Bullock exhibited sculpture at the Royal Academy from 1804 and continued to do so after he arrived in the capital until 1816, when presumably the growth of his furniture business occupied all his attention. He was president of the Liverpool Academy between 1810 and 1811. His sculpture had distinct quality. In Liverpool he had also been briefly in partnership with Joseph Gandy, who had trained as an architect under James Wyatt, and was known as 'the English Piranesi' for his architectural fantasies, which he exhibited at the Royal Academy almost continuously between 1789 and 1838. Gandy also, in complete contrast, published designs for cottages of marked simplicity. Bullock seems to have been related to William Bullock, who owned the Liverpool Museum; both men had the same London address in 1813–Grecian Rooms, Egyptian Hall, Piccadilly (this building was completed in 1812)–until George Bullock moved, by 1815, to Tenterden Street. Bullock had developed two marble quarries in Anglesey, which produced stone with colours resembling porphyry and verde antique. This is the 'Mona marble' which gave its name to the London premises.

The *Repository's* illustrations of Bullock's work underline his importance as well as confirming his versatility. Bryan Reade, whose researches were the first to rescue Bullock from almost complete obscurity, rightly describes him as the man 'whose style dominated fashionable furniture design in the years after Waterloo'.[63] Significantly, five issues of the *Repository* in 1816, the first full year of peace, devote their 'Fashionable Furniture' section to Bullock. The February issue shows a 'Drawing-room Window-curtain' in addition to the cabinet 'in our native woods relieved by inlaid metal ornaments'. In May appears a view of part of the Tenterden Street manufactory with a collection of Grecian furniture consisting 'of a sofa, monopodium, footstool, pictures and drapery, affording a specimen of harmonious decoration and colouring'. There are cabinets attached to the sofa in the form of elegant pedestals for portfolios and manuscripts, surmounted by 'fine specimens of the Mona verd-antique marble' and 'enriched by bhule [*sic*] and or-molu'. A 'Mona Marble Chimney-Piece' is the subject in the October issue, with the note that this marble had 'so considerably increased in reputation and fashion'. These chimney pieces were specialities of Bullock's firm and were often decorated with ormolu. An 'English Bed' by Bullock in the November number was selected, so runs the text, 'for the tasteful simplicity that pervades it'. This was no doubt an answer to the fashionable ornate French beds of the time, a challenge indeed to the example illustrated by the *Repository* in the previous April, when it was described as reflecting 'the reciprocal exchanges of British and French taste'. In December there is another plate showing drawing-room window curtains.

Between the September 1817 issue and its launching of the Elizabethan style and the final illustration of Bullock's work there is a gap of almost seven years, for it is not until June 1824 that a group of drawing-room furniture—table, chairs and footstools—is shown. All are in the Grecian taste, 'continued with much taste by the chief upholsterers of the day', to be executed in rosewood, partly gilt, with ornaments in carved satinwood. The publication of this plate six years after Bullock's death coincided with the determined reaction in the 1820s in favour of the Classical taste.

It is not an uncommon occurrence in the course of researches into the history of English furniture to unearth the name of a cabinet-maker and designer who was obviously of considerable importance in his own day but who has been almost completely forgotten since. Once the importance of such a man has been confirmed, the next step is to try to trace his furniture. In the case of Bullock, who fits into this category, the veil was lifted a little by reference in the letters of Maria Edgeworth who saw 'fine tables of Bullock's making, one of wood from Brazil—Zebra wood—and no more to be had of it for love or money' in April 180 ft of timber.[67] Bullock used larch on the spot, light in colour and cabinet of 1815–20 with 'G. Bullock' branded on the fore-edge of each drawer.[65] It is made of rosewood and is inlaid with brass and with other woods. But for the recent discovery of furniture by Bullock, which adds considerably to our knowledge, we are indebted to the researches of Anthony Coleridge.[66] Important identified pieces are in Scotland, where Bullock had wealthy clients. Bills from his firm survive at Blair

Octagonal table, *c.* 1818, rosewood, with brass and ebony inlay of floral and leaf design, in the manner of George Bullock.

Section of brass inlay, thyrsis and bacchic mask.

Castle, Perthshire, where he was patronized by the fourth Duke of Atholl between 1814 and 1819. The 'planting Duke' was widely known for his interest in forestry, particularly for his cultivation of larch trees. Louis Simond, whose travels in Britain in 1810–11 have been noted, recorded that the Duke had 'not mere patches, but whole mountains clothed with trees' and that a single larch, sixty years old, had yielded 180 ft of timber.[67] Bullock used larch on the spot, light in colour and simply figured. The State Drawing Room at Blair Castle has his two best-known pieces in this timber–a pair of dwarf cabinets with panelled doors enclosing drawers and shelves. They are decorated with buhl-work in continuous strips of floral and foliate motifs against an ebonized background; these run across the top and bottom of the front, and frame the central panels on the doors. Each of these central panels is made up of four oyster pieces and each cabinet has a top of polished Glen Tilt marble from the local quarries. For the two cabinets the firm originally charged £120–the account was dated February 1819, after Bullock's death–but this was reduced to forty guineas each. No reason was given for this reduction–it may be due to the fact that the Duke had been charged £45 in 1817 for a similar cabinet (now lost) and objected to paying more for the present pair–but Georgian furniture-makers' accounts, including those submitted to the royal family, abound in alterations from the original to lower prices. The two Glen Tilt marble tops cost £10. 17s.

Other pieces of larchwood furniture made by Bullock for the Duke were a sofa table and three circular tables, of which all except one of the tables survive at Blair Castle. Their price was six guineas each in the bill of December 1817. 'Bog oak from the Isle of Man' was used by Bullock for two tables which he supplied in 1814. One cost £21; it has a pillar and tripod base, and a circular top inlaid with brass ornament in the repetitive foliate pattern associated with Bullock. The other table, four-legged with rectangular top, cost fourteen guineas. It was originally a worktable, but has lost its blue velvet bag. Its top bears an inlaid panel of Glen Tilt marble. The wood for these two tables may have connection with the fact that the Dukes of Atholl were hereditary Lords of Man prior to the Jacobite Revolt of 1745, when they lost their title. A third table of ebonized wood, supplied by Bullock in 1814 at a cost of eighteen guineas, has its octagonal top inlaid with a pattern of varied marbles.

It is very probable that Bullock's influence did much to further the use of British marbles in furniture-making. He himself combined the functions of sculptor and entrepreneur of marble quarries. A whole field of research surely lies open for a study of his chimney-pieces, about which almost nothing is known at present. As noted above, in May 1816 the *Repository* commented on Bullock's use of Mona verd-antique

marble as part of his designs of library furniture. This is an early reference to the return to fashion of marble in English furniture. The lighter pieces of furniture of the Hepplewhite and Sheraton periods had put marble out of favour, but with the revival of heavier and stronger furniture marble from all parts of Britain, together with fluorspar and coloured stones – these native varieties, like native timbers, suited the patriotic sentiment of the times – were now in general demand for the tops of tables, commodes, cabinets, pedestals and washstands. Bullock employed the two popular methods of complete slabs and varied specimens made up into chequered patterns. Mosaic work was also in favour, usually with ornaments of English flowers. Marble was so

Dwarf larchwood cabinet decorated with buhl-work, supplied to Blair Castle, Perthshire, by George Bullock, 1819.

prominently displayed as a component of furniture at the Great Exhibition that it stimulated the use of slate, among other cheaper substitutes.

Bullock's name has been associated with the furniture supplied to Abbotsford, the famous home of Sir Walter Scott.[68] Bullock was a personal friend of Scott, who refers to him many times in his letters with obvious warmth. Between 1816 and 1818 Bullock collaborated with William Atkinson, the architect who was a pioneer of the 'baronial' style, on the interior decoration of Scott's house. Bullock designed for Scott a cast of Shakespeare's bust at Stratford-on-Avon, which was set on a fine cabinet and was described by Scott in a letter of 1816 as 'positively the most elegant and appropriate piece of furniture which I ever saw. It has been the admiration of all who have seen it, and that has been half Edinburgh'. But precise evidence concerning Bullock's responsibility for other Abbotsford furniture is unfortunately lacking. The evidence has been examined in detail by Dr James C. Corson, Honorary Librarian of Abbotsford. It is clear that Bullock supplied Scott with material from his antiquarian depository for his collection of arms and armour, and also sent doors and windows to the house; it is also evident that Bullock's death on 1 May 1818 interrupted the arrangements for the supply of furniture. In an unpublished letter of 15 May 1818 Daniel Terry, the actor and playwright who was a close friend, writes to Scott giving him an account of Bullock's death and of the work completed in his workshop. He refers to doors and windows but not to furniture. Scott writes to Terry three days later:

'There was much furniture, grates, sideboard, dining tables, etc. which our poor friend was to have furnished and which may perhaps be still got from his warehouse better than elsewhere.'

Well over a year after Bullock's death Scott was still dealing with his firm, for in a letter of 19 September 1819 he paid 'Messrs. Bullock and Coy.' an outstanding bill of £430 with a note in the covering letter that 'the sideboard came safe and is extremely beautiful'. Dr Corson's conclusions are that William Atkinson designed the dining-room sideboard and wine cooler, and that Bullock's firm made the dining-room tables, the cabinet to hold extra leaves, and the cabinet for Shakespeare's bust. It is likely, of course, that the firm may well have made the pieces designed by Atkinson, as indeed appears to be the case with the sideboard. All the dining-room pieces are in light oak. The sideboard and dining table—the latter is of the 'Imperial' extending type—have plain turned legs and their simple design is different from that of other furniture definitely associated with Bullock. Tradition states that the table was made by Bullock from old oak trees on the estate of Drumlanrig Castle.[69]

BUHL-WORK

The 'English buhl' produced by Bullock was another instance of the force of French influence, for this was the first time that English craftsmen had undertaken any considerable imitation of the famous technique of inlay in brass and tortoiseshell (and other materials) perfected by A. C. Boulle (1642–1732), *ébéniste* to Louis XIV. Boulle furniture had never gone out of fashion in France; it continued to be made throughout the eighteenth century and had indeed undergone a distinct revival just prior to the Revolution. Some fine examples of this decorated furniture were bought by the Prince Regent for Carlton House and some excellent pieces were later in Brighton Pavilion. The Prince's purchases set a fashion among members of the English aristocracy, and English craftsmen seized the opportunity offered by the new market. English imitation of the French technique appeared early. In 1810 George Oakley of 8 Old Bond Street supplied the Prince Regent with 'a capital mahogany pedestal library-table inlaid with Buhl bordering' for £84. In 1815 the French craftsman, Louis Le Gaigneur, established a 'Buhl factory' at 19 Queen Street, Edgware Road, and in the same year sold 'a buhl library table' to the Prince Regent for Carlton House for the sum of £250. This may refer to one of a pair of

Card table, *c.* 1810, rosewood, the top decorated with crossbanding of cut-brass scrollwork, the frieze inlaid with *contre-partie* brass; inlaid brass scrollwork on the base.

The post-1800 revival of marquetry furniture: a commode of *c.* 1820, rosewood veneer on mahogany and pine, decorated with boulle panels and gilt brass ornament.

Knee-hole writing table veneered on pine with *contre-partie* boulle marquetry of pewter, brass, copper and shell; made by Louis Le Gaigneur, a Frenchman, of the 'Buhl Manufactory', 19 Queen Street, Edgware Road, London, c. 1815

signed tables now at Windsor Castle. They are the same in form and decoration as a signed knee-hole writing table in the Wallace Collection. The latter, rectangular in shape, is supported on eight square canted legs, four on each side of the knee-hole, and is in full Louis XIV style. Another English producer early on the scene was Thomas Parker, Buhl Manufacturer of Air Street, Piccadilly. In the late 1830s Town and Emanuel, 103 New Bond Street, advertised themselves on their trade card as 'Manufacturers of Buhl Marqueterie, Reisner and Carved Furniture'.[70]

Bullock's dwarf cabinets typify the Louis Quatorze forms that were adopted, very naturally, for buhl-work. Large commodes of early eighteenth-century French inspiration are among other fashionable pieces of the later Regency. George Siddons, in the 1830 edition of his *Cabinet-Maker's Guide*, refers to buhl-work as 'a term of modern date' and follows with full directions which, he trusts, 'will soon enable the ingenious mechanic to accomplish that which has hitherto been monopolized by foreigners', with the conviction that 'British artists will equal if not outdo their rivals'. He defines the method as 'inlaying with turtle or tortoiseshell, with brass or silver'.[71]

Rosewood library table, *c.* 1815,
pillar and base in *contre-partie*
boulle marquetry in the manner of
Louis Le Gaigneur.

Clifford Musgrave has analysed the pattern of English brass inlay-work in two main categories. In the earlier stage spaced-out groups of patterns are found, usually small foliate and floral forms or classical motifs. Sometimes these occur as a small chain or, again, in a larger open grouping, but still employing a relatively small number of patterns. Later, under the influence of the Louis Quatorze vogue of the later 1820s and afterwards, the patterns become more elaborate and are designed in continuous rows, with the use now of arabesques and chinoiseries reminiscent of the designs of Bérain, the most influential designer of the later part of Louis XIV's reign. The continuous row or strip of brass is sometimes composed of the foliate and floral ornaments of the earlier phase, but now in more delicate form, running round, for instance, the top or frieze of a table.[72]

By 1850 buhl-work was particularly associated with china cabinets, commodes and small tables. Turtleshell, mentioned by Siddons, was used for cheaper work; otherwise red or green tortoiseshell and brass remained the chief materials.

Brass had certainly established itself as an important cabinet-making material in the first half of the century. Its cheapness and durability,

Opposite top 'Marqueterie Centre Table', Plate 16 in R. Bridgens's *Furniture with Candelabra*, 1838. This design, the top decorated with marquetry of English flowers in a border of acanthus leaves, bears a close relationship with the walnut table at Ickworth, Suffolk (*see* jacket illustrations).

Right Boulle decoration persisted into the 1840s, when case furniture took on rounded forms; this English boulle cabinet has four gilt bronze-mounted Gothic pinnacles.

Opposite bottom Marquetry of flowers decorates this walnut cabinet of the mid-century. The craftsmanship is of a very high standard.

recommended by Sheraton in his *Cabinet Dictionary* of 1803, had particular appeal during the war years, and at the time it made an attractive contrast to the fashionable dark glossy woods. First used in simple lines or stringing round drawer fronts and edges of tables, it had largely supplanted woods for this purpose by about 1812. Later it was put to a wide variety of uses on furniture – as colonnettes, trellis work, galleries, lion paw feet, lion mask handles, etc. – quite apart from the patterned inlay-work referred to above.

MARQUETRY

Marquetry, 'now lately revived in our cabinet work' as Siddons wrote in 1825, was, like 'English buhl', another English counter to the challenge of French buhl-work.[73] In the 1830s and 1840s there was a fashion for marquetry of leaf designs in holly, which developed into floral and foliate work of detailed character. This work was mentioned in pattern books until the time of the Great Exhibition, when a number of leading firms exhibited marquetry furniture.

Richard Bridgens, in his *Furniture with Candelabra*, 1838, illustrates, on Plate 16 in the section headed 'designs in the Grecian style', a 'marqueterie centre table' with circular top and pedestal base with scrolled feet. There is a remarkably close resemblance between this design and a table now in the Drawing-Room at Ickworth, Suffolk. The top of finely figured walnut has a marquetry decoration of English flowers in the centre and a continuous leaf design round its edge. The floral pattern is also found on the base. The quality of the craftsmanship throughout this piece is very high.

Henry Whitaker's *Treasury of Designs*, 1847, illustrates several examples of marquetry. It is recommended as suitable decoration in four designs of tables, and on the front panels of a chiffonier in Louis Quatorze style. On one table top, for which the best ground, it is suggested, is walnut on a body of amboyna or maple, the figure of a swan is shown, composed of mother-of-pearl and ivory. Whitaker adds in this instance (Part 1, fig. 4): 'everything of the sort being exceedingly

Table, carved mahogany, the top decorated with marquetry, designed by Henry Whitaker for the Conservative Club, 1844.

Detail of the table top, with rose, thistle and shamrock decoration.

well executed at the present day, it would be superfluous to say more'. In the case of another table, a 'Fancy Coffee Table and Loo Table' (Part 16, fig. 4) in the Elizabethan style, the text states that it is 'calculated to receive marquetry ornaments with advantage'.

Although carving proved the outstanding decorative technique at the 1851 Exhibition, marquetry furniture of obvious quality was shown. Trollope and Sons, Banting, Snell and Co., Smee and Son, Gillow and Co., and Dowbiggin were among the eminent firms who exhibited such furniture. Trollope and Sons had a complete bedroom suite–bedstead, wardrobe, drapery table, toilette glass and washstand–'inlaid in marqueterie worked with woods in their natural colours'.[74] In general tables were clearly the favourite pieces for this decoration. There certainly seems no evidence for the contention that marquetry passed into abeyance between about 1830 and 1855.

JOHN B. PAPWORTH

John Buonarotti Papworth (1775–1847), architect, landscape gardener and designer of furniture, glassware, metalwork and other 'art works', achieved a considerable reputation as one of the most prolific and versatile designers of the period between 1815 and his retirement in 1846.[75] His work bridges the gap between late Georgian and early Victorian

[176]

design. No man of the time presaged more clearly the dichotomy of mid-century taste – on the one hand eager interest in and understanding of new materials and processes, and on the other love of eclectic ornament under the spell of prevailing historicism. He won great acclaim from his contemporaries. He was eight times vice-president of the Institute of British Architects, which he helped to found in 1834, and was the first director of the new Government School of Design in 1837–8. His work was known in Europe and America – he complained in Paris in 1824 that many of his designs were plagiarized there – and in 1820 he was granted the title of 'Architect to the King of Wurtemburg'. From 1825 he developed the Montpellier and Landsdowne estates in Cheltenham, and between 1825–30 he laid out the Brockwell estate for John Blades at Dulwich, in Regency Greek taste at its best.

Papworth was an artist of ability and exhibited at the Royal Academy on a number of occasions. Nine portfolios of his drawings, now in the library of the Royal Institute of British Architects, illustrate his facility in figure as well as in architectural subjects. He became the friend of the publisher Rudolf Ackermann, redesigning his premises at 101 Strand, and was a regular contributor to the *Repository of Arts* between 1812 and 1823. Seventy-six coloured plates from the *Repository* were published separately by Ackermann in 1816 under Papworth's name as *Select Views in London*, and in 1818 a series of papers and plates previously contributed to the *Repository* by Papworth were published as *Rural Residences* (there was a second edition in 1832). In literary work he was a prolific as in architecture and design. In addition to his contributions to the *Repository* he published, among many other writings, a standard technical treatise on dry rot in buildings, and descriptions of buildings in H. W. Pyne's well-known works. In 1826

The Library, Cranbury Park, Hampshire, with fittings designed by J. B. Papworth, *c.* 1831.

he edited, with copious notes, the fourth edition of Sir William Chambers's *Treatise on Civil Architecture*, the standard English work on the use of the Classical orders. His all-round skill was amazing. He was the first architect to use the 'severed column' as a monument, and it was his drawing of a 'Tropheum' to record the battle of Waterloo that led his friends to acclaim him as a second Michelangelo and induce him to add 'Buonarotti' to his name.

So much for Papworth's versatility. We know far more about him than about any other designer of his period, for he was fortunate in his biographer, his son Wyatt, the founder of the Architectural Publications Society and the editor of that Society's *Dictionary of Architecture*.[76] This biography is quite remarkably free from the pious and effusive eulogy that is so characteristic of the usual run of Victorian biographies. Published in 1879, it is firmly based on family papers, which are freely quoted, and includes an autobiographical fragment left by J. B. Papworth himself. What is puzzling, though a natural enough result of the neglect, until recently, of the study of the furniture design of the immediate post-Georgian period, is the almost complete dearth of identified furniture by Papworth in spite of the abundant evidence of his great activities as a designer. Apart from Boodle's Club, for which Papworth designed furniture, including that of the Reading Room in 1821, and where the present suite in Grecian taste and that in the Dining-Room may be assigned to him (although the accounts do not appear to have survived) and the library furniture at Cranbury Park, Hampshire, where he was concerned with the fittings about 1831, there is nothing to show for his many busy years. Yet Papworth's special concern with furniture design was commented upon by the architect C. R. Cockerell, when making a speech on the occasion of Papworth's retirement in 1846, and presenting him with a silver inkstand. He referred to

'the changes of taste in the various departments of manufactured art, which had all benefited in turns by Mr. Papworth's employment of them from his own designs (especially furniture)'.[77]

Fortunately Wyatt Papworth's biography makes quite clear the variety and eclecticism of his father's furniture designs. Papworth's own early career also provides a clue to his future designs.

He was originally intended for a medical career, but turned to architecture on the advice of Sir William Chambers who employed Papworth's father, the leading stuccoist of the day, at the Office of Works, and who recognized the boy's artistic talents. Papworth's professional and artistic training proceeded side by side. He learned drawing from the sculptor John Dare, and perspective from Thomas Malton. He exhibited at the Royal Academy from 1791 and entered the

Academy Schools in 1798. He meanwhile spent two years in the office of John Plaw, the designer of Picturesque cottages, three years in practical instruction with the builder, Thomas Wapshott, and a period with Sheringham of Great Marlborough Street 'in the study of internal decoration (and fresco work) as then practised, it having been lately introduced from France by Mr. Sheringham and was making its way into general use'. The picture begins to take shape. Papworth's training was firmly rooted in the Classical tradition; his best known buildings, those at Cheltenham, are excellent examples of late Classical elegance. Through Plaw he gained working knowledge of *cottages ornés* and their interiors, expressions of the romantic Gothic revival within the framework of the Picturesque. Sheringham, who had brought French craftsmen to work under Henry Holland's direction at Carlton House, gave Papworth valuable experience of French Neo-Classicism in the early 1790s.

Papworth always took the view that the design of articles in common use was properly within the province of the architect. He made this clear as witness before the Select Committee on Arts and Manufactures in 1835. When asked if he thought that there was 'sufficient intelligence in art exhibited in such works as furniture in this country', he replied: 'I think not, unless designed by the architect himself. If he will not give his attention to it, the taste of the furniture is not good in this country, or not so good as it might be.' On this same occasion he took the opportunity of praising the work of Percier and Fontaine and of condemning the Rococo revival of the 1820s for not being, as it claimed to be, the grand style of Louis XIV, but the spurious designs of his successor.[78]

Papworth's furniture designs were, no doubt, responsive to the demands of his patrons. Though he numbered members of the royal family and of the aristocracy among these, his clients were mainly bankers, industrialists, prosperous tradesmen and business men, who represented a relatively new and increasingly important class. He designed a great deal of furniture for them, in some instances for their business premises as well as for their private residences. Shop fronts, showrooms, factories, warehouses and workshops were all designed by him, with their interior equipment. New materials and constructional methods, the products of the industrial age, were quickly taken up. He was a pioneer in the design of new shop fronts, using the plate glass produced by improved manufacturing processes in place of the standard small panes of Newcastle crown glass. The new gas lighting, for which Papworth designed fitments, enabled larger and brighter window displays to be made.

As a designer of furniture Papworth was closely associated with three leading London firms: W. and E. Snell of 15 Hanover Street, Long Acre, cabinet-makers and upholsterers (with a royal appointment at the beginning of Victoria's reign); George Morant, decorator, of New Bond Street; and John Blades, glass manufacturer, of Ludgate Hill. For all three firms, Papworth also designed new showrooms and workshops. He is known to have designed workshops between 1830 and 1832 in the Grays Inn Road for G. and T. Seddon, and large open sheds, including the veneer drying sheds, for the same firm in 1836. These must have been large premises, for they were later used as a hospital. It is uncertain, however, whether he designed furniture for Seddons.[79]

For many years Papworth's closest commercial links were with Snells. He altered their premises in 1823, supplied furniture designs for them between 1824 and 1830, and between 1829 and 1835 designed their extensive workshops in the Belgrave Road. No furniture made by this firm appears so far to have been identified, but they are known to have specialized in the French Empire style. It seems reasonable to credit Papworth with designing in this style, not only through his connection with the firm, but also because of his expressed admiration for Percier and Fontaine and his dislike of the Rococo.

Papworth began designing glassware for Blades in 1816 and continued to do so for many years. His designs included a large Gothic lantern and lamp for Lord Grosvenor at Eaton Hall, Gothic lustres, a church chandelier, a glass chair of state for the Shah of Persia (1822) and an elaborate sherbert service for the Pasha of Egypt. He made a very important contribution to the development of chandeliers when he suggested to Blades lustres of long oblong drops full of prismatic colours, and these became so much appreciated by the public that the small and long, oval- or diamond-shaped drops went out of fashion. In April 1823 the *Repository* published an illustration by A. C. Pugin of Blades's Upper Show Room, which had been designed by Papworth in 1821. The view shows these lustres with long stalactite pendants hung from a canopy and base on a gilt metal framework.

Very little is known of Papworth's relationship with Morant. Wyatt Papworth records that his father had first met Morant when they were both pupils of Sheringham and later supplied Morant with many designs for decoration between 1808 and 1818. About 1817 Morant sent Papworth a specimen of the imitation of maple wood. This indicates Papworth's interest in the current fashion for staining and graining woods to imitate fashionable timbers, but whether this interest extended to furniture, or was directed only towards shop fronts and interior decoration, cannot be ascertained.

In 1820–2 Papworth designed the furniture and building of Leigham House, Brixton Hill, for J. G. Fuller, one of the proprietors of Boodle's Club, where he designed the Reading Room furniture in 1821 and other furniture in 1823. For John Allnutt of Clapham Common he designed dining-room furniture in 1821 and also, in 1825, a gas lamp – 'one of the earliest introductions of this light into a country dwelling'—and a carpet.[80] He did a great deal of designing in several houses owned by James Morrison, later MP for Inverness, and also built warehouses for Morrison's firm in Milton Street, London, designing the furniture in the chief rooms. The eclectic character of Morrison's furniture is evident from his letters to Papworth. He writes in 1838:

'I send you a writing desk as a specimen of Buhl work, and I want you to design for me merely the case of a inkstand for the Gallery. I should think that it may be in Turtle or Tortoise-shell, inlaid either with brass or pearl and with gilt or silver ornaments.'[81]

Concerning another house, Basildon Park, Hertfordshire, Morrison writes in 1842:

'The more I think of your new Indian notion for the so-called Chinese Room, the more I like it. May you be as happy as you were with the Etruscan. Pray get on with designs for Tables, Chairs or Seats, and Sofa, as well as Blinds . . . not, of course, forgetting the Picture frame made by Ackermann.'[82]

Furniture was also designed by Papworth for John Blades's house, Brockwell Hall, Dulwich (1824–9) and for Park Hill, Streatham (1830–5).

According to the *Dictionary of Architecture* (1853–92) many of the examples of furniture in the Grecian style pictured in Loudon's *Encyclopaedia* of 1833 were copies of articles designed by Papworth.[83] It was obvious that Papworth had long worked in this style, for drawings of Grecian dining- and breakfast-room furniture made by him in 1814 were published in 1823 to illustrate Peter Coxe's poem *The Social Day*.[84] As noted above, in 1824 Papworth saw imitations of his designs in Paris, and at his retirement Cockerell stated that his 'designs (especially furniture) . . . had been begged, borrowed and stolen in all directions'. Twice at least Cockerell's farewell speech to Papworth makes pointed references to his furniture designs.[85] In Papworth's correspondence not all references to styles may necessarily apply to furniture; they may equally apply to interior decoration. But there is a strong presumption that they would include furniture. To the styles mentioned above we can also add designs for rustic garden furniture, appropriately enough for a landscape gardener, and we also know that some of his silver and metalwork designs were in Egyptian taste.

Above State Bedroom, Osborne House. Another good example of the good taste of the best of mid-century furniture.

Right Osborne House. Prince Albert's roll-top desk and the stool are true successors to Regency prototypes; the whatnot and harmonium are Victorian pieces. All the furniture is restrained and of good quality, reflecting mid-century conservative taste.

CHAPTER 4

THE ROYAL
FURNITURE-MAKERS

There seems to be little convincing evidence to support the contention that after the death of George IV in 1830 the court lost its position as leader of furniture fashions, or that its taste tended to be some ten years or so behind that of London society generally. Certainly neither William IV nor Victoria could match George IV's knowledge and discernment—or his extravagance—as a collector, but then only Charles I among English monarchs can rank with George IV as a patron of the arts. After 1830 the royal craftsmen revealed in their identified work a full awareness of current trends, which they interpreted with great skill. For their part the royal family were very influential in promoting the trend towards domestic comfort, which is one of the distinguishing features of early Victorian furniture. William IV's dearest wish was for a home that was to be comfortable; he wished it to be plain, without touch of gilding, which he disliked exceedingly.[1] That was why he was fond of Brighton Pavilion, where the domestic comfort and intimate scale of the rooms had special appeal for him and Queen Adelaide. But he equally appreciated the grandeur of the Pavilion's State Apartments on the occasion of royal entertaining. Victoria made a similar distinction between her private family life and official functions. And in one important respect Victoria gave a clear lead in the matter of taste. This was in the appointment of a professional designer, a lead that was to be followed extensively by commercial firms later in her reign. The first important designer of this kind was Ludwig Gruner, who was born in Dresden and after periods of residence in Milan and Rome came to England in 1841. His work in connection with the garden pavilion at Buckingham Palace in 1844 has already been described. For the 1851 Exhibition Gruner designed a number of articles exhibited by the Queen and the Prince Consort, including a jewel case in Cinquecento style, carpets, a garden seat and a candelabrum. Gruner's appointment was due to Prince Albert, to whom he acted as artistic adviser.

A royal appointment was the fulfilment of every furniture craftsman's ambition. It was a recognition of professional work of the highest calibre, and obviously firms that were granted this special status, stood to profit considerably from the opportunity for the business expansion it offered.[2] Some of the royal firms were highly successful businesses. Charles Elliott, who was first appointed to the royal service in 1784 and had premises in New Bond Street, is said to have left a fortune worth

Queen Victoria's jewelry chest designed by
Ludwig Gruner in Cinquecento style and
exhibited at the Great Exhibition, 1851.

nearly £500,000 at his death in 1832, having set out for London sixty
years earlier with only a shilling. He was succeeded as royal cabinet-
maker by William Francis, his brother-in-law and partner, and the firm
continued in the royal service until the end of Victoria's reign.[3]

The names of all the royal furniture craftsmen appear in the Lord
Chamberlain's accounts preserved in the Public Record Office, London.
The Lord Chamberlain was responsible for appointing and, if necessary, discharging the craftsmen, for ordering furniture and upholstery
from them, for directing them to the various tasks of decorating or re-
decorating, and, finally, for making payment to them when the work had
been satisfactorily completed. Firms' charges were carefully scrutinized
and were amended if they were deemed excessive. Until 1828 the Lord
Chamberlain's jurisdiction was most comprehensive, extending to all
the royal households and buildings, the royal yachts, the residences
abroad of ambassadors and colonial governors, the Houses of Parliament
and government offices, and he was responsible for any requirements

in connection with such royal occasions as coronations, weddings and funerals and with the ceremonies of the royal orders, such as the Order of the Garter. The demands were clearly becoming burdensome. During George IV's reign the quarterly lists of the sums paid to craftsmen for furnishing were divided into two categories: 'Ordinary Service', which included the royal buildings–Carlton House, Brighton Pavilion, Hampton Court Palace, St James's, Buckingham House (as Buckingham Palace was then known), Kew Palace, Kensington Palace and various cottages on the royal estates; and 'Extra Service' for all other requirements. Relief came after 1828 when the Office of Woods and Works (known as the Office, and later the Ministry of Works) assumed responsibility for the Houses of Parliament and public offices–a responsibility which was to increase considerably as government departments proliferated during Victoria's reign. Unlike the Lord Chamberlain the Office of Works put out each commission to tender.[4]

Two other significant changes occurred early in Victoria's reign: one was the great increase in the number of royal furniture craftsmen; the other was the Queen's employment of local firms, an innovation that broke the long monopoly of London firms in the royal service. During the Georgian period it was the custom for the royal family to employ only a small group of craftsmen. Until about 1830 these normally included two cabinet-makers, an upholsterer, a joiner, coffer-maker and clockmaker. As occasion arose, depending largely on the dictates of fashion, a carver and gilder, a lamp- and lustre-maker, a seamstress and embroiderer were added to the list. All these employees were centred in the capital. The inclusion of the joiner and coffer-maker in this small circle illustrates the archaic procedure that was retained at court well into the nineteenth century. These were the two oldest types of furniture craftsmen to appear in the royal records, their initial appointments dating back to Tudor times, and their ancient office entitled them, alone among their colleagues, to wear a special livery, for the upkeep of which they received a small annual payment from the Lord Chamberlain. The joiner had preserved his old function of making chairs of state, including thrones for the monarch, and ceremonial chairs for ambassadors. The coffer-maker, the oldest of all royal furniture craftsmen, had long lost his prime task of making and decorating standards, chests and coffers and other pieces of furniture, and by Stuart times had been reduced to making utilitarian travelling equipment and storage furniture, such as laundry baskets, for royal use.[5]

By 1850 the increase in specialization and the much wider scope of the commissions undertaken for the royal family were reflected in fundamental changes in the number and types of craftsmen and the kind of work on which they were employed. The coffer-maker disappeared from the records. Part at least of the function that he performed was now assumed by the trunk-maker, an appointment which was filled for some years after 1832 by Samuel Pratt of New Bond Street, the patentee of wire springs in 1828, and, in 1826, of swinging beds in ships to prevent seasickness.[6] Joiners were now principally concerned with interior fittings, and were classed with carpenters; they seem to have lost their time-honoured function of making chairs of state, though occasionally a chair-maker appeared in the Victorian records (chiefly, apparently, as producer of cheaper, utilitarian seats). Cabinet-makers and upholsterers still formed the largest group of craftsmen, though it was fashionable, at least for a time, to drop the title of cabinet-makers and classify them simply as 'upholsterers', a change in nomenclature that typified the increased importance attached to upholstery. It was the royal upholsterer, Edward Bailey, who made the chair of state for Victoria's wedding at the Chapel Royal, St James's in 1840, and his sketch of the chair, with a note that it had met with Her Majesty's approval,[7] showed that it had a high rounded back, thick padded arms and heavily fringed seat upholstery, the only visible woodwork being the curved frame of the back and the gilt claw feet. Among the other royal craftsmen the old names of joiners, carvers and gilders and clockmakers still appear, but there are more carvers and gilders than ever before, further indication of changing taste towards carved and gilt furniture and interior woodwork. The most striking changes are in the new appointments, including buhl manufacturers and restorers of buhl-work, ormolu workers, 'scaglioliers', gold and silver lacemen, japanners, carpet manufacturers, timber merchants, composition ornament makers, Tunbridge ware manufacturers, designers, furniture printers (i.e. upholsterers supplying printed fabrics), decorators, portable-furniture makers and turners. Of course, there was no novelty about many of these names, for they represented instances of old crafts, such as gilding and turning, which had formerly been carried out under the direction of cabinet-makers. Turning, for example, was a very ancient craft, but the appearance of turners as independent firms illustrated not only the increasing specialization of the period but a change of function, for they supplied kitchen equipment of all kinds. Indeed this development on their part was already clear in the eighteenth century, as is shown by the trade cards of many turners.[8] Again, whereas the large Georgian firms such as Chippendale's were responsible, partly through sub-contracting, for supplying practically all the household equipment, now in many cases the goods—carpets, for instance, and kitchen utensils—came direct from specialist firms. And the above list shows also how decorative processes, which used to be done by the major firms themselves or through contractors, were part of the same developments and had become the function of specialists acting independently. The inclusion of buhl and Tunbridge ware manufacturers, furniture printers and portable-furniture makers indicates concessions to fashionable demands. In this connection Silver and Co. of Cornhill, London, who were portable-furniture makers to the royal family in 1846, were the firm who made cabin furniture for emigrants to New Zealand (see Chapters 6 and 7). They later supplied furniture to Windsor Castle.[9]

At the beginning of 1837, the year of Victoria's accession, the Lord Chamberlain was employing some thirty firms in the furnishing and decorating of royal households.[10] Among these firms, if we exclude the few engaged solely in glazing and paperhanging, were eight upholsterers and cabinet-makers, five turners, two japanners, two joiners, three clockmakers, three carpet manufacturers, three carvers and gilders, and two lamp- and lustre-makers. The eight upholsterers (the general term now in use) were Thomas Banting of Pall Mall, Edward Bailey of Mount Street, William Francis of New Bond Street, H. L. Goertz of Windsor, Anne McBean also of Windsor, T. and G. Seddon of Grays Inn Road (this was the address of their new workshops), John Saunders of Brighton, and Thomas Turner of New Bond Street. The five turners were Allnutt and Son, C. H. Bridges, M. Mascall, Richard Ordway and J. Thompson. The first three were described as 'turners and matlayers', and Ordway as 'turner and brush-maker'. The two japanners were George Cooper and Sons of Windsor and C. W. Vick of Brighton. The joiners were John Marshall of Soho Square and Robert Tebbott of Windsor. The three clockmakers were Edward Buckwell of Brighton, William Hanson of Windsor, and most celebrated of all, B. L. Vulliamy of Pall Mall. The three carpet manufacturers were H. H. Blackmore of Burdensball near Wilton, Papworth and Co. of Old Bond Street, and Watson, Wood and Co. also of Old Bond Street. The three carvers and gilders were William Baker of King Street, Bloomsbury, James Henderson of New Bond Street, and James Spencer of Knightsbridge. The two lamp- and lustre-manufacturers were well known: Hancock and Rixon of Pall Mall East and Perry and Co. of New Bond Street.

The addresses of these firms are sometimes given in the accounts; where they are not, they can usually be verified from other sources such as directories, a straightforward matter if the firm is a well-known one. But in the case of the lesser-known firms whose addresses are not found in the accounts, one cannot necessarily take for granted that they are the firms with the same names in directories, though there is usually a strong presumption that they are. The royal turners, for instance, remain in some obscurity; Allnutt and Ordway appear to be London firms with addresses in Piccadilly. In general the list of names and addresses of the royal craftsmen indicate the preponderance of London firms and the fashionable furniture-making areas in the capital, and the

Hall chair, carved mahogany, designed by Henry Whitaker, *c.* 1845 and made by Holland and Sons for Osborne House; monogram 'V.A.' on back (*see* p. 120).

'A satinwood and gold Easy Chair french legs' supplied by Holland and Sons to Osborne House in 1845 for £15.

growing number of provincial firms in royal employment. Certainly, of the firms specializing in furniture and upholstery, Banting, Francis, Bailey and Seddon must rank as the outstanding names in the opening year of the new reign.

By 1850 or shortly afterwards more and more provincial firms were brought into the royal service as the Queen extended her building and furnishing projects.[11] H. L. Goertz continued to supply the royal family at Windsor until the end of the century. Another Windsor firm with a long record of royal service were Cleave and Underhay, who succeeded Tebott as joiners in 1850 and kept their appointment for well over thirty years. Henry Lovegrove, upholsterer of Slough, appeared in the records in 1853. The Queen's new house at Osborne, Isle of Wight, led to the employment of a number of local firms.[12] Osborne was designed by the Prince Consort with the advice of Thomas Cubitt, who acted in a double capacity as builder and joiner; much of this firm's joinery can be identified from the Osborne Papers at Windsor Castle and consists of tables, dressers, cupboards, etc. in the servants' quarters, as well as shelving, mouldings, etc. The house was built between 1845 and 1848 at Victoria's own expense and had a great influence on buildings, not only in England, but also in Canada and the United States and even on the Continent in France and Germany, another pointer to the pervasive influence of royal patronage.[13] The main furniture for the house came from the leading London firms of Holland and Dowbiggin, the local firms supplying the 'secondary' furniture required for the servants' quarters. It was stipulated that the estimates of local firms should be scrutinized closely to make sure that their goods conformed to the quality and prices of similar goods supplied by Dowbiggin.[14] Already in 1847 three Isle of Wight firms were being paid for articles delivered and work done at Osborne: Francis Pittis of Newport; George Marvin of East Cowes, both upholsterers; and P. Christensen of Newport, clockmaker. Pittis was later succeeded by Avery and Co., to be joined by Edwin Joyce, gilder, and John Redfern and George Woodyear, both upholsterers.

Balmoral was leased in 1845 by the Queen, but was not rebuilt until after 1850. There were, however, some furnishings required soon after the house was leased, and the first of the Scottish firms to be employed were James Allan and Co., upholsterers, of Aberdeen and William Beattie and Sons of Edinburgh, joiners. They were soon joined by a number of other Edinburgh firms and these, in contrast to the local firms employed at Osborne, were of outstanding reputation and supplied the principal furnishings. They included Robert Bryson and Sons, clockmakers; Smiths and Co., lamp- and lustre-manufacturers; Charles Trotter, upholsterer; shortly succeeded by Potts, Cairnie and Ray and James Morrison, upholsterer.

Above Set of 13 mahogany dining tables, 150 ft long and 8 ft wide, supplied to Windsor Castle by Thomas Dowbiggin in 1846 for £378 14*s*.

Left 'A satinwood and gold commode carved front and mouldings', a fine piece supplied by Holland and Sons to Osborne House in 1845 for £57 8*s*.

Circular table of rosewood veneered on mahogany, parcel gilt, stamped 'Holland and Sons', Osborne House.

'A satinwood and gold loo table w. shaped and carved pillar and angle base' supplied by Holland and Sons to Osborne House in 1845 for £46 14s.

The Royal Furniture-Makers

Right 'An ornamental Pier Table with brackets richly gilt . . . £14 5s.; a fine silvered plate of glass with circular top. . . . £34 3s. 6d.; an overmantel frame for do. . . . £10 4s.' Supplied by Holland and Sons to Osborne House, 1845.

Below 'A satinwood and gold writing table w. shaped and carved standards' supplied by Holland and Sons to Osborne House in 1845 for £42 5s.

Bottom Bench in former Pages' Waiting Room, Osborne House; mahogany with carved rosettes; central stretcher with double lotus-leaf carving; claw feet. Stamped 'Holland and Sons'.

CHAPTER 5

INTERIORS

By the beginning of the nineteenth century a revolution was occurring in the arrangement of furniture within the house, particularly in state and reception rooms, but not necessarily only in the grandest houses. Picturesque disorder was replacing precise symmetry, thus upsetting centuries-old tradition. The long-established arrangement was to leave the centre of the room as free of furniture as possible and to place seats with their backs against the wall, alongside side tables, candle stands and, from the Tudor period onwards, clocks and mirrors. Medieval woodcuts and paintings which illustrate interiors show that chests were often arranged end to end around the wall, leaving an unencumbered centre, a system which may very well have been influenced by monastic interiors. By 1500 the chests were gradually replaced by benches which skirted the whole room.[1]

In the seventeenth century the formal character of interiors was even more strongly emphasized by Baroque decoration, particularly so in France and Holland, the two countries whose furniture was greatly to inspire English design in the generation after the Restoration in 1660. The engravings of Abraham Bosse, illustrating many types of Dutch interiors *c.* 1635–40, prove that it was customary to place chairs in a long line against the wall. There may have been, in the opinion of some scholars, additional impetus to such arrangement from the influence of Chinese interiors, but the most important overriding influence, which was to establish the practice widely, came from the ceremonial formality at the court of Louis XIV. Here architecture, interior decoration and furniture were part of a unified scheme. Chairs and other seats formed an essential part of the wall decoration. The French distinguished between *chaises courantes*, which were allowed to be moved about freely, and *chaises meublantes*, which formed part of the architecture. Hence the story of the rebuke which Louis XIV administered to Madame de Maintenon, when she pulled a chair forward from the wall, that she was 'spoiling the architecture'.[2]

Formal symmetry in the interior was the mark of good taste in eighteenth-century England. Even the exact location of each piece of furniture was carefully planned, as deliberately thought out as the dimensions of the room, the spacing of the windows, the decoration of the walls and ceiling, the position and size of the fireplace, the symmetrical positions of doors (which often entailed the creation of a 'dummy' door to create balance in the room), and the pattern on the carpet. Indeed the well-known correlation between the ornament of the ceiling and the design of the carpet, which was especially fashionable in the Adam period, was only feasible when the centre of the room was left bare. The placing of chairs against the wall explains why their backs were so often left undecorated, a point which has puzzled modern observers when so much skill has obviously been lavished on the decoration and upholstery seen from the front. This formal arrangement is evident in paintings of eighteenth-century English interiors, as in the second of Hogarth's series, *Marriage à la Mode*. Failure on a servant's part to preserve this tidiness was quoted by Adam Smith in 1759 (*The Theory of Moral Sentiments*) as an example of negligence meriting reprimand:

> '*When a person comes into his chamber, and finds the chairs all standing in the middle of the room, he is angry with his servant, and rather than see them continue in that disorder, perhaps takes the trouble himself to set them all in their places with their backs to the wall. The whole propriety of this new situation arises from its superior conveniency in leaving the floor free and disengaged.*'[3]

Smith in this particular passage is concerned with utility as 'one of the principal sources of beauty' and, by association of ideas, with the pleasure or conveniency which the utility of any object suggests. Thus, he argues, the conveniency which ultimately recommends the placing of chairs against the wall to leave the floor free 'bestows upon it the whole of its propriety and beauty'.

At no time in the eighteenth century was there greater preoccupation on the architect's part with furniture than in the period from 1760 to 1800. Robert Adam's drawings in the Soane Museum illustrate his concern with the synthesis between his decoration of a room and the location of its furniture, and show the minute care which he devoted to designing furniture intended to be on or against the wall. It is now equally well known that leading cabinet-makers were able to design furniture in Adam's houses (and in other Neo-Classical interiors) independently of the architect. In fact the pattern of patronage at this time was normally to commission one architect and a number of cabinet-makers to make furniture from both the architect's and their own designs. There was doubtless a great deal of collaboration between all parties concerned. Sometimes the architect insisted on it. In 1773 Sir William Chambers complained to Lord Melbourne, when he was building Melbourne House, that Chippendale, who was designing furniture independently for the house, was not producing designs that fitted in satisfactorily with the architect's schemes. He prevailed on Lord Melbourne to insist on closer co-operation between the two, for 'I wish

Opposite
Top Etruscan Room, Osterley House, with
formal arrangement of chairs and pole screen.
Bottom The Library, Osterley House. Though
the arrangement of library furniture could be
less formal, as much space as possible was left
clear in the room.

The careful arrangement of 18th-century furniture; the Eating Room, Osterley House,
Middlesex showing the formal placing of chairs
around the walls.

to be a little consulted about the matter as I am really a very pretty connoisseur in furniture'.[4]

Informality in interiors has been so much the rule for almost two centuries that it is difficult today to reconcile oneself to the arrangement that had prevailed for so long. Few houses of the eighteenth century retain their furniture intact, and even in those that have, subsequent rearrangement has often completely changed the original intended appearance of the interior. A striking instance of the restoration of furniture to its original location is provided at Osterley Park, Middlesex, a house where, as it happens, Louis Simond in 1811 left a record of his impressions of the rooms when the original formal arrangement had been newly abandoned. The staff of the Department of Furniture and Woodwork of the Victoria and Albert Museum have restored to its original position the furniture which was listed in the house in an inventory of 1782. The result to modern eyes is startling. In the Eating Room, for instance, there was no dining table permanently sited in the

centre of the room. For a meal, several small tables with gate-legs and folding leaves were set up in the room; when not in use they were stacked, not against the wall, but actually outside in the corridor. The lyre-back chairs of the room now stand back against the wall and reveal a remarkable, and hitherto undetected, correspondence between their carved anthemion and scroll decoration and similar ornament on the plaster panels above. The same kind of relationship between the decoration on the back of chairs and that on the wall is seen also in the Library and the Etruscan Room. The Drawing-Room, now cleared, shows off the fine carpet and the related ceiling decoration admirably.[5]

It was in June 1811 that Louis Simond, the French-American, visited Osterley and recorded his dismay at what he saw:

[195]

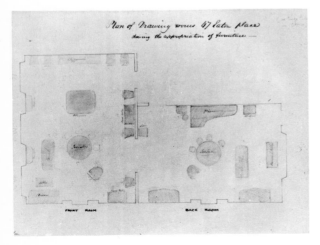

'*Tables, sofas and chairs were studiously* dérangés *about the fire-places, and in the middle of the rooms, as if the family had just left them, although the house has not been inhabited for several years. Such is the modern fashion of placing furniture, carried to an extreme, as fashions are always, that the apartments of a fashionable house look like an upholsterer's or cabinet-maker's shop.*'[6]

Jane Austen's novels mirror changing fashions. In *Persuasion* (written 1815–16 and published in 1818) she describes how fashionable taste in the arrangement of furniture was moving in the direction of pro-fusion and disorder, to the delight of the younger generation and the dis-may of the older. The two sisters in the novel, on a visit to the great house, find themselves in the old-fashioned square parlour, 'to which the present daughters of the house were giving the proper air of confusion by a grand piano forte and a harp, flower-stands and little tables placed in every direction. Oh! could the originals of the portraits against the wain-scot, could the gentlemen in brown velvet and the ladies in blue satin have seen what was going on, have been conscious of such an overthrow of all order and neatness! The portraits themselves seemed to be staring in astonishment.... The Musgroves, like their houses, were in a state of alteration. The father and mother were in the old English style, and the young people in the new.'[7]

The proliferation of styles naturally added to the confusion. In *Our Village*, in which the descriptions of furniture in Egyptian taste have been referred to, Miss Mitford writes of Rosedale Cottage that 'every room is in masquerade' and mentions the anomalies that arise when the furniture is moved about: 'the mitred chairs and screens of the chapel, for instance, so very upright and tall, and carved and priestly, were mixed up oddly enough with the squat Chinese bronzes, whilst by some strange transposition a pair of nodding mandarins figured among the Egyptian monsters'.[8]

This complete change in the established conventions of arranging fur-niture from 'all order and neatness' on the one hand, to 'the proper air of confusion' on the other, is well illustrated from the original source in two sets of drawings by London cabinet-makers, separated in time by some eighty years. Both sets are concerned with the disposition of furniture in the drawing-room, the place where traditionally formality reigned and which Robert Kerr in 1864 could still describe as 'in most respects the chief room of the house' distinguished for 'refinement of elegance'. Some ink and wash drawings of *c.* 1760 by William Gomm of Clerken-well Close, a lesser-known maker, dealing, one can assume, with middle-class clients, show all the furniture ranged against the walls, and the centre of the room left completely bare.[9] A pencil drawing by Banting and Son, 'showing the appropriation of furniture' for the large drawing-room—actually a double room—extending over most of the first floor at 47 Eaton Place, London and leased by the Hervey family in 1840, sketches in, as well as the chairs, a chiffonier, a piano stool, a whatnot and divans all ranged against the walls, a loo table with four chairs, easy chairs and a centrally sited couch in each of the two main sections of the room, and a large ottoman in one section.[10]

The Private Suite, Queen Victoria's Sitting Room, Osborne House. By 1850 the formal arrangement of furniture had been abandoned, as this room shows.

Opposite
Top The Drawing-Room, Osterley House. Here the placing of furniture around the walls allowed full appreciation of the correlated design of ceiling and carpet.
Bottom 'Plan of Drawing rooms 47 Eaton Place showing the appropriation of furniture'. A pencil sketch of Banting and Son's furniture, *c.* 1840.

Combined writing and games table, *c.* 1830, of novel circular form, mahogany; brass plate inscribed 'J. Wilson, 18A Wigmore Street, London' (active 1817–39).

Rosewood davenport, *c.* 1820–40, with keyboard xylophone by Chappell and Sons; an example of fashionable combined furniture.

Riding-boot stand, unusual upright form, *c.* 1830. Made of beech, all sections screw into each other; the boots are slotted into the central section and are secured to the pegs at the top.

'Rocking' cradle after a design in Sheraton's *Cabinet Dictionary*, 1803. Possibly made by William Hollinshed, early 19th century.

CHAPTER 6

PATENT FURNITURE

The first half of the nineteenth century saw an extraordinary development in the application of mechanical processes to furniture and in the adoption of new materials for both furniture and upholstery. This is reflected in the number of patents concerned with furniture-making taken out at the Patent Office.[1] Not all mechanical devices or new materials, of course, were patented, and not all registered patents seem to have been put into production. The word 'patent' itself acquired a fashionable connotation and was widely abused, like the word 'contemporary' in the mid-twentieth century, being often applied indiscriminately to any piece of furniture with a new gadget or attachment, or to any material with a semblance of novelty about it. Nevertheless, the increase in the number of official patents illustrates how furniture craftsmen were as concerned as craftsmen in other industries with new devices, substances and constructional methods.

Only four patents under the heading of furniture and upholstery were granted before 1760, all in the seventeenth century. By the end of 1800 the total was thirty-seven, and by the end of 1810, fifty. The total of 100 was reached by the end of 1829, fifty registrations occurring between 1811 and 1829. The 200th registration took place in 1848, and by the end of 1850 the number was 220. A graph would show a steady rise between 1800 and 1825, then a progressively steeper one to 1850.

Mechanical devices were applied to furniture to produce mobile and compact pieces, often ingeniously fulfilling two or more functions. Some of the earlier designs of Thomas Sheraton, like that for a 'Harlequin Pembroke Table' in his *Drawing Book* of 1791–4, in which a small structure fitted for writing materials could be made to rise from the body of the table by the use of weights and springs, are excellent examples of furniture of this kind.[2] To the traditional training of the cabinet-maker in drawing and knowledge of the Classical orders, a new course of study was now added. This was made clear by Thomas Martin, writing in 1813 in *The Circle of the Mechanical Arts*: 'as it is the fashion of the present day, to resort to a number of contrivances for making one piece of furniture serve many purposes, "a bed by night, a chest of drawers by day", it becomes necessary on this account, as well as on many others, that the complete cabinet maker should be acquainted with the principles of mechanics'.[3]

The main reason behind this urge towards space-saving furniture was

Rosewood patent adjustable wing chair, mid-19th century; ratchet for adjusting slope of back is seen at side. This type of chair, with various means of adjustment, was very popular in the period 1800–51.

A finely made weighing chair by W. and T. Avery of Birmingham, *c.* 1850.

Mahogany revolving bookcase, *c.* 1810, with four graduated tiers on twin turned columns based on a table stand; three curved and tapered legs inlaid with rosewood.

the unprecedented increase in the country's population, which more than doubled between 1751 and 1821, and doubled again between 1801 (the year of the first census) and 1851 (the year of the Great Exhibition). There was a remarkable acceleration in the 1780s which led to a 50% increase in the two decades 1801–21. While in 1750 there were only two cities in Britain—London and Edinburgh—with a population of over 50,000, in 1801 there were eight such cities, and in 1851 no less than twenty-nine, including nine with a population of over 100,000. Until relief came from the railways and the consequent growth of suburbs, large cities, and most of all London, which was by far the largest, felt enormous pressure on their living space, and congested conditions were the lot of even many of the comfortably-off classes. Most Londoners were tenants, living near their place of work and occupying rooms let out by householders who normally occupied part of their premises themselves. The cramped way of life, resulting from a population explosion with little opportunity of building expansion, can readily be imagined. Hence the urgent need for adaptable, portable and space-saving furniture.[4]

Already by 1815 it was clear that these conditions had inspired the labours of many patentees.[5] They included Anthony Eckhardt, who patented a portable table and chair in 1771; Thomas Gale, who patented a folding bedstead in 1772 which closed up to resemble a bookcase or wardrobe; and Robert Campbell, who produced combined library steps and table ('first made for the king') in 1774. In 1798 Day Gunby patented a system of 'entire new weights, bolts and springs' to operate desks, tables, chairs, etc. This patent was developed by the well-known firm of Seddon, Sons and Shackleton, who used it to produce a desk with concealed lead weights inside panels forming the supports; by pulling cords, the operator could raise at will from the top of the desk a small nest of drawers and pigeon holes, or a reading desk with two drawers and candle rests. In 1802 Robert Walker patented adjustable claws on dining tables with the object of saving 'a great proportion of the room or space occupied by tables of the present make'. A circular bookcase, with shelves fixed to a central shaft, intended to save wall space, was patented by Benjamin Crosby in 1808. Thomas Figgin's 'Palenquin Couch' of 1812 formed, according to its own specification, 'by day a handsome couch; in the night, when turned up, a handsome bed'. Extending dining tables were the subjects of a number of patents, including those granted to Richard Gillow (1800), Richard Brown (1805), George Remington (1807) and William Doncaster (1814). Gillow, member of the famous London and Lancaster firm, stated in his specification that his invention used 'wooden or metal sliders in dovetail T or square, or cylindrical, or other grooves, with or without rollers', all this being 'calculated to reduce the number of legs and pillars and claws of dining and other tables and to facilitate enlargement and reduction in size'. Both

Brown and Remington employed a system of lazy-tongs for their tables, while Doncaster used hydrostatic bellows.

Patents for metal fittings for furniture sprang from the important technological advances that were occurring at this time in the metallurgical industries, which produced greater quantities of improved metal at cheaper rates. Stamped ornaments on plated metal, much used as backs for drawer handles and keyholes on late Georgian furniture, replacing expensive, hand-chased plates, had a long history going back to John Pickering's patent of 1769, improved 1777 by the two Birmingham brass-founders, John Marston and Samuel Bellamy. Birmingham was now to play an increasingly important part in furniture-making. In 1812 John Steinhauser patented his metal tubes 'sliding successively for uprights of fire screens, music stands, reading desks and candelabra', followed by John Bennett's metal dovetail joint 'for portable and other furniture', Samuel Pratt's wire springs (1828), of which more will be said later, and Benjamin Day's metal picture frames (1828). A significant trend may be noted in the number of patents for castors. Five of these had been registered by the end of 1816 and ten by the end of 1838. Then the number doubled to twenty by 1850—surely an index of the growing weightiness of seat furniture in the early years of Victoria's reign.

Several patents were for metal bedstead frames and metal joints for fastening wooden frames. In his *Cabinet Dictionary* of 1803 Sheraton specifically mentions that patent bedsteads 'are contrived as much as possible to prevent the harbour of vermin and therefore have brass joints'. More hygienic beds and bedding resulted from the general improvements in medical knowledge and sanitation, which inspired the production of invalid furniture. The long Revolutionary and Napoleonic Wars of 1793–1815, resulting in large numbers of wounded and disabled army and navy personnel, further stimulated the production of ingeniously contrived furniture for invalids. This was not all narrowly specialized furniture, for most of it was intended to be used in the home and can thus be rightly classed as domestic furniture. Most of the mechanical features and new materials which distinguished this kind of furniture could be adapted for household usage in many different ways.

The greatly increased interest in sanitation and personal hygiene was largely due to the investigations into 'putrid fevers' by Dr John Hunter and the work of Dr Lettsom, Dr Stanger and Dr Rowley among the London poor. Much closer attention was also being paid to the care of invalids following the growing acceptance of Dr Lettsom's view that most diseases were mitigated 'by promoting instead of restraining the indulgence and care of the sick'.[6] The problem of beds and hygiene—an important one when it is remembered that as late as 1814 Tiffin and Son held a royal appointment as 'Bug-Destroyers to His Majesty'—was

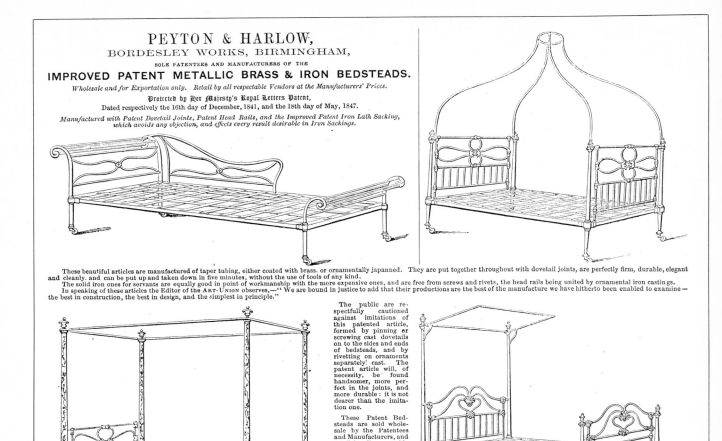

'Improved Patent Metallic Brass and Iron Bedsteads' advertised by Peyton and Harlow, Bordesley Works, Birmingham, 1849.

tackled first of all by introducing metal joints to wooden frames, then by discarding wood altogether in favour of metal.[7] The best method was to use hollow tubes of brass, iron and steel, which were light and cheap as well as clean. Seven patents for such tubes were registered between 1812 and 1831, including one by William Day in 1826 for extending tubes, a very convenient device for altering the dimension of beds (and also of seat furniture). Samuel Pratt of metal-spring fame patented metal rods for bed hangings in 1825, while for beds which retained their hangings

Thomas Breidenback in 1827 patented a close-mesh metal wire for testers, sackings, bed enclosures and coverings to obviate 'the annoyance of mosquitoes and other vermin'.[8]

General conversion to metal beds was well on its way by the date of Victoria's accession. Loudon in 1833 strongly advocated metal beds of all kinds, assuring his readers that iron bedsteads were 'to be found in the houses of people of wealth and fashion in London, sometimes even for best beds'.[9] The process was hastened by the patents granted to two prominent Birmingham firms in the 1840s – to R. W. Winfield in 1841 for metallic bedsteads, and to Peyton and Harlow in 1847 for metal tubes for beds.[10] Both firms gained distinctions at the Great Exhibition in 1851. Peyton and Harlow won their prize medal for japanned metallic bedsteads. Two examples appear in the *Art-Journal Illustrated Catalogue*, which praised their lightness and elegance. One of those shown has a simplicity that is an excellent example of the union of technological skill with a competent grasp of design. Winfield's exhibits in 1851 on the other hand illustrate the widening division between this basic simplicity and fashionable decoration. His firm were awarded the council medal for their brass foundry work, a metallic bedstead with taper roller pillars, and chandeliers. The *Art-Journal Illustrated Catalogue* devotes three pages to these exhibits, with special comments in praise of a bed in Renaissance style and of the well-known 'angel cot', which has often been illustrated since as one of the worst instances of the ornateness of the time and of the insipidness of the associationist theory. Yet it is typical of the period that there should be no illustration of, or comment on – and no particular general interest in – Winfield's rocking chair of

Above Two iron bedsteads exhibited by Peyton and Harlow of Birmingham at the Great Exhibition, 1851, as shown in the *Art-Journal Illustrated Catalogue*.

Left Tester bedstead in brass and japanned iron with the label of R. W. Winfield and Co. Queen Victoria's Bedroom, Brighton Pavilion.

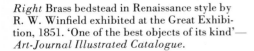

Above The brass 'Angel Cot' exhibited by R. W. Winfield at the Great Exhibition, 1851. 'The body and frame of the cot are very elegant'— *Art-Journal Illustrated Catalogue*.

Right Brass bedstead in Renaissance style by R. W. Winfield exhibited at the Great Exhibition, 1851. 'One of the best objects of its kind'— *Art-Journal Illustrated Catalogue*.

tube metal, which was also at the Exhibition and which showed in its unusual simplicity of design and control of material both a startling contrast to the other exhibits and an approach far ahead of its time.[11] With its carefully balanced curved supports and uprights it foreshadows the metal furniture designed by Marcel Breuer and other Bauhaus designers after the First World War, and has many affinities with the Thonet furniture which the British public also saw for the first time at the Crystal Palace.

'Beds, sofas and machines' for invalids were the subjects of a number of patents by 1850. Their object was to raise the patient from a lying to a sitting position, or raise his legs, or lift him completely clear. These inventions had in common various forms of levering mechanism, usually worked by a worm-gear. The mattress and board were divided into three movable segments related to the back, thighs and legs, and the appropriate section was raised to suit the patient's needs. Though some of these patents were obviously too complicated for general use, such as George Paxon's bed of 1812 which could perform, according to its specification, no less than ten distinct movements through a special framework over the bed, the ingenious arrangements by which surfaces could be extended and contracted, raised and lowered (normally by means of one operating mechanism—a shaft and handle) were soon applied to other pieces of furniture. Special attention has been paid to the 'sofa or machine for the ease of invalids and others' which was patented by Samuel James in 1813. This was an elegant Regency sofa; a toothed quadrant worked by a handle lifted half the mattress into a completely upright position; a smaller toothed bar, worked by another and smaller handle, raised the rest of the mattress into an inverted V. This piece has been described by Siegfried Giedion as marking an important stage in the development of furniture, for it exemplifies the introduction of an era of adaptability into furniture design and shows how processes applied originally to one specialized sphere of operations could easily be transferred into others, for 'furniture suitable for the informal posture between lying and sitting was first used for the sick'. The importance of James's invention could probably be matched by contemporaries working in the same field, but their general result was to herald innumerable versions of seat furniture of which Minter's 'reclining chair', patented in 1830, with 'self-adjusting leverage of the back and seat', is but one example among very many.[12]

Mechanical ingenuity applied to the production of compact and versatile furniture received further stimulus in England from the need to supply travellers of all kinds. In the early years of the century the demand came mainly from members of the armed forces who were away on campaign or on a long sea voyage; or from civil servants, administrators and the like who were on government business; or from the families of serving officers who were required to move about the country. Sheraton (*Cabinet Dictionary*, 1803) refers to this demand as follows: 'In encampments, persons of the highest distinction are obliged to accommodate themselves to such temporary circumstances, which encampments are ever subject to. Hence every article of an absolutely necessary kind must be made very portable, both for package, and that such utensils may not retard a rapid movement. . . . And it will be observed that most of the things which are of this nature, will suit a cabin of sea voyage.' It is significant that Sheraton should use the word 'utensils' to describe these strictly utilitarian and necessary pieces of furniture. Once peace was established in 1815 there was a great increase in general overseas travel, which included voyages to fast-developing distant markets and to colonial areas such as South Africa, Australia (and somewhat later to New Zealand), India and the West Indies. In addition to the ex-

Brassbound mahogany military chest in two parts, mid-19th century. Compact, protected furniture of this kind was made for army officers during the Napoleonic Wars and was also used widely afterwards for travellers.

panding export trade in furniture to markets all over the world there was need to satisfy the special demand for emigrants' furniture. It was then the custom for shipping owners to let empty cabin space for a voyage, and those emigrants who could afford it naturally fitted their cabins with as much furniture as they could, both for the long outward voyage and for future use in their new homes ashore. There were, among the many kinds of furniture that were made to fold and pack easily, a number of patents designed for the special requirements of sea travellers, such as a bed to prevent seasickness (Samuel Pratt, 1826), a table for ships (Hugh Evans and William King, 1827) and 'a buoyant bed for seamen, cork included' (William Dickinson, 1827).[13]

In some of these latter specialities ingenuity was undoubtedly misplaced, but in general such furniture was designed with everyday usage in mind. In 1809, for instance, James Hakewill's patent for tables, chairs and stools that would 'pack together and fold easily' was declared to be applicable for 'domestic, military and naval service'. Travelling beds of all kinds, often complete with posts and arched framework for the hangings, which could all be folded and stored in a very small space, had been increasingly popular since the end of the previous century. One example, a chair-bed of about 1790, bears the label of Thomas Butler of 13 and 14 Catherine Street, Strand. Butler's trade card describes him as 'sole proprietor of the patent articles', a title which presumably means (since he does not appear in the official list of patentees) that he acquired rights of production and sale from inventors. His labelled bed, when set up, has elegant turned posts and legs and an end section, which can also be used as a chair, in solid, attractively figured mahogany. The mattress is made in three sections. This piece is characteristic of the precision of construction and slenderness of form necessary for the smooth functioning and portability of much of this travelling furniture.[14]

Unlike Butler, a number of London shop owners selling patent furniture at this time were actually patentees themselves. These included Robert Campbell of Little Marylebone Street; Thomas Waldron, patentee of a bedstead made without nuts and screws, of Catherine Street; and Robert Daws, inventor of 'recumbent easy chairs' (1827), of Margaret Street, Cavendish Square.[15] The most famous name was that of Richard Gillow. But Gillows were complete house furnishers whose patent extending dining table was but one of a very large number of diverse pieces. In contrast there were in the early nineteenth century a number of London firms specializing entirely in patent and invalid furniture. Among these was Pococks of Southampton Street, Strand, whose founder has emerged from complete obscurity owing to the recent publication of details of his career.[16]

William Pocock was born in Buckinghamshire in 1750 and, fatherless at the age of seven or eight, made his own way in the world. He became a

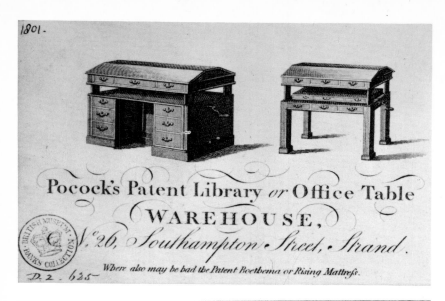

Advertisement for William Pocock's 'Patent Library or Office Table.' Trade card dated 1801.

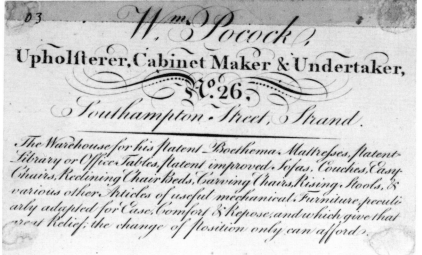

Front and back of William Pocock's trade card, illustrating the 'Patent Boethema or Rising Mattress'.

Advertisement for Pocock's self-acting dining-tables, boethema, 'Merlin's Reclining and Gouty Chairs', and patent sofa beds.

Patent Sympathetic and Self-acting Dining Tables,
FOR GENERAL USE,

Which One Person can, with Ease and Facility, enlarge or diminish to the size required, in a Manner perfectly new. The self-acting Tables also are completely novel and striking. The Construction so astonishingly simple, and the Scale so variable as to suit either the Cottage Orneé, the festive Board of the hospitable Mansion, or the extensive Entertainments of the Nobility and Men of Fashion. Can be made to unite with a fashionable Sideboard, and form an elegant Piece of Furniture for a Dining-Room.—See ✱ PLATE, Nos. 4, 5, 6, 7, and 9 : And yet can be made so portable as to go with the Baggage of a Regiment for the Officers' Mess.

The Sympathetic Dining Tables very much exceed all others yet offered to the Public, as will be seen upon the first View of its Movements in changing from one Size to another ; which one Person performs with as much Ease and Facility as two Persons can any other, except the Self-acting Tables, which are the true Ne plus ultra; nor can it be reasonably expected they will ever be excelled.—The Persons sitting at this Table, if they wish to enlarge it, need only draw one of the Ends of the top towards them, and the other will recede from them, till there is room sufficient for another Leaf between, when one instantly rises and fills up the Space, without any assistance from the Person enlarging it. In Fact it needs only to be seen to be approved, being completely simple and effectual to all the Purposes intended, and cannot be put out of Order.

The Patent Bœthema, or Rising Mattresses,

Are for the Use of Invalids to raise them up in their Beds ; or for any Person accustomed to sit up while in Bed ; can be laid upon any Bedstead, and is so constructed as to be applicable to a Sofa. —See PLATE 1, 2, and 3.

Merlin's Reclining and Gouty Chairs,

Are so improved as to have an elegant and modern Appearance ; and Persons by the Use of the Footstools can recline in them or travel from one Room to another.—See PLATE, Nos. 8 and 10.

The Patent Sofa Beds,

Make a comfortable and convenient Sofa and Bed, suitable either for Camp or Barracks, or on Board a Ship, or even for an elegant Drawing-Room ; and yet are very portable by folding into a very small Compass for the Convenience of Carriage. They have been highly approved by distinguished Officers of the Army and Navy.

We also manufacture curious Treble Reflecting Looking-Glasses of new Construction—Library Tables to rise to suit either a sitting or a standing Posture for Reading or Writing—Go-to-Bed Chairs to assist infirm Persons in going to Bed and getting up—Cradle Beds to change and remake the Bed without disturbing the Invalid—Vibrating Pendulum Beds to swing and give gentle Exercise, or lull them to sleep ; and many other Inventions too numerous to mention in our present Limits.

And also every Article of Cabinet or Upholstery Furniture, from the plain and useful to the most costly and magnificent, and pledge ourselves the Goodness of the Workmanship and Materials, either in the general Line of Furniture, or those we make by exclusive Privilege of His Majesty's Patent, shall be of the best Quality, and have no Doubt of being as successful in giving full Satisfaction to those LADIES and GENTLEMEN who may yet honour us with their Commands, as those we have been already favored with.

carpenter in London where he obtained the freedom of the Carpenters' Company by redemption (i.e. by purchase) in 1782. He took up cabinet-making by way of the flourishing building business which he established in Essex about 1786. He was registered as the patentee of an extending dining table in 1805. Some time before that, from 1802, his showrooms in Southampton Street are recorded in the London directories. His trade cards illustrate two kinds of furniture: a 'patent elevating library or office table', which had a canted top with drawers that could be raised clear of the desk proper so that the user could work standing up, as was the case with the so-called 'shipmasters' desks' of this time; and the 'boethema' or rising mattress.[17] Both pieces worked by the simple principle of turning a handle at the side. The cards refer to Pocock's premises and stock thus: 'the Warehouse for his Patent Boethema Mattress, Patent Library or Office Tables, Patent Improved Sofas, Couches, Easy-Chairs, Reclining Chair Beds, Carving Chairs, Rising Stools and various other Articles of useful mechanical Furniture peculiarly adapted for Ease, Comfort and Repose, and which give that great Relief, the change of Position can afford'.

A large double-page advertisement of Pocock's furniture, with ten illustrations and a brief description of each and an explanatory text on the back, has come to light among Foreign Office papers concerned with the British Embassy in Spain in 1814, its presence among these documents being perhaps explained by its interest to army officers in the Peninsula.[18] In this advertisement the boethema appears again (its name is taken from the Greek word for relief or help), both for invalids' use and adapted as a 'patent elevating sofa'. A 'sympathetic' dining table, illustrated in five sketches, could seat from four to twelve persons; it could be made with or without flaps, and have either pillar and claws or straight tapered legs. In the latter case it was designed to stand beneath a sideboard. It was this 'sympathetic' table that was patented by Pocock in 1805. It could be extended by one person, pulling a handle at either end. The movement was effected by an ingenious arrangement of ropes and pulleys within the framework of the table; these could be replaced by cogged wheels engaging with racks if the table were particularly heavy. The text of the advertisement explains that a development of the 'sympathetic' table, known as the 'self-acting' table, went a stage further, for when the two leaves of the top separated, another leaf rose automatically to fill the gap. The rest of the advertisement is concerned with a number of invalid pieces, including 'Merlin's reclining and gouty chairs', and 'patent sofa beds'. The latter are described as 'suitable for camp or barracks, or on board a ship, or even for an elegant drawing-room, and yet are very portable by folding into a very small compass for the convenience of carriage. They have been highly approved by distinguished officers of the army and navy.'

Advertisement for William Pocock's 'Improvements in Furniture and various Inventions for Invalids', *c.* 1814.

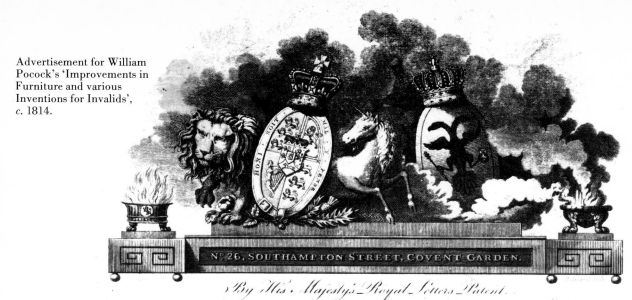

No. 26, SOUTHAMPTON STREET, COVENT GARDEN.

By His Majesty's Royal Letters Patent.

POCOCK'S Improvements in FURNITURE & various Inventions for INVALIDS.

1 — Patent Reclining Bedstead that can be had in any Bedstead

2 — Patent Elevating Sofa upon the same useful principle.

3 — Patent Reclining Chair, Mattress or Bedstead, that will raise Invalids to a sitting Posture in their Beds

4 — Patent Sympathetic Table, to dine from 4 to 12 Persons.

5 — Dining Table on the same principle shut into a small Compass.

6 — End View of the same Table.

7 — Patent Sympathetic Table upon one Pillar & Claw extended to the length for 12 Persons.

8 — A Patent reclining Easy Chair with double Footstools

9 — Patent Sideboard & Sympathetic Dining Table.

10 — An Invalids Chair that reclines in the Back, upon Wheels, with reading Desk &c

(*Most of the above Inventions,*)
have been *honored with* His Majesty's *immediate* Patronage.

Mess. Pocock's manufacture every Article of Cabinet & Upholstery Furniture, & fit up Houses with Economy, on the shortest notice, & in a superior style of Elegance & Fashion.

SOUTHAMPTON HOUSE, No. 26, SOUTHAMPTON STREET,

COVENT GARDEN.

Patent Camp or Barrack Sofa-Beds, that fold into a very small Compass.

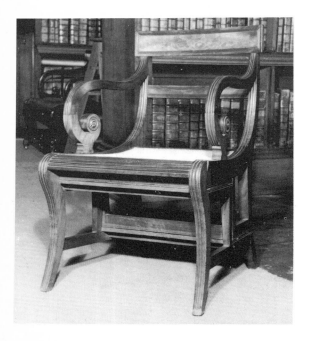

'Patent Metamorphic Library Chair', combined library chair and steps in mahogany, made by Morgan and Sanders and illustrated in Ackermann's *Repository of Arts*, July 1811.

Pocock's 'Reclining Patent Chair' of the 'Merlin' type described in the advertisement is illustrated in Ackermann's *Repository of Arts* in February 1813. It has an adjustable back, two footstools, deep buttoned upholstery, and a Greek key-pattern decoration on its frame. But the rest of the ornamentation is very far removed from the simplicity of so much of this early mechanical furniture. The seat is decorated with two distorted monopodia, the adjustable reading-stand rests on a curious snake support, and the extended foot-rest is supported on a small winged stand. All this is in complete contrast with the simple and functional character of the rest of Pocock's furniture. Pocock died in 1835, aged almost eighty-five. He was active until the end, but his cabinet-making business in London wound up about 1824, largely through the mismanagement of his son John. It may be that this date indicated some sort of loss of fashionable prestige for 'patent' furniture, for the most celebrated London firm of the time in this line of business, Morgan and Sanders, closed down in 1822.

This firm had their premises at Trafalgar House, 16 and 17 Catherine Street, Strand. Much of their earlier furniture is illustrated in Ackermann's *Repository of Arts*, which shows, in August 1809, a coloured engraving of their ware-rooms and states that in their premises 'formed of six houses united, are daily employed nearly one hundred mechanics, besides other necessary servants. . . . Above ten times as many are . . . in the employ of Morgan and Sanders in different parts of London and its environs.' This is an interesting reference to the number of outworkers employed by a large London furniture firm. Their stock, we are informed, consisted of 'patent sofa-beds, chair-beds, brass screw four-posts and tent bedsteads, newly invented Imperial dining-tables, portable chairs, Trafalgar sideboards and dining tables, Pitt's cabinet globe writing table, and numberless other articles'. Many of these pieces are illustrated in their trade card. The Imperial dining table could 'seat from four to twenty persons or any greater number, the whole shuts up in the space of a large Pembroke table, the feet are completely out of the way, and the whole may be packed in a box only ten inches deep'. Their 'Patent Metamorphic Library Chair', a combined chair and library steps, is illustrated in the *Repository* in July 1811. The firm supplied Nelson's cabin furniture for the *Victory* and received a large order just before the battle of Trafalgar in 1805 to furnish his house at Merton, Surrey, for which they made the 'Trafalgar patent sideboard'. According to a circular letter on the back of one of their trade cards in the Banks Collection, British Museum, they were at one time 'sole managers and promoters' of the business of Thomas Butler and were his intended successors until unjustly supplanted by Thomas Oxenham. Butler, already noted as the supplier of chair-beds, specialized in 'articles particularly adapted for travelling and exportation', his designs being executed 'in the Egyptian, Etruscan, Greek and Chinese manner'. Another trade card contains a public warning against plagiarisms of their furniture. In an advertisement in the *Windsor & Eton Gazette* on 15 August 1812 addressed to 'the nobility and gentry of this and adjoining counties' the firm 'engage to complete orders to any extent from their extensive ready-made stock' in a matter of days, even the furnishing of a whole house.[19]

Much of the patent furniture produced in the last generation of the Georgian period, whether officially registered or not, can reasonably be taken as representing functional design at its best, far ahead of its time and the most progressive in Europe. It was simple, practical, compact, adaptable and refined in form, related in the most direct way to the demands of its environment and inheriting the classic furniture-making skills of the Hepplewhite and Sheraton eras. The use of mechanical devices, which marked this alliance between the cabinet-maker and engineer, added precision to furniture; its proper functioning was impossible unless the wooden framework matched the meticulous accuracy of the mechanism. This new approach in design encouraged both the production of fresh forms of furniture appropriate to the early stages of the Industrial Revolution, and a simplicity of construction which eschewed unnecessary ornament.

In an age when the forms and decoration of furniture were governed to an extraordinary extent by diverse and often conflicting concepts of design, it is important to note that the simplicity and precision of patent furniture fulfilled the requirements of an aesthetic theory which, since at least the middle of the eighteenth century, had been developed by a number of influential writers and which equated utility and fitness for purpose with beauty. In 1759, for instance, Hogarth writes in his *Analysis of Beauty*: 'The bulks and proportions of objects are governed by fitness and propriety, it is this that has established the size and proportion of chairs, tables and all sorts of utensils and furniture.'[20] This point was taken up by Adam Smith, the celebrated political economist, in 1759 in *The Theory of Moral Sentiments*, in part IV of chapter 1, which is entitled 'Of the Beauty which the Appearance of Utility Bestows Upon the Productions of Art'. He states that: 'the fitness of any system or machine to produce the end for which it was intended bestows a certain propriety and beauty upon the whole and renders the very thought and contemplation of it agreeable'. He adds a note on the association of ideas—a clear announcement of this theory long before the Victorian age with which it is usually connected—thus: 'The utility of any object . . . pleases the master by perpetually suggesting to him the pleasure of conveniency which it is fitted to promote. Every time he looks at it, he is put in mind of this pleasure.'[21]

This same theory received perhaps its widest propagation through the

Cabinet safe, *c.* 1850, in burr walnut with single drawer above.

influential *Essays on the Nature and Principles of Taste* by Archibald Alison, first published in 1790 and reissued in 1810:

'In the mechanical arts, the object of which is utility, this utility is itself the principle by which we determine the perfection of every production . . . that this quality in forms is productive of the emotions of beauty, every one must probably have perceived. In the forms of furniture, of machines and of instruments in the different arts, the greater part of their beauty arises from this consideration; nor is there any form which does not become beautiful where it is found to be perfectly adapted to its end.'[22]

Alison developed the theory of the association of ideas further than anyone had previously done. The conflict between this theory and that of the propriety and beauty of functionalism outlined above is one of the main causes of the breakdown in the quality of furniture design, which was all too apparent in the second quarter of the nineteenth century. By 1850 the lead in the production of adaptable, simple and mechanized furniture had clearly passed to the United States, though in many respects English vernacular furniture kept alive the traditions of the past while pointing the way to future developments.[23] The very mechanical skill which had equated functionalism with beauty and had helped to give furniture simplicity and grace of form provided the forces that produced material abundance on an unprecedented scale. The Industrial Revolution was the 'provider of comforts' and thus brought an element of self-indulgence to social life.[24] On former occasions in English history self-indulgence was the prelude to ostentation, but never before had so many English people had the opportunity of occupying a place of their own and of stocking it with so many goods. It was inevitable that an important new consideration in the design of furniture should be a growing emphasis on comfort, both as a measure of the physical benefits of the Industrial Revolution and as a reward for the virtuous toil which produced such abundance.

Until the 1860s the words 'comfort and ease' recur constantly in the literature dealing with furniture, furnishings and interior decoration as the accepted requirements of everyday life. When Mr Pickwick announced his retirement at the final dissolution of the Pickwick Club, he told his fellow-members: 'The house I have taken is at Dulwich. . . . It has been fitted up with every attention to substantial comfort; perhaps to a little elegance besides.'[25] This emphasis on comfort, with elegance of much lower estimation, reflects the challenge to refinement of form and good proportions, which came from extended use of new materials in the novel conditions of the time. The problem facing furniture designers was clearly seen in a letter received in 1823 by the architect and designer J. B. Papworth, from his client A. Galloway:

Opposite Chess table made in 1833 by Bullon of Bury St Edmunds, the top decorated with drawings after Piranesi.

*'I wish you would think of a chair that would be easy to sit in and yet
not heavy. Remember it is a room constantly in use, and it is of the
greatest importance that the chairs be comfortable. Can't you unite
novelty, elegance and the comfort of a lounging chair? The one shown
us at Snell's was neat and pretty, but we have seen many very like it and
it would not be easy to the back.'*[26]

This increasing comfort in the home was accompanied by, and was no
doubt the cause of, the decline in the studied formality of rooms and
furniture, which had been one of the most widely accepted social von-
ventions of the Georgian era.

A change of emphasis is perceptible in the nature of the patents
registered in the 1830s and onwards. They were more concerned with the
appurtenances of the home and much less with compact furniture.
Twenty patents, for example, were granted between 1836 and 1850 (out
of a complete total of thirty-three such patents registered by the end of
1850) for window blinds, including the roller and Venetian varieties.[27]
Upholstery came in for a great deal of attention, not only for bed furnishings, but for curtains, cushions and fabrics generally. Upholstery
materials of all kinds were now more readily available than ever before.
The enormous output of the Yorkshire woollen mills meant increasing
quantities of cheap fabrics available for the home. In 1828 Samuel Pratt,
Camp Equipage Maker of New Bond Street, took out a patent for wire
springs in beds, cushions, etc. It was this patent which more than anything else seems to have stimulated the fashion for deep-sprung upholstery on easy chairs, sofas and the many varieties of seating furniture
made for drawing-rooms, boudoirs and private rooms. Upholstery now
tended to hide so much of the framework of these seats, whose depth,
conditioned by the requirements of the new springs, led to the widespread use of short stumpy legs, that their former elegant outline and
good proportions were largely lost. The depth of the seat was greater
when springs were used in preference to horsehair or feather stuffing,
and the accompanying curves were accentuated by the buttoned upholstery then in fashion.

Pratt's springs were spiral shaped, of iron or steel twisted into circular
coils (in the familiar hourglass form) or triangular coils. Loudon's *Encyclopaedia* (1833) illustrates a spring of this kind and describes its use
in the following passage, in which there appears to be a clear reference to
Pratt's patent:

*'Wire springs for stuffing are nothing more than spiral coils of wire,
fig. 704, generally an eighth of an inch in diameter for mattresses and
smaller for cushions, carriage seats, etc. The springs are placed side by
side, on interlaced webbing, strained to a frame of the intended bed,*

Opposite Fly chair, painted white with gilt
enrichments, designed by Philip Hardwick in
1834 and made by W. and C. Wilkinson for
Goldsmiths' Hall. An example of the 'old French
style'.

cushion or seat; they are then all confined by cords to one height and covered by a piece of ticken or strong canvass [sic], strained tightly over them. On this is spread a layer of curled horse-hair, and an upper cover of ticken is then put over the whole, and nailed down tight to the under side of the wooden frame with tacks. For our own part, we prefer beds made with these spiral springs to any other; not only from their greater elasticity, and the equal diffusion of the support which they afford to the body, but because, from the quantity of air among the springs, they can never became so warm as beds stuffed with any of the ordinary materials. The effect of spiral springs as stuffing has long been known to men of science; but so little to upholsterers that a patent for using them in stuffing was taken out, some years ago, as a new invention. Beds and seats of this description are now, however, made by upholsterers generally and the springs may be had from Birmingham by the hundred weight.' [28]*

The search for comfort explains, as the above references to seat furniture demonstrate, the development of the most significant feature found on all types of early Victorian furniture, viz. the introduction of the important structural change of the curve, both in woodwork and upholstery and in all the prevailing 'historic' styles. It can be seen in the rounded outline of sideboards, chiffoniers and sofas and in perhaps the best example of all, that well-known contribution to chair design, the Victorian balloon-back. Until well into the 1860s comfort held first place among the considerations occupying architects and designers generally. The Reports of the Juries in the International Exhibition, 1862, could state categorically that 'household furniture . . . must above all things be useful and comfortable. . . . It would be an absurdity to sacrifice convenience to elegance. It is only when all the conditions of utility and convenience have been attended to, that the aid of art begins to be called for.' [29] And in 1864 Robert Kerr, the architect, writing in *The Gentleman's House*, put the order of values for a gentleman building a house as 'quiet comfort for his family and guests; thorough convenience for his domestics; elegance and importance without ostentation'. Kerr claimed that the elements of comfort were more clearly understood in England than in any other country, one reason for this being 'our large share of the means and appliances of easy living'. [30] It was the latter that had brought to all classes what Loudon called 'their natural right of enjoyment'.

CHAPTER 7

THE STRUCTURE OF THE FURNITURE INDUSTRY

ECONOMIC ORGANIZATION

In spite of assertions that are frequently made to the contrary, there were surprisingly few changes in the structure of the English furniture industry in the period 1800–50. There were, of course, significant repercussions which inevitably followed the growth of population, its geographical redistribution, and the rise of great cities in the North and Midlands with the advent of the Industrial Revolution. All these factors led to an increase in production and, in some instances, in the scale of working, but increased productivity and growth of scale do not necessarily imply alteration in the type of organization. There are certainly no signs within the period under review of the establishment of the factory system in the modern sense of fully mechanized mass production. In fact the complete production of furniture by mechanical means, by which every stage in the process of manufacture is carried out by machinery with the end product under the general supervision of the industrial designer, is not a nineteenth-century phenomenon at all. Its full introduction had to wait until the twentieth century. Many of the features of the furniture industry that are commonly supposed to have been established in the early nineteenth century as a result of industrialization—such as large-scale workings, piece-work and out-work, well-developed retailing, the sub-division of labour and sub-contracting—were all quite clearly present, in various stages of development, in the eighteenth century, and in some cases can be traced back to an even earlier period.[1]

The following summary, which forms the opening section of a history of Victorian furniture, may be considered a fair sample of the conclusions that have been reached as a result of the study of nineteenth-century techniques:

'The radical changes in furniture-design that came with the nineteenth century were accounted for to a great extent by the altering social and economic conditions of the country. The changes in furniture, though gradual at first, were by the accession of Queen Victoria well established, little of the eighteenth century remaining, either in style or method of production. . . . Such a change did not happen overnight and the first two decades of the nineteenth century still saw a *continuation of the traditional system of handicraft. Thereafter, greatly increased production, helped by the use of wood-working machinery, had the inevitable consequence of separating the maker from the customer. Until 1800 the crafts of furniture-making had altered fundamentally very little throughout the centuries and tradition was the all-important factor in the handicrafts from medieval times to the end of the eighteenth century.'[2]*

The first sentence of this summary is unexceptionable; the rest must be treated with considerable reserve. To maintain that by 1837 there was little remaining of the eighteenth-century method of production of furniture, that after about 1820 greatly increased production was separating the maker from his customers, and that prior to 1800 the furniture crafts had altered fundamentally very little since medieval times is to ignore the evidence provided by the study of furniture-making in eighteenth-century London, the greatest single furniture centre by far in the country. On a national basis the scale of working in furniture remained decidedly small during the first half of the nineteenth century, for the census returns of 1851 applying to cabinet-makers and chair-makers showed that firms in England and Wales employed 5·1 workers (this assumed that all proprietors could be counted as workers), and that over 90% of the firms with over 60% of the workers had less than ten workers each. There was thus no sign at all of a factory revolution in furniture at the time of the Great Exhibition.[3]

In spite of the growth of provincial urban furniture firms with their expanding markets, London's traditional predominance in the English furniture industry was strongly maintained, and has indeed been maintained with remarkable consistency to the present day. It remains the central theme to any study of the organization of the industry. As one of the world's greatest furniture-making areas it retained its enormous advantages: its own expanding market; its easy access to imports of its bulky raw materials, now arriving in ever increasing quantities; its key position in national and international communications, particularly in relation to its extensive export trade; and its ability to gain from the government contracts, which were a special feature of the nineteenth century. It would be impossible here to give a detailed account of the London furniture industry in the eighteenth century—this has been done elsewhere[4]—but a short summary is essential to show that the pre-1800 industry, so far from being one of relative simplicity, regarded as the classic period of the craftsman-customer relationship before the coming of industrialization, was, on the contrary, one of extreme complexity. Very many types of economic organization were to be found, subject to endless variations and sub-divisions as one merged into the other.

A London cabinet-maker of the eighteenth century, for instance, might be a craftsman-shopkeeper who was responsible for making on his own premises the furniture which he sold to the public; or a capitalist-shopkeeper, i.e. a dealer or retailer or trading capitalist, who retailed the furniture that he bought from craftsmen outside his premises, often also supplying it to other dealers for sale in different parts of the country or abroad; or a working master who was not a shopkeeper but had his own workshop where he made furniture for the shops or for other craftsmen, or did repair work; or, finally, one of the numerous journeymen who worked at home as out-workers by the piece for the shops or masters, or were wage-earners under other craftsmen or dealers.

The London shopkeepers who were retailers only, acquiring their stocks from outside makers, were a familiar part of the scene in the eighteenth century and indeed this type of shopkeeper can be traced back to at least the Tudor period. In his classic study of the domestic system in industry, George Unwin, quoting the example of the twentieth-century dealer in Curtain Road who buys furniture from the workshop of a Shoreditch cabinet-maker and sells it to a provincial shopkeeper, states that this may be regarded as a survival in the furniture trade 'exemplifying the type of industrial organization which predominated in the days of Shakespeare and Milton'.[5] Early Georgian observers took the system for granted. The anonymous author of *A General Description of All Trades*, 1747, writes of cabinet-makers, 'many of their shops are so richly set out that they look more like Palaces and their Stocks are of exceeding great Value. But this Business seems to consist, as do many others, of two Branches, the Maker and the Vendor; the Shop-keeper does not always make every sort of Goods that he deals in, though he bears away the Title'.[6] The same author notes similar trends among turners and upholsterers, the latter being from early times dealers in miscellaneous goods, including second-hand wares, and experts in appraising household furnishings. These developments explain the activities of even the most fashionable firms who were undertakers, auctioneers and valuers as well as suppliers of the best furniture on the market. The numerous trade cards issued from the early years of the eighteenth century by the smaller London shops (but not by fashionable craftsmen, who avoided advertising of this kind as smacking too much of mere trade) made quite clear from their wording the difference between the craftsman who 'makes and sells' furniture, and the retailer who 'sells' only.[7] Well before the end of the century the value of the traditional seven years' apprenticeship was seriously questioned if at the end it was to lead only to shopkeeping. On the other hand, retailing could be a lucrative career, and large shops were taking on apprentices for high premiums, not to train them in the craft of furniture-making, but to instruct them in the business side of shopkeeping.

Trade cards of Joshua Taylor and Sons of the Minories, illustrating the range of activities of a craftsman-shopkeeper *c.* 1830.

Receipt for goods bought of J. Davis, Great Russell Street, Bloomsbury, craftsman-shopkeeper, dated 15 March 1819. The furniture in the bill would be made on the premises; other items (decanters, etc.) would be bought from outside suppliers.

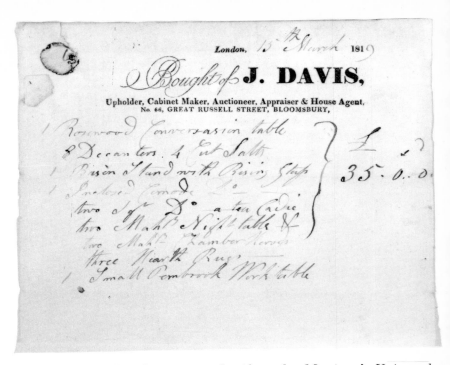

The first London directory to classify trade, *Mortimer's Universal Director* of 1763 (its scope is indicated by its sub-title of *The Nobleman and Gentleman's True Guide to the Masters and Professors of the Liberal Polite Arts and Sciences*) carefully points out that its list of cabinet-makers 'contains only such as either work themselves, or employ workmen under their direction; and that not one of those numerous Warehouses which sell ready-made Furniture, bought of the real artist, is to be met with in this work; the plan of which is to direct the merchant and private gentleman to the fountainhead in every department'.[8] Although the *Universal Director* establishes the important distinction between the shops which superintended the making of the furniture that they sold on their premises, and those which retailed furniture bought from outside sources, actually both kinds of shops were purveyors of ready-made goods. One wonders indeed how much eighteenth-century furniture was made to specific orders. Until recently interest and research have been chiefly concerned with the study and identification of the specially made outstanding sets of furniture in great houses, and this may have encouraged the belief that most good quality furniture must have been made to the customer's direct order, but evidence shows that by the mid-century it was normal for the upper classes to patronize shops for ready-made furniture. To take one example of many, William Linnell of 28 Berkeley Square, the fashionable carver, cabinet-maker and upholsterer, had in his 'cabinet shop' at the time of his death

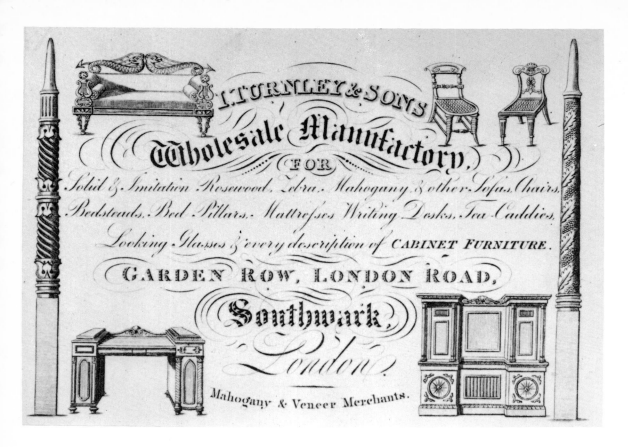

Two trade cards of Turnley's Wholesale Manufactory, Southwark; the pieces illustrated indicate the styles of the second quarter of the century.

Contrasting types of organization: *right* a dealer's warehouse in Lambeth; *below* a craftsman's shop in Covent Garden (J. Walker is recorded as working 1774–1814).

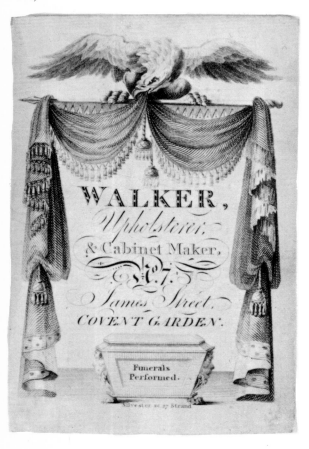

in 1763, among many other items, '222 Marlborough feet for Tables and Chairs' and '79 pr. of Mahogy. arms for Chairs' ready to be assembled later. Similar shops had also a permanent stock of furniture, including rout chairs, that could be hired out.[9] Ready-made furniture kept the employees busy between large commissions, and the pattern books, such useful guides to prevailing fashions, must have been a considerable help in this method of keeping the working staff together. In the competitive furniture-making world of the capital the loss of skilled craftsmen could be serious. Most serious of all to a firm's standing was the departure of the foremen, the real workshop organizers, some of whom are known to have set up their own shops in close proximity to those of their former employers, no doubt taking away some of their customers and perhaps some of their employees as well.

The most fashionable London furniture firms had always been concentrated in well-defined areas. The fashionable topographical boundaries had a certain fluidity about them, for the firms concerned were, in a long-term sense, migratory, following the movement of the upper classes to the western and northern suburbs and searching for larger premises. Just as the firms had moved by about 1750 from the once fashionable area of St Paul's Churchyard and the City to Soho, Covent Garden, Long Acre and the main centre, St Martin's Lane, so by about 1800 they were establishing themselves in the districts which were the chief centres until 1850–Oxford Street, Tottenham Court Road, Old

[222]

and New Bond Street, Pall Mall and Mount Street, the last-named becoming particularly prominent with firms such as Dowbiggin (later Holland and Sons), Tatham and Marsh and Edward Bailey, all of whom obtained royal appointments.

London directories issued between 1800 and 1850 show an increase in the number of firms with two addresses, denoting the separation of workshop and showroom, but this again was not a nineteenth-century phenomenon. Charles Pryer, Manufacturing Cabinet-Maker and Upholsterer, advertised on his trade card at the end of the eighteenth century two addresses—No. 472 Strand and 'his Manufactory, Paradise Row, Chelsea'.[10] About the same time George Oakley, who had an upholder's shop in St Paul's Churchyard, opened a second shop in Old Bond Street. His first premises were described as a 'Chair and Cabinet Manufactory', the second as a 'Magazine of General and Superb Upholstery and Cabinet Furniture', with a 'constant supply of every kind of fashionable Furniture, compleat and ready for immediate Delivery'. This was an excellent example of a high-class warehouse of ready-made furniture, for in 1807 Oakley, who had obviously developed a flourishing business, was described as 'famous for goods of the latest fashion', and he, Gillow and Elliott were picked out as the 'chief makers and sellers' of furniture and upholstery in London.[11] Gillows had established this pattern of business in a wider sense by opening a branch in Oxford Street in the 1760s and supplying it for a time with furniture made in their original centre in Lancaster.[12]

At the beginning of Victoria's reign *Pigot & Co's Alphabetical Directory of London*, 1838, included, among others, the following prominent firms with two addresses: Jackson and Graham, 37–38 Oxford Street and 18 Newman Street; William Smee and Sons, 6 Pavement, Finsbury and 34 Little Moorfields; William and Edward Snell, 1 Belgrave Road, Pimlico and 27 Albemarle Street, Piccadilly; Samuel and Henry Pratt, 47 New Bond Street and 19 Cockspur Street; and Taprell and Holland, 19 Marylebone Street and 6 Silver Street. In 1843 the last-named, now styled Holland and Sons, had the same premises in Marylebone Street and a manufactory at 38 Broad Street. They moved into Mount Street in 1852. Pigot's 1838 *Directory* also showed that Seddons had, in addition to their well-known shop in Aldersgate Street, new workshops in Grays Inn Road. These had been designed for them between 1830 and 1832 by the architect J. B. Papworth, who added large drying sheds in 1836.[13]

According to the evidence which has so far come to light Seddons were the largest furniture firm of the eighteenth century. The account left by the German visitor Sophie von la Roche, after her visit to the Aldersgate Street premises in 1786, states that Seddon employed 400 apprentices (this number would include journeymen), who were engaged in a building with six wings in all aspects of cabinet-making and upholstery.

Trade card, *c.* 1830, of another Walker of Skinner Street, Holborn advertising his Bedding Manufactory and Furniture Warehouse, where 'Merchants and Captains supplied'. The imposing coats of arms may be taken as advertising only.

It has been calculated from further evidence based on two fires at Seddon's premises that he employed some eighty workmen in 1768 and nearly 300 in 1783.[14] While it seems clear that firms continued to increase in size during the half-century after 1800, there is no evidence to hand that any firm exceeded Seddon's figures of 1786. The firm of Holland were employing 350 workmen according to the census of 1851.[15] In his report on the furniture and decoration at the Paris Universal Exhibition of 1855 Matthew Digby Wyatt makes special mention of Jackson and Graham as a firm which had grown into an important manufactory within the last fifteen years. The number of employees in the early 1850s, including females, averaged about 250, and the weekly wage bill was about £400. There was to be a considerable interval of time before a distinct increase in numbers was evident. About 1877 Jackson and Graham were said to be employing between 600 and 1,000 workers, according to the season and the demand for furniture, with a weekly wage bill of almost £2,000.[16]

The nineteenth century saw one of the major developments of the London furniture industry; the growth of the East End ready-made trade with the mass concentration of the cheaper trades in Shoreditch, Bethnal Green and Stepney. By 1861 these areas had 31% of the total of London's furniture workers (at this same date the important West End high-class furniture area of St Marylebone, St Pancras and the City of Westminster had almost 28% of the total workers).[17] The East End's emergence as a major furniture area was clearly a development of the later part of the century, with a powerful impetus from the immigration of Russian and Polish workers in the 1880s. The build-up had certainly begun before 1850, when Shoreditch and Hoxton were losing their former market-garden character with the eastward expansion of London. From early in the century working masters' (or piece-masters') shops had grown up in and around Tottenham Court Road and Euston Road, providing in the first instance good-quality ready-made furniture for the retailers.

A rapid extension of this contracting-out system followed the advent of large retail stores in Tottenham Court Road after about 1840, Maple's, for instance, in 1841. These stores at first produced their furniture in their own workshops, but after 1850 contracting-out, extending over a wide field and embracing the growing East End trade, became the rule, especially during and after the 1870s. This East End trade included skilled craftsmen making ready-made goods for the main stores, but sub-contracting and the division of labour were carried out to a most complex degree and gradually developed into the sweating system among the less skilled workers. These post-1850 developments were already apparent in the second quarter of the century, according to Henry Mayhew, writing in 1861. The small working masters of the East

A 'garret-master' or cheap furniture-maker bargaining with an East End retailer; an illustration in Henry Mayhew's study of skilled and unskilled labour in London, 1851.

End, whom he calls 'garret-masters'–'their own employers and their own workmen'–were at that time the principal suppliers of the 'slaughter houses, black houses and linen-drapers', as the big retailers were variously known to the trade.[18]

MACHINERY

In spite of the general quickening tempo of mechanization in the period 1800–50 the furniture industry was curiously unaffected by machinery except for the simplest processes. Yet woodworking machines of all kinds had been invented before 1800 by Sir Samuel Bentham, the naval architect and engineer. While in Russia he had invented a planing machine as early as 1781, and on his return to England he patented, by 1793, a comprehensive range of woodworking machines for planing, moulding, rebating, grooving, mortising and sawing, covering, in fact, every woodworking process that is still in use. From 1791 he used the house of this brother Jeremy Bentham, in Queen's Square, Westminster, as a manufactory for woodworking machinery.[19]

The furniture trades preferred to continue on traditional lines, the structure of the industry lending itself smoothly to greatly increased output based on hand skill and thereby, no doubt, encouraging a conservative outlook. Hand craftsmanship certainly began to show signs of declining standards by 1850, but these can be attributed to the general adoption of routine processes on the basis of the division of labour. The decline was certainly not due to the advent of machinery into furniture-making–though it did affect the standards of other branches of the

Examples of woodworking machinery *c.* 1850. These machines were used for industrial processes but adaptations prepared timber for furniture-making.

Another industrial process: preparing timber for steaming and bending.

decorative arts, such as pottery, metal, textiles and wallpapers—and indeed this aloofness of furniture from mechanized processes emphasizes perhaps more than any other factor the largely unchanged character of the industry before 1850. The increasing specialization of hand methods in furniture as the domestic system extended provided little incentive for the introduction of machinery, which was regarded as late as 1874 as an uneconomic proposition by a writer in the *Furniture Gazette*.[20]

Until the 1870s the mechanical saw, useful in the preliminary processes of preparing the timber for the craftsman, was the only woodworking machine which can be considered to be in general use. There were various shaping machines in use and, after 1845, carving machines. But even the mechanical circular saw—and this applied also to the planing machine—was slow in establishing itself, only making real headway in the mid-1830s, and then only in larger urban areas. In most of the country the traditional sawpit, operated by the 'top sawyer', the expert and master, and the 'bottom sawyer', whose work in the pit below was a byword for drudgery of the worst kind, continued in wide use. In his reference to Jackson and Graham quoted above, M. D. Wyatt adds that 'a steam engine, and machinery for various purposes connected with cabinet-making' had recently been installed by the firm and had resulted in a considerable saving in costs without affecting the level of wages. Wyatt's particular reference to steam power seems to indicate that its introduction by the firm was a distinct novelty. He refers also to the firm of Holland and Sons, who also were 'now introducing machinery to a large extent', but these developments again take us into the second half of the century.[21]

It is true that mechanical methods greatly increased the production of the decorative details which could be added to furniture. These help to explain the growing elaboration of the early Victorian furniture, the trimmings, for instance on furniture of the so-called Elizabethan style. George Fildes in 1844 commented on the handsome and cheap 'elaborate open work' in panels on Elizabethan furniture which were produced by machinery, and Henry Whitaker in 1847 noted how this same strapwork decoration was facilitated by carving companies. A rotary cutter (or toupie) was used for Gothic and Elizabethan decoration, its special advantage being its speedy method of chamfering. Turned work, of course, the traditional mechanical process, could always be adapted for applied ornament. Thomas King in 1835 referred to rosettes turned by the lathe and then channelled into leaves, 'being a considerable saving in the expense of carving'.[22]

Steam-driven machines for cutting veneers were in use in the early nineteenth century. A detailed description published in 1829 refers to several mills employing these machines in the vicinity of London, and gives details of Messrs Watson's works at Battersea, which installed Brunel's machine, patented in 1805. The writer explains the high cost of veneers sawn in the traditional manner. Only highly skilled sawyers could produce unbroken veneers of equal thickness and the wood itself, carefully chosen for its figure and colour, was bound to be expensive. Machine-cut veneers considerably diminished the cost and vastly extended the market for veneered furniture, down to 'those classes of the people who, not long ago, had even the favourite articles of their furniture in deal or in the coarser woods'. Another effect was to prolong the life of furniture, for the foreign woods that were used for veneers were more resistant to worm than English woods, and their use improved the appearance of furniture. This is the description of the machinery in Watson's mill:

'Their apparatus is driven by steam, and consists of a number of circular saws, the largest of which is eighteen feet in diameter. One side of those saws is a plane kept perfectly true by a strong and well bound frame work, to the circumference of which the saw is attached. The teeth of the saw are rather large than otherwise, in order that they may not clog with the saw-dust, and thus tear the finer veneers; and it revolves with considerable velocity. The log of timber which is to be

cut into veneers is fastened upon a frame, with the piece in the direction in which it is to be cut, in a vertical position. The frame that carries forward the log is moved at a rate which may be varied according to the quality of the timber that is cut. It has a rack on the under part, in which a pinion works. In cutting coarse stuffs, such as the soft and straight-grained mahogany, of which the bottoms of drawers, and other internal works of an inferior kind, are made, the log moves forward, and the veneer is cut at the rate of about one foot of length in four seconds. Allowing the depth of the log to be two feet, the quantity of veneer taken off would, by one of these machines alone, be two hundred and forty square feet in an hour. Where the wood is harder, or of more value, the motion is considerably slower; but, even then, the quantity cut by one machine as compared with that which sawyers would cut in the same time, is, independently of the saving of wood, and the superiority of the veneers, almost incredible to anyone who has not actually witnessed the operation.

The circular saw of eighteen feet diameter, at Messrs. Watson's mill, makes thirty-two revolutions in a minute. We observed a veneer of a log of mahogany, four feet six inches long, by thirty-three inches wide, cut in eighty seconds. The smaller saw, at which inferior timber is cut, has a quicker revolution, called a tumbling motion; and by this we noticed a veneer of a piece of mahogany six feet six inches long, by twelve inches wide, cut in twenty-five seconds.'[23]

The writer goes on to make the important note that 'those who are reckoned respectable cabinet-makers do not, in general, wish to have more than eight or nine thicknesses out of the inch; but those who manufacture furniture for occasional sale, and are in consequence indifferent as to the quality of the timber, and the durability of their work often have the inch cut into fifteen or sixteen thicknesses'. One can see in this distinction much more than the established craftsman's preference for well-tried methods and reluctance to adopt the new-fangled. The growing custom among producers of cheap furniture of covering inferior material with thin outer sheets of more expensive and showy woods was beginning to give veneers a new and pejorative meaning. Dickens's *Our Mutual Friend*, published in parts in 1864–5, is usually quoted as an example of this secondary meaning with his description of Mr and Mrs Veneering as types of flashy social parvenus. But the reference to veneering as a term of contempt is much earlier than mid-Victorian and was indeed established by the beginning of Victoria's reign. Almost thirty years before *Our Mutual Friend* Dickens made the reference clear in *The Pickwick Papers*, 1836–7, in 'The Bagman's Story' (Chapter XIV), when the old chair exclaims in offence, 'That's not the way to address solid Spanish mahogany.

Dam'me, you couldn't treat me with less respect if I was veneered.'

Carving machines came into prominence in London in the 1840s. The quest for cheap and rapid methods of carving reflected the general revival of this craft at the beginning of Victoria's reign. The revival is of particular interest, as hand carving was in a poor state in the early years of the century. In 1813 Thomas Martin in *The Circle of the Mechanical Arts* wrote: 'There are only eleven master carvers in London and about sixty journeymen (though at one time there were six hundred). Many of the latter are now very old. They make no shew of their work and live in private houses. Carving in wood has long been in the back-ground as a branch of the arts.'[24] The increasing use of carved ornament on furniture—essential for the historical styles—and the manufacture of 'old' pieces by assembling genuine fragments into hybrid furniture, stimulated a renewed interest in the hand craft. The London carver W. G. Rogers, who was one of the few to be trained during the Regency, showed considerable virtuosity, which gained him royal patronage. His reputation reached its height at the Great Exhibition at which the Queen exhibited his celebrated boxwood cradle, purchased by her in 1850 for £330. Roger's two sons continued his work and hand carving, in which Prince Albert showed a keen interest, maintained much of its renewed vitality until the end of the century. W. G. Rogers himself was greatly influenced by the work of Grinling Gibbons, and his purely decorative carvings have a certain delicate charm, but his carving on furniture is obviously based on the elaborate bulbous Elizabethan ornament in favour at the time.[25]

Five patents were taken out between 1844 and 1848 for carving machines, but by far the most successful was Thomas Brown Jordan's of 1845. He was awarded the Isis medal by the Society of Arts for his machine, and this was presented to him by Prince Albert at a special visit to his Lambeth workshops. Jordan's machine was a realtively simple one. It had two main sections: an upper one with the tracing and cutting tools, the latter worked by steam power producing between 5,000 and 7,000 revolutions a minute; and a lower iron table for the pattern and the blocks of wood for carving. The one fixed tracer and the rotating cutters were worked vertically by a foot pedal in an ingenious adaptation of the turner's lathe. The cutters carved the blocks as the tracer moved over the pattern, so that the original model was copied to the last detail.[26]

Ministry of Works records show that the architect Charles Barry carried out tests in 1845 on two carving machines with a view to their possible use for the carved panels and ornaments required for the new Houses of Parliament. The machines under review were those of Samuel Pratt and of Taylor Williams and Jordan (the official name of Jordan's firm). Barry reported that Pratt's machine was 'more properly a bosting

Model of T. B. Jordan's woodcarving machine, patented 1845, used for repetitive carved work on furniture and also for duplicated panels in the House of Lords.

or moulding machine', and recommended Jordan's for the proposed work, after submitting a detailed account of its working and concluding that it produced 'perfect copies of the work requiring to be imitated'. The duplicated panels and other carving in the House of Lords were made on Jordan's machine in 1848.[27]

For furniture the machine carried out repetitive work which had to be finished by hand in the cabinet-maker's shop. There was usually no undercutting by machine, though an improved version of Jordan's patent did allow some undercutting to be done. Machine work was responsible for the deep, bold relief carving that was a feature of so much of the furniture of about the mid-century.

THE PROVINCES

Furniture historians and collectors have tended to concentrate on the products of fashionable London firms and those of the chief provincial cabinet-makers who followed London styles.[28] The study of English provincial furniture in its widest sense of the urban, rural, regional and vernacular aspects of furniture-making outside London, the principal centre of fashion, is still largely undeveloped. We now know enough to question the long-held and over-simplified division between London and 'country' furniture, the former representing fashionable refinement and stylistic leadership, setting the standard of technical competence, and imitated with varying degrees of success by leading makers in the larger provincial cities, the latter reflecting traditional, unsophisticated and utilitarian furniture of a general uniform and undifferentiated character. But considerable research remains to be done before a full and accurate picture appears.

There is growing interest in vernacular furniture, both urban and rural, and this is revealing a strong tradition of distinct regional characteristics based on solid pegged construction in local woods, turned members in chair-making, and mannerisms of ornament which occasionally show simplified influences of elements from fashionable pieces, free, of course, from any trace of the advanced decorative techniques of veneering, marquetry and gilding. Until recently vernacular furniture has been regarded as relatively unimportant, and the task of identification of regional features has been made difficult by the wide dispersal of those vernacular pieces which have survived destruction by furniture's many enemies, including accident, fire, worm and sheer neglect. Some pioneer work on the subject from the American side by John T. Kirk suggests links between early American and seventeenth-century English regional furniture–between, for example, Connecticut Valley and East Anglian types–and this could obviously be a promising line of research.[29]

Opposite
Cheval fire screen, *c.* 1835, with needlework panel showing Richard I and Blondel. The spiral turned uprights (late Stuart in style) and the strapwork on the frame are in the Elizabethan style.

Oak armchair, *c.* 1840, with modern upholstery, in the Gothic taste of the early Victorian period.

Scottish cabinet-makers were prominent in the second quarter of the century; a rosewood cabinet with the label of John Scrimgeour, Perth, 1845.

The most fruitful findings to date by English scholars are concerned mainly with northern English and particularly Yorkshire furniture, through the researches made by and under the direction of Christopher Gilbert and Lindsay Boynton. Christopher Gilbert's studies of oak furniture from Yorkshire churches and, in a broader field, of town and country furniture in Yorkshire, extending to part of Lancashire and northern Nottinghamshire, and his two specialized studies of Broughton Hall near Skipton, Yorkshire, with reference to the furniture supplied there by provincial firms from 1788 onwards, and of Pratts of Bradford, prominent in the Victorian and Edwardian periods, all present important information gained through careful investigation of documentary material as well as of surviving pieces of furniture. Under the direction of Lindsay Boynton the University of Leeds has presented admirable studies of Yorkshire firms.[30]

Provincial towns had long had cabinet-makers and upholsterers capable of supplying the needs of the local gentry. The wealthy families who ordered their best furniture from London often completed their furnishing from local sources. The Purefoys of Shalstone near Buckingham bought furniture from Belchier of St Paul's Churchyard and Baxter of Covent Garden, but obtained their chairs from a Bicester chair-maker.[31] This was in the 1730s, and the custom persisted well into the nineteenth century, even when the provincial industrial cities were expanding enormously in population. The census returns of 1801 and 1831 reveal that between those two dates Sheffield and Birmingham doubled their population, Leeds increased from 53,000 to 123,000, Liverpool from 82,000 to 202,000, and Manchester and Salford from 95,000 to 238,000. There is still, however, little detailed evidence of the growth and business working of the furnishing firms before 1850, with the exception of Leeds.

An examination by Christopher Hutchinson of furniture firms in Leeds (at least 1,500 of these have been traced as active between 1700 and 1910) shows a particularly rapid rise in their number from twenty in 1800 to seventy-five in 1850. By this date the population had risen to some 175,000, and the city's business prospects were proving an attraction to craftsmen from other parts of the country, thus beginning the reversal of the trend that for so long had made London the magnet to men of ability and enterprise.[32] This rise in the number of firms can be connected not only with the extraordinary growth of the city's population, but also with its advantages as a centre of communication by river, canal and later (nearer 1850) railway. Clearly the period 1800–50 was a time of transition, during which these firms were struggling to win parity of esteem with London, for while during the late Regency and the early years of Victoria's reign important local families like the Gotts and Tempests were ordering furniture from prominent Leeds firms, among whom were Kendell, Constantine, Bullman and England, the goods which they supplied seem to have been for servants' quarters and the less fashionable rooms.

John Kendell is known to have made furniture for Harewood House between 1818 and 1822 and to have repaired chairs there, possibly those previously supplied by Chippendale. The evidence indicates that this firm was still then fulfilling the traditional role of provincial crafts-men in supplying the secondary needs of wealthy clients, 'missing the cream of custom', as did leading contemporaries, until they came into their own in the 1860s. One of the greatest provincial firms of the later part of the century, Marsh and Jones of Leeds, acquired Kendell's business about 1864. It was then that they supplied furniture worth £4,000 to Titus Salt junior of Saltaire, and indeed the most detailed bill of a major Victorian furnishing firm which has so far been published concerns this commission and is dated 1866.[33] Another distinguished provincial firm, James Lamb of Manchester, began working about 1840, but did not achieve eminence until the 1860s when, like Marsh and Jones, they employed the London designer Charles Bevan.[34] Thus, as in so many other aspects of furniture-making, the half-century 1800–50 saw important but not yet decisive changes in the relationship between London and the provinces as suppliers of fashionable furniture. It was not until after 1850, when local pride reached its height to be commemo-rated in the great new Town Halls and civic universities, that furniture firms in the main industrial cities rose to prime importance. This, no doubt, explains the even more rapid growth of furniture firms in Leeds from the seventy-five in 1850 to 120 in 1860 (for a rise in population of 35,000). Very much the same sequence of development occurred with Pratts of Bradford, a firm which survives today. Founded in 1799 as an individual concern, this firm became a partnership about 1845, and after 1850 launched on a successful career with constantly expanding business, relying almost entirely on hand processes of manufacture (except for the installation of veneering machinery in 1865) until well into the 1870s.[35]

York provides an excellent example of a city of well-established cultural traditions, with a steadily increasing population lacking the rapid rise of the great industrial centres. The census returns give York's population as 26,620 in 1831, 28,842 in 1841 and 40,359 in 1851. Directories reveal an ample establishment of furniture-makers catering for a prosperous, middle-class clientele of quite different character from the largely working-class market in Leeds. Parson and White's *Directory of the Borough of Leeds and the City of Leeds and the Clothing District of Yorkshire*, published in 1830, shows that York then had twenty-three cabinet-makers and upholsterers, eight carvers and gilders, one chair-maker and thirteen furniture-brokers (total, forty-five). In 1841 there were thirty-six cabinet-makers and upholsterers, nine carvers and gilders, two chair-makers and twenty furniture brokers (total, sixty-seven). In 1851 this total had risen to eighty, according to the *General Directory and Topography of Kingston-upon-*

Hull and the City of York, made up of forty-three cabinet-makers and upholsterers, nine carvers and gilders and twenty-eight furniture brokers.

The carvers and gilders indicate a demand for the more luxurious types of furniture, while the comparatively large number of furniture brokers, the dealers in second-hand furniture, represent an important and flourishing trade to supply the needs of customers of lower social ranking. Kingston-upon-Hull in 1846 had thirty-seven cabinet-makers and upholsterers and thirty furniture brokers for a population of some 66,000.

The post-1850 story of York's furniture-makers is in direct contrast to that of Leeds. By the end of the century there was a steady decline in their numbers, some fifty firms appearing in the Directories in 1891 for a population of almost 67,000. The reasons for this await investigation. The explanation may lie in the development of large-scale production in Leeds (and other cities) and of the railways; both factors could well account for cheapness, wider choice and speed of delivery as they serve to emphasize how traditional furniture-making had been in York for the first half of the century.[36]

WINDSOR CHAIRS

After 1800 rural furniture-making, based on family concerns, continued, as could be expected, on traditional lines. Adam Smith's village craftsman, who was 'not only a carpenter, but a cabinet-maker or even a carver in wood'—Smith's example of the way in which the division of labour was limited by the extent of the market—could be found in villages throughout England as he can still be found today. But even in remote country areas a certain degree of specialization was possible; at the end of the century Ernest Gimson took lessons in chair-making from Philip Clissett, the Herefordshire craftsman with a life-long experience in making the tall, ladder-back, rush-seated chairs which Gimson and the Cotswold School were to make so fashionable.[37]

The most significant development in rural furniture-making in the early nineteenth century was the concentration of Windsor chair manufacture in High Wycombe, long famous as the centre of an area where beech (the 'Buckinghamshire weed') grew in abundance.[38] In the 1720s Defoe had commented on the vast quantities of this timber, which reached London from Buckinghamshire (to be used, of course, for many other purposes than furniture-making).[39] The beginning of the rise of small chair manufacture in Wycombe is traditionally put at 1805, when Samuel Treacher, a farmer, established a chair-making business in the town as a winter occupation for his farm labourers, and Thomas Widgington, a chair-maker of Wycombe, taught Treacher's employees how to assemble chairs from parts made by the 'bodgers' in the neighbouring woods. Though this tradition is commemorated by a stained-glass window in Wycombe Town Hall, its dating is largely discounted by L. J. Mayes, the historian of the High Wycombe chair industry, for he has evidence of a flourishing chair-making trade in the town before 1800.

Directories prove that the industry was progressing considerably between 1823 and 1830, but the biggest spur to production came somewhat later with the introduction of the Wycombe chair vans. These travelled extensively with their loads of chairs, to be sold at first as the occasion arose. Later, as the van loads became more widely known, orders were taken for further supplies. The first recorded pioneer in this

Above Windsor chair, *c.* 1800, of traditional bow-back form with stylized splat and cow-horn stretcher.

Left An elegant comb-back, *c.* 1830, straight legs with pad feet.

'Comb-back' Windsor chair, *c.* 1835, cabriole legs.

Opposite Advertisement of *c.* 1865 of Edwin Skull of High Wycombe, showing his numerous versions of Windsor chairs.

Right The standard form of kitchen Windsor chair, *c.* 1840.

Far right Another version of a mid-century Windsor.

Below left More sophisticated versions of Windsor chairs were made at High Wycombe *c.* 1850. This example of a balloon-back has painted decoration.

Below right Rocking-chair Windsor, *c.* 1850.

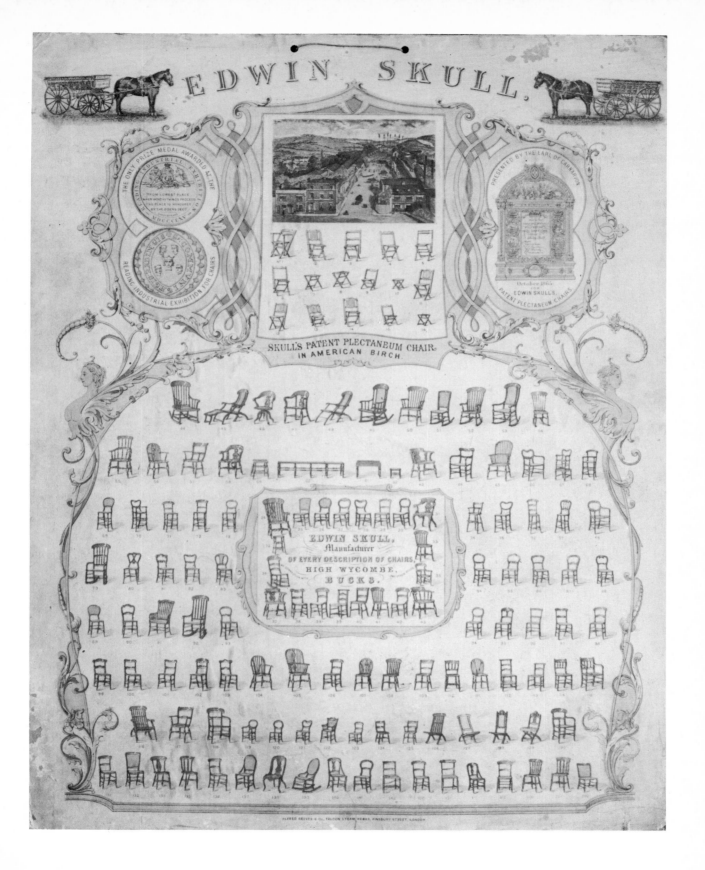

EDWIN SKULL,

SKULL'S PATENT PLECTANEUM CHAIR.
IN AMERICAN BIRCH.

EDWIN SKULL,
Manufacturer
OF EVERY DESCRIPTION OF CHAIRS,
HIGH WYCOMBE,
BUCKS.

marketing and advertising project was Benjamin North, whose *Auto-biography* shows that he began his travels in 1836 with a van-load of chairs made by the chair-maker, Randel, of Thame.[40] He covered the West Country, Midlands and East Anglia. In 1837 he began to travel for Thomas Harris and reached the industrial cities as far north as Sheffield and Leeds. During the opening years of Victoria's reign this local chair industry was tapping a rapidly expanding market, and when North set up his own business in 1853, his market was a national one.

High Wycombe did not, of course, have a monopoly of production of Windsor chairs. These ancient traditional stick-back chairs were made in all parts of the country. Loudon in 1833 refers to them as 'one of the best kitchen chairs in general use in the midland counties of England', and he describes the staining process employed by the Windsor chair manufacturers in the neighbourhood of London. He makes no mention of High Wycombe, which was clearly only emerging as a principal centre of manufacture before 1850.[41]

'Stick-back' Windsor chair, *c.* 1800, of yew and elm, stamped 'T. Simpson, Boston'.

OVERSEAS TRADE

One very important aspect of the organization of the English furniture industry, which only recently has been attracting due attention, is the export trade in furniture. In direct contrast to other branches of furniture-making the history of this trade is backed by reasonably full documentation in the official statistics which have survived from the late seventeenth century. These prove that since late Stuart times English furniture was exported to a world-wide market vased on all the trade routes opened and exploited by English shipping. London remained the predominant centre of the trade which made England Europe's greatest exporter of furniture in the Georgian and Victorian periods.[42]

In the early nineteenth century England's overseas trade expanded considerably. For her furniture, furnishings and household goods generally there was, of course, a valuable sustained demand from her colonies. The American market was by no means lost with the creation of the United States; cultural ties were to prove more lasting than political ones, and indeed the first English ships to leave the port of London in 1783 bound for the new republic had many consignments of furniture among their cargoes.[43] By 1850 there was a growing demand for furniture from the newer colonial areas of Australia and New Zealand. India, where there had been relatively few British residents before 1800, was also attracting more furniture by the mid-century as its white population increased in numbers. South Africa was another expanding market. The older colonial area of the West Indies was traditionally a very good customer for furniture from home, a position it was to maintain until those twin supports of the sugar industry and planters' prosperity, slavery and protection, were eroded by emancipation and free trade.[44]

But colonies were only part of the story. The official figures show clearly that there was a brisk trade in English furniture to many foreign countries—to practically all parts of Europe, to the coast of Africa 'from Morocco to the Cape of Good Hope', to the 'Southern Continental States' (i.e. the young and growing republics of South and Central America) and, as noted, to the United States. In the seventeenth and eighteenth centuries all the trading routes were treated by Customs officials under four main divisions: Short Sea Trades (i.e. Northern Europe), South Europe and Mediterranean, Long Distance Trades (i.e. all routes outside Europe) and the quaintly named 'Foreign Coasting Trade' (i.e. Ireland, the Channel Islands and the Isle of Man). Expanding trade after the Napoleonic Wars made such divisions obsolete, and they were replaced by the main continental areas, in which there was a constant increase in the number of countries importing furniture.[45]

[241]

A brief survey is necessary of the statistical evidence behind the trade. The Custom House Accounts remain the chief source. A series of volumes, *The States of Navigation, Commerce and Revenue* (Customs 17/1–30), give abstracts of imports and exports for Great Britain as a whole for the period 1772 to 1809. This source does not distinguish, as earlier volumes do, the exports from London and those from the out-ports (i.e. all ports excluding the capital), but London's share in the trade is recorded separately in another series, Customs 8/1–46, covering the years 1812 to 1837. Overlapping these to some extent are the most important volumes of all for a study of the nineteenth century – the 109 ledgers (Customs 9) which stretch from 1812 to 1899 and give exports under the heading of 'Furniture (Household): Cabinet and Upholstery Wares'. They show the value of the trade to each importing area and add useful summaries of the value by continents. Further information can be gleaned from other sources, particularly Board of Trade returns and Colonial Office collections, which sometimes prove useful in expanding the bald statistical evidence of the Customs returns, for these, valuable as they are, cannot be regarded as fully complete and are subject to a number of qualifications.

Export figures for furniture come under a general heading and do not attempt to break down the returns into types of goods. This would be an impossible task for what are intended to be general summaries. From the existence of separate headings in the Customs accounts we know that furniture did not include clocks, carpets or looking-glasses (the latter are entered under 'Glass'). 'Bedsteads or other Furniture of Iron' and furniture made of brass were also excluded. It is also clear that the value of the trade is that of officially registered cargoes and does not cover the furniture that was bought in England and taken abroad as the personal possessions of its owners. When it is remembered that a great deal of furniture was purchased by foreigners to take home for their own use, and that emigrants from Britain often took furniture with them to stock their new homes in the colonies, it can be seen how inadequate the trade figures are. Inadequate, that is, in one sense; in another they make the dimensions of the trade even more impressive, especially when it is realized that the recorded value of exported furniture normally represents wholesale prices, and that the final value must have been much higher. It is impossible to measure, in either quantity or value, this 'private' non-recorded trade, but there is no doubt that it must have been considerable.

The value of the furniture exports, the extent to which English styles were influential abroad, and information of purchasers from documentary and other sources, all give some indication of the kind of furniture that went overseas. It is abundantly clear that by 1800 English furniture had long established a very good reputation for its excellent craftsmanship and attractive design. Between 1711 and 1762 Dutch cabinet-makers at The Hague had to submit an 'English cabinet' as their masterpiece for admission to their guild.[46] In Germany, Norway and Denmark in the eighteenth century leading craftsmen took the title of 'English Cabinet-Maker' as a prestige symbol, the most famous example being the German, David Roentgen, one of the most important furniture-makers of the century, who styled himself *Englischer Kabinettmacher*, though there is no evidence that he ever visited England.[47] By 1788 Hepplewhite could write with complete justification in the preface to his *Guide* that 'English taste and workmanship have, of late years, been much sought for by surrounding nations'. Just seven years before, in 1781, Carsten Ankers had been made director of the Royal Furniture Magazine in Copenhagen, and under his guidance English furniture styles were absorbed by Danish craftsmen, some of whom had been trained in London.[48] Throughout the century English furniture spread its influence widely in Europe, from Scandinavia in the north to Spain, Portugal and Italy in the south, and east to Poland and Russia. Even France, for so long the dominating force in European furniture design and decoration, was showing distinct English influences in chair-design and in the use of mahogany just prior to the Revolution. There is thus no question of the high standing of English furniture among foreigners, and its impact on colonial furniture can be taken for granted.

Very little of exported English furniture was in what may be termed the luxury class. There had always been a certain amount of furniture of very high quality exported for private commissions in Europe, such as the fine suite of japanned furniture sent to Spain about 1740 by Giles Grendey of Clerkenwell, London.[49] And clearly furniture of this quality was sent out to furnish the homes of colonial governors or of rich plantation owners. But wealthy families in Europe were accustomed to get their most splendid furniture from France, as the English aristocracy did in the Georgian period. The special appeal of English furniture was to the European and colonial middle classes—the professional men, officials, merchants, smaller landowners and industrialists—with whom English merchants and officials had close links, which often (as in the case of trading families) developed into personal ties for several generations and fostered cultural relations. Dutch and Norwegian shippers, to quote only two examples, often took furniture home with them from London for themselves or to fulfil special orders from their friends. Sea captains found furniture and other English goods for household use convenient for filling the holds of their ships after unloading their cargoes. American visitors to London on business had often found pieces of furniture at the request of their friends back home. Furniture of this kind was also exported or taken abroad for the use of the numerous class of British officials, civil servants and military and naval personnel who resided overseas or were completing long spells of duty. There was also a great deal of cheaper, more utilitarian furniture which was exported, as the prices make clear.

English furniture seen in houses abroad undoubtedly stimulated interest among the owners' friends and visitors. Further orders would reach England. English styles were adapted, if not directly copied, by native craftsmen with the English pieces as their guide, or with the aid of London pattern books. These books had a very wide currency in Europe; they were well known in Poland, for instance, in the last two decades of the eighteenth century.[50]

In the early nineteenth century the number of London furniture firms advertising goods specially made for export continued to increase. Morgan and Sanders's trade card advertised a 'very convenient and highly approved of SOFA BED, contrived on purpose for Captains' Cabins and Ladies and Gentlemen, going to the East or West Indies, with every other Article necessary for Voyages and Foreign Climates'.[51] 'For Exportation' became a frequent addition to trade cards and advertisements as more and more firms geared their production to the export market. During the Napoleonic Wars there was inevitably a bias towards the needs of serving officers and government officials travelling abroad, often with their families.

The furniture trade flourished triumphantly during the long French wars (1793–1815), despite temporary recessions. This was, of course, a tribute to British naval supremacy and also convincing proof of the high regard that was universally paid to English furniture. A general abstract of cabinet ware exports 'to all parts of the world' in 1800 (Customs 17/22) gives the total value as £38,401. These exports were from Great Britain as a whole, but all the evidence, from earlier and subsequent records, leaves no doubt that London was the main source. The 1800 total was shared out thus: Europe, £16,959; Africa, £477; and America, £20,965. Of the European total, south Europe accounted for £3,275, north Europe for £8,928 and the 'Foreign Coasting Trade' for the rest. Half of Africa's small total went to the Cape of Good Hope (£236). In America the chief markets were the British West Indies (£7,371) and the 'Conquered Islands' (£8,620)–an interesting addition to the list of purchasers. The United States came some way behind with £3,561.

The trade's successful emergence from Napoleon's Continental System of 1806–7 is clearly illustrated in the figures for 1812 (Customs 8/1). What is revealed is not a state of recovery but one of buoyancy and expansion. London exported furniture to eighteen recorded destinations in Europe to the value of well over £24,500. These were not all individual states, for Portugal (£1,379), the Azores (£528) and Madeira (£1,569) were listed separately, though under one government as was also the case with Spain (£1,803) and the Canaries (£2,447). In the north Norway's figure was £1,942 and Sweden's £1,224. There was a small amount to Russia (£34). No exports were recorded to Denmark, and only £7 to Holland. There was even an entry – a very puzzling one – of £148 to France itself. In the Mediterranean area £7,994 recorded to Gibraltar and £4,838 to Malta no doubt denoted exports to be passed on to other sources. All this was in addition to Britain's coastal trade, in which the value of London's exports amounted to £6,713, and that of the outports (whose exports of furniture to the Continent were very much smaller than London's) to no less than £10,123. By far the largest share here went to Ireland – £14,120 altogether, £5,805 from London and £8,315 from the outports.

The cabinet ware in 1812 from London in the East India Company's 'Private Trade' (the official description of the trade which was handled as a special privilege by the Company's officers on outward voyages) amounted to £3,867. More furniture was going to Africa, principally to the Cape (£2,036) and Senegal (£581). The West Indies, British and foreign and including Bermuda and the Bahamas, remained a lucrative market (total exports of furniture from London were valued at well over £16,000 and from the outports at over £4,000). The United States' total was £2,868, but here the outports' contribution of £2,439 was considerably larger than London's £429. Important newcomers were in central and southern America: Buenos Aires (£1,758), Brazil (£1,206) and Honduras Bay (£836). These were London exports, to which the outports added £1,201 to Brazil.

The story of the trade in the thirty-five years between the peace of 1815 and 1850 may be conveniently summarized by reference to the position in 1830, 1840 and 1850 – respectively the end of the Georgian period, the opening phase of Victoria's reign, and the mid-century. In 1830 the total value of the exports of 'Cabinet and Upholstery Wares' from the United Kingdom (effectively this meant England, with London the principal centre) was £55,892 (Customs 9/17). In 1840 the total was £78,124 (Customs 9/27). By 1850 the £100,000 mark had been passed, the actual total in that year being £102,283 (Customs 9/39). The value had thus almost doubled in twenty years. The break-down of these figures by continents is shown in the following table:

	1830	*1840*	*1850*
Europe	19,450	19,084	38,430
Africa	2,979	6,799	10,755
Asia	4,399	22,349	19,891
America	29,064	29,892	33,207
Totals	55,892	78,124	102,283

Asia at this time included all Australasian territories.

In 1830 Europe and America had the lion's share of the exports, thus preserving the general pattern of the eighteenth century. In Europe the furniture reached all parts, but in only three foreign countries France, Tuscany and the Netherlands–did the value exceed £1,000, France being the best customer with £3,013. A number of countries, however, were running them close, including the Hanseatic Towns, Portugal, Spain, Gibraltar, the Ionian Isles and Turkey (which then included continental Greece). The European figures, it must be noted, still included those of the Channel Islands (£4,488) and the Isle of Man (£1,922), but not Ireland. In America the British West Indies (£16,108) retained their predominant position as the biggest importers of all. The United States accounted for £4,290; the 'British Northern Colonies'–a new and growing market–for £4,978 (this was mainly Canada, £2,344); and the 'Southern Continental States', now six in number, for £3,273, Brazil remaining the most prominent (£1,499). Africa's total was chiefly made up by the Cape (£1,170) and Mauritius (£1,244). Under 'Asia' were found the 'East Indies and China' (£2,268) and the new Australian settlements, among which the chief importers were 'Van Dieman's Land' (i.e. Tasmania–£1,356) and New South Wales (£559). Only £8 was registered for 'New Zealand and the South Sea Islands'.

In 1840 the four principal foreign markets in Europe were France (£2,167), the Hanseatic Towns (£1,461), Russia (£1,093) and Tuscany (£1,014). The exports to Russia were recorded as £746 to her 'Northern Ports' and £347 to her 'Ports on the Black Sea'. All these areas, however, fell well behind the Channel Islands (£5,557) and the Isle of Man (£3,053). The significant gains in the area designated Africa were mainly due to the Cape (£3,397), followed by the 'Coast from Morocco to the Cape of Good Hope' (£1,256), Mauritius (£1,012) and 'Egypt, Ports of the Mediterranean' (£424). But Asia showed the most remarkable advances, the key here being provided by the Australian colonies. New South Wales (£10,371), Van Dieman's Land (£4,162), 'Swan River' (£1,042) and South Australia (£1,692) made up practically three-quarters of the recorded total. Of the remainder the East India Company's territories accounted for £4,482, and New Zealand–1840 was the year of the Treaty of Waitangi and the beginning of British sovereignty–for £559. The American market was still dominated by the British West Indies, with £15,814. The exports to the British Northern Colonies were valued at £5,901, of which Canada's share was £2,601, followed by New Brunswick with £1,273 and the group of Nova Scotia, Cape Breton and Prince Edward Island with £1,502. Exports to the United States were £3,265 and to the Southern Continental States £4,474 (Brazil's share was £1,965).

The increase in exports recorded to Europe in 1850 were mainly explained by the very large share absorbed by the Channel Islands–

£16,154. But there were now seven foreign countries with imports at over £1,000: France (£5,837), Turkey (£3,643), Holland (£2,696), Belgium (£2,195), the Hanseatic Towns (£1,726), Norway (£1,274) and Spain (£1,141). In Africa, where the list of receiving countries was growing steadily, what were now termed the 'British Possessions in South Africa' accounted for £5,416 – over half the total. Other important customers here were Mauritius (£1,156), Egypt (£1,043) and Sierra Leone (£962). In Asia the Australian colonies, now five in number, did not reach the 1840 values, but nevertheless made up most of the total of the area. The figures were: Western Australia, £634; South Australia, £2,673; New South Wales, £3,122; Victoria, £3,667; and Van Diemen's Land, £1,698. New Zealand's total was £1,487, and the East India Company's, £5,137. There was an interesting amount of £790 recorded to China. In America the decline of the British West Indies was now quite clear. Their imports amounted to only £5,377, but in their place were those of the British Northern Colonies (£11,100), the United States (£7,539) and Central and Southern America (£8,384).

Emigrants from Britain to the colonies in the early nineteenth century followed traditional procedure in taking their own furniture with them. The colonization of New Zealand provides us with detailed information on this point. In 1857 Charles Hursthouse, a New Zealand colonist who had travelled extensively in North America, South Africa and Australia, published a guide book in two volumes for prospective emigrants under the title of *New Zealand or Zealandia, the Britain of the South*.[52] As emigrants hired empty cabin space on their outward voyage, it was obviously to their advantage to furnish the cabin with the furniture which they would require in their new homes as well as for the many weeks at sea. Serviceable, space-saving articles were particularly useful. In addition to household necessaries such as cutlery, glasses, curtains and carpets, etc., Hursthouse recommends travellers to take with them a table, a set of chairs, a chest of drawers or chiffonier, iron bedsteads, a bookcase or cupboard, a washstand, shelves and a mirror. Detailed instructions are given for packing this equipment, which was allowed to go freight free, into cases to get it on board and transport it at the destination. Hursthouse adds a touch of sentiment in recommending emigrants to take their own family pieces if possible: 'the sight of an old article of furniture . . . lends a homely charm to the new house in the new land', especially 'a good cottage cabinet piano', quoting the example of an established settler who later exchanged his old piano, which he no longer required, for fifty acres of land. Another good reason was that such furniture, which could command only knock-down prices if sold in England, had a ready sale in New Zealand 'at two-thirds more' than its value. Among the London warehouses which specialized in providing all types of cabin furniture and fittings Hursthouse names

Brown of Leadenhall Street. This was the Joseph Brown who had taken out a patent in 1838 (no. 7799) for beds, sofas, chairs, etc. 'to render them more suitable for travelling and other purposes, particularly on shipboard', followed by another patent in 1852 for swinging furniture 'for the prevention of seasickness'. Such furniture was exercising the ingenuity of a number of inventors who were lured by the boom in emigration.

A modern study by a New Zealander (S. Northcote-Bade, *Colonial Furniture in New Zealand*, 1971) makes use of documentary material, contemporary sketches and identified surviving furniture to describe and illustrate the early examples brought from England.[53] The sketches show a cabin in which the furniture has been specially fitted and another which has ordinary furniture chosen for its compactness. In the latter example the cabin, which measures 9 ft by some 12 ft, has two settees (used as beds during the voyage), a piano, piano stool, a Pembroke table, a chair of about 1840, a wardrobe, a washstand, a stand and shelves. Some of the earliest surviving imports are extendable settees adapted as beds. One example, of beech, with back and seat of canework, has detachable side pieces to prevent the sleeper from rolling out of bed. This piece, which arrived in New Zealand in 1843 and was made by S. W. Silver of London and Liverpool, is now in the Dominion Museum, as also are a pair of oak chests, further imports of 1843, which have hinged tops folding backwards to join together and form a knee-hole desk.

Furniture which reached New Zealand from England well before the date of recorded exports was that taken out by missionaries from as early as 1814—a further illustration of the way that recorded furniture forms only a part of the story. 1814 is the date of the first missionary settlement, soon to be followed by many others. The missionaries, educated men of some standing, could claim to be the earliest colonists in New Zealand and builders of the first permanent homes. They have left documentary material which has helped to identify their possessions, and these have proved to be, on the whole, of good quality. A mahogany bookcase with Gothic glazing bars in late eighteenth-century taste, reputedly brought over by a missionary in 1814, is judged to be the oldest surviving piece of English furniture imported in this way into New Zealand. Kemp House, Kerikeri, built by the Church Missionary Society in 1818–19, is the oldest surviving wooden house in the country and retains much of its original furniture, including a late Regency Pembroke table and dining chair. After 1840 fashionable furniture was exported for government residences. Documents in the National Archives, Wellington, include an estimate of 1839 of £630 for furnishing part of Government House, Auckland, and an inventory of the furniture there in 1841 shows that it was completely furnished in latest style. A bill of lading of 1849

Jewel case on stand in French taste by J. M. Levien, exhibited at the Great Exhibition, 1851 and illustrated in the *Art-Journal Illustrated Catalogue*. Decorated with Sèvres plaques.

reveals the contents of nine cases of furniture shipped to Government House, Wellington, by the leading London firm Holland and Sons, who had been appointed royal cabinet-makers in 1846.

Australia and New Zealand were now colonial areas, and it was understandable, as they busied themselves with building Victorian cities, that they relied to a considerable extent on supplies of furniture from the homeland, and that their own furniture-makers, once established, followed English fashions very faithfully. In this respect they differed somewhat from other areas of British settlement. In Canada, South Africa and the United States, for example, English furniture, though widely admired and imported, had to compete with furniture of other traditions, respectively French, Dutch and American. New Zealand was unique in producing a cabinet-maker of distinction who played an intimate part in forging even more closely the links with England. This was the German, Johann Martin Levien, who, after travelling round the world, set up business in Wellington in 1840. He left for London in 1843 and never returned. His mission, backed by the New Zealand Company, was to publicize and promote the sales of New Zealand timbers. He had a successful career in London. In addition to obtaining commissions from wealthy clients to fit up rooms with the new woods, he sold goods quantities to leading London cabinet-makers, including Gillow and Dowbiggin (the business associate of Holland and Sons), and showed pieces at a number of exhibitions.[54]

Lady's worktable made of various New Zealand woods and decorated with marquetry by J. M. Levien, 1858.

Top of lady's worktable, the butterfly in the centre of mother-of-pearl.

[249]

India was another area with a long history of skilled craftsmanship, and the growing number of British residents were accustomed to add furniture of native production to the pieces which they had brought from home. In a three-volume study of 1835, entitled *Scenes and Characteristics of Hindustan, with Sketches of Anglo-India Society*, Emma Roberts writes that for new residents 'little is wanted besides the furniture which has been used for the cabin on board ship, and that little can be immediately supplied from the bazaars'. But she adds that once the newcomers have settled in they can buy elegant Indian furniture. There was also a certain amount of English furniture always available at auction sales when residents sold their homes before returning to England, or when army officers and officials moved to other parts of India.[55]

ENGLISH INFLUENCE IN THE UNITED STATES

The United States are a case apart, for they clearly provide an example of an area where the trade statistics (which make an unimpressive record between 1800 and 1850) are far from being a true summary of the situation. Here was a country where the furniture styles had the most intimate connections with those of England through imports, personal purchases in London, immigrant craftsmen and pattern books. Political independence did not snap the close cultural link between the two countries that had been forged for almost two centuries, and if American craftsmen during that period had developed their own fine standards of workmanship, marked by important regional characteristics of style and decoration, their products remained English furniture with an American accent.

Adam's version of Neo-Classicism had arrived somewhat late in America, about 1780, delayed by the outbreak of hostilities in 1775. Thereafter the style in America spread through the pattern books of Hepplewhite and Sheraton, to be continued into stricter archaeological versions through those of Hope and Smith. In both the forms of furniture and the use of Classical motifs English influence is evident. There was, however, strong competition from French influence after the outbreak of the French Revolution in 1789, when the internal troubles in France and the subsequent long wars drove many French craftsmen to emigrate to the United States. But there was also renewed English emigration to America after independence, and an analysis of American regional styles after 1800 indicates that in general English influences were of fundamental significance, while French influences were secondary.

French craftsmen were particularly prominent in New York at the conclusion of the war of 1812–14 between Britain and the United States.

Cabinet of mahogany, satinwood, holly and ivory, Baltimore, USA, *c.* 1800. This piece shows the influence of the pattern books of Hepplewhite and Sheraton.

New York had been the main centre of attraction for the *émigrés* and their outstanding cabinet-maker, Charles-Honoré Lannuier, who began working there in 1803, made pieces of high quality in the latest French styles.[56] His work was characterized by the use of ormolu mounts and inlay in metals. But the versions of Empire furniture which were made for a small group of wealthy purchasers were not representative of the general run of furniture production. Even so, a great deal of furniture was also imported from France. Indeed, in the opinion of one American writer, in 1850 'nine-tenths of imported cabinetwork came from

Left Girandole looking-glass, Boston, USA, *c.* 1800; very similar to Regency looking-glasses.

Right A fine American version of Regency taste; mahogany armchair, *c.* 1810, attributed to Duncan Phyfe.

Above Mahogany card table by J. Brauwers, New York, *c.* 1815.

Right Pier table in French Empire style; rosewood veneer, brass inlay and ormolu mounts; dolphin feet and swan supports. One of nine pier tables known to have come from the shop of C. H. Lannuier, New York, *c.* 1815.

Sideboard with tambour doors, mahogany of fine figure, attributed to the workshop of John and Thomas Seymour, Boston, *c.* 1800–10.

France'.[57] In addition, ornamental metal mounts were among other imports from France. Much of the furniture, however, exhibited a skilful blending of the two traditions. This is seen in a mahogany card table in that great repository of American furniture, the Henry Francis du Pont Winterthur Museum, Wilmington, Delaware. This table bears the label of Joseph Brauwers, 'Ebenist from Paris, with the Richest Ornaments just imported from France'. The base is in distinct Sheraton tradition, but the pedestal of four pillars and the metal mounts are in French taste.

In Massachusetts, both in Salem, the rising centre of American craftsmanship where Samuel McIntire was the best-known carver, and in Boston, where John and Thomas Seymour were the outstanding cabinetmakers, English influence strongly persisted, as it did also in Philadelphia and Baltimore. In Baltimore this influence was so strong that the elegance of its furniture has been described as at times confusingly close to English style. In this connection it is important to note that a number of leading American cabinet-makers, including the Seymours, were of British extraction. Among them was Duncan Phyfe, the most celebrated cabinet-maker of the time, who worked in New York from 1795 until his retirement in 1847. He worked through successive versions of the Classical style, beginning with work of Sheraton inspiration and proceeding to the severe interpretation of the French Empire. What may be termed the intermediate phase of his stylistic development, from about 1810, was based upon English Regency taste. This is clear from drawings of chairs, preserved in the Winterthur archives, which Phyfe made for a Philadelphia client in 1816 and which shows legs of both sabre and cross-framed types and, in one instance, an adaptation of the lyre-back.[58]

Above Mahogany lyre-back chair, reeded decoration on frame, carved paw feet; from the workshop of Duncan Phyfe, New York, *c.* 1810–20.

Right Mahogany chair in Sheraton style, attributed to John Seymour, Boston, USA, *c.* 1800; an American version of a design in 1802 edition of *The London Chair-Makers' and Carvers' Book of Prices.*

Far right Chair in Empire style, painted gold with green and black decoration; Baltimore, USA, *c.* 1815–20.

Above Circular centre table, mahogany with top of intarsia marble; brass inlay; carved paw feet. Made by A-G. Quervelle, Philadelphia, *c.* 1830. Similar to designs in George Smith's *Guide*, 1826.

Right Rosewood chair and stand. New York, *c.* 1850. The chair combines Rococo curves with traces of Gothic decoration. The stand has scrolled apron which resembles arcading in the chair back; finials on the supports.

Below American sofa, *c.* 1820, in the Empire style; inlaid brass Greek key pattern on seat rail; carved dolphin feet with foliage.

By about the mid-century, there were significant changes in American furniture styles. A. J. Downing, the American writer whose works were to have widespread influence on architecture and interior decoration, writes in his *Architecture of Country Houses* (1850), with special reference to furniture, that 'most of our patterns are of Parisian taste. There is, at the present moment, almost a mania in the cities for expensive French furniture and decorations.' He describes the Grecian or modern style as 'most generally used in private houses' and then

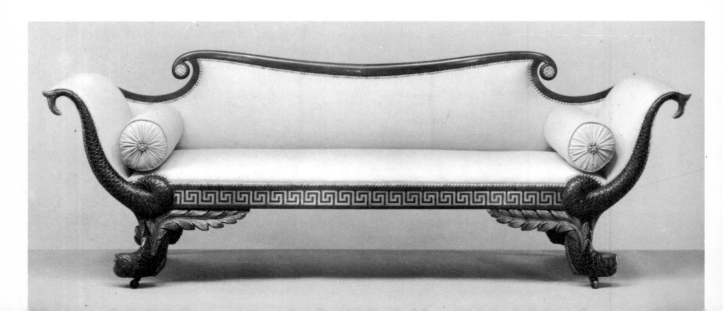

confirms that 'modern French furniture, and especially that in the style of Louis Quatorze, stands much higher in general estimation in this country than any other'. He also refers to Gothic and Elizabethan styles. His words may be taken to mark the height of French fashions and at the same time indicate the growing vogue for historical revivals.[59] The richness of American furniture at the beginning of Victoria's reign impressed English visitors. James Silk Buckingham MP, founder of the artistic and literary review *The Athenaeum*, who began a tour of the United States in 1837 which he later described in three volumes, *America, Historical, Statistic and Descriptive* (*c.* 1841), admired the 'costly and gorgeous furniture' in the principal houses in New York and concluded that 'on the whole the number of large, commodious and elegantly furnished private dwellings in New York is much greater in

American furniture in Gothic taste: oak wheel-back chair by A. J. Davis, *c.* 1841; mahogany secretary, New York, *c.* 1835; rosewood chair by John Jelliff, Newark, *c.* 1855.

proportion to the whole population than those of London and approaches nearer to the ratio of Edinburgh or Paris'. Lady Emmeline Stuart Wortley, in her *Travels in the United States, etc. during 1849 and 1850* (three volumes, 1851), was equally impressed: 'some of the private mansions in New York have quite imposing and palatial appearance, and are very magnificently furnished'.[60]

The revival of historical styles, coinciding with the beginning of the mass production of furniture in America, was of English inspiration, and the all-important key to the situation was the continued influence of English pattern books. Indeed the imports of English furniture can be regarded as supplements to imports of English printed designs. So close were these stylistic ties that pattern books and trade manuals were published simultaneously in both countries. This again upheld established tradition, as seen in *The Cabinetmakers' Philadelphia and London Book of Prices*, published in Philadelphia in 1796. G. A. Siddons's *The Cabinet-maker's Guide*, the popular English manual, was published in 1825 in both London and Greenfield, Mass. This book greatly influenced J. Stoke's *Complete Cabinet Maker and Upholsterer's Guide*, published in England in 1829. This had an American edition in Philadelphia in 1852 and had subsequent reissues until as late as 1906, a striking instance of Anglo-American accord in the matter of techniques and decoration. The first American pattern book was *The Cabinet-Maker's Assistant*, published by the Baltimore craftsman John Hall in 1840. In this the preface states, 'as far as possible the style of the United States is blended with European taste'. The 'sub-classical' taste of contemporary English designers is emphasized, denoting the end of the archaeological phase, and Joseph Down's verdict is that the *Assistant* 'smoothed out heavily carved surfaces of mahogany into massive undulating curves presaging the intricate, wiry forms of the pseudo-Louis xv taste now known as the Early Victorian'.[61] The end of the third decade of the century has been taken as a good starting point for what may be generally termed 'American Victorian' furniture.

The Gothic, Elizabethan and Rococo revivals in America echoed the designs of King, Bridgens, Whitaker, Taylor, the Nicholsons, Wood and other English designers. Loudon's *Encyclopaedia* of 1833 was another source. In his work cited above Downing shows two Gothic bookcases taken from Loudon's designs and also illustrates a bed and canopy from those of Henry Wood, whose pattern books of furniture and draperies appeared in England in the mid-1840s. Downing describes the Gothic as 'rarely seen in this country', and of the Elizabethan he says 'at the present moment, among lovers of highly characteristic and expressive design, it is still more admired than that in any other taste'. It seems that neither Gothic nor Elizabethan furniture attained great popularity in America, with the exception of the mass-produced cottage furniture

Rosewood chair with Gothic decoration; designed by A. J. Davis, *c.* 1830.

American mahogany dining chair, *c.* 1830, with vase-shaped splat.

Another variety of American dining chair of *c.* 1830; mahogany, with legs of sabre form.

The Rococo revival was fashionable in America by 1845 as seen in this rosewood chair of *c.* 1850 attributed to John H. Belter, New York. The back is carved with oak leaves and acorns and vine decoration.

American version of the Elizabethan revival: rosewood and mahogany chair, *c.* 1850, with intricately carved back and spiral turned uprights and front legs.

in Elizabethan style. The Museum of the City of New York has a chair of *c.* 1845 in Elizabethan taste. Made of rosewood and mahogany, it has spiral-turned uprights and front legs, and an elaborately carved and pierced back, reminiscent of Daniel Marot's designs of the late seventeenth century.

The Rococo became the most dominant of these historical revivals in America, although it flourished distinctly later than in England, from about 1845 until well into the second half of the century. John Henry Belter, the foremost exponent of the style, first appears in New York directories in 1844, and with his elegant designs executed mainly in laminated rosewood, a process which he later patented, he was to succeed Duncan Phyfe as the city's most fashionable cabinet-maker. The ground was thoroughly prepared for even greater English influence. Typical of the 1850s was George J. Henkels's *Catalogue*, issued from the City Cabinet Warehouse, Chestnut Street, Philadelphia, of 'furniture in every style comprising Louis XIV, Louis XV, Elizabethan and Antique' with Gothic ornamenting for wainscoting and vestibules. With the advent of Eastlake and Morris designs later, there was a substantial increase in the imports of furniture from England which rose, for instance, to the value of over £48,000 in 1890.[62]

ENGLISH INFLUENCE IN EUROPE

Even when allowance is made for the inclusion of the Channel Islands and other areas of the old 'Foreign Coasting Trade' in the total for Europe, the exports of English furniture to the Continent have a special significance in the way they illustrate successful invasions of countries with long-established national traditions and high standards of craftsmanship from which intense competition could be expected. Historians of English furniture have concentrated attention on the great value of the trade in the last half of the nineteenth century to the almost complete neglect of study of the period 1800–50. The figures of the later nineteenth century are certainly impressive. In 1890, for instance, total English furniture exports reached the very considerable value of nearly £650,000. Europe's share was over £121,000, of which France accounted for £40,057 (she had taken even more–£72,313–in 1885).[63] But these substantial statistics are not, of course, a beginning, only an acceleration, although admittedly a very decided one. Continental historians have also concentrated on the post-1850 situation. There is a dearth of information on the preceding period, particularly on the three decades 1820–50. As has been shown, the story of the trade generally between 1800 and 1850 is one of sustained progress, continued even during the war years, and maintained at a regular level in the 1820s and 1830s (exports to Europe totalled £17,106 in 1837, the year of Victoria's accession), then rising in the 1840s to £31,941 in 1845 and to 1850's total of £38,430.

There were two main fashionable styles on the Continent before 1850, the Empire and *Biedermeier*, both widely disseminated.[64] The Empire style, reflecting the close parallel between Napoleon's Europe and that of Imperial Rome, brought the widespread interest in antiquity to a climax. *Biedermeier* was of middle-class origin, current in Germany and Austria between 1815 and 1848. It adopted a simplicity of line and decoration which emphasized function. Its modest approach, with plain surfaces and little use of metal-work decoration, was a reaction to the Empire style. Current also on the Continent in this period, as in England, were historical revivals, dominated by a romantic medievalism. This Gothic revival in France produced the so-called 'cathedral' style.

Although the Empire style was widespread in Europe, its extent and duration varied from country to country. Where French military or political domination was complete, the style took a firm grip; this was the case in Italy, Holland and Denmark. Spain was exceptional in that she developed her own version of the Empire style. This had flourished when Spain was France's ally until the national revolt against French rule in 1808, and continued even after the restoration of Ferdinand VII in 1814. The 'Fernandino' style persisted until the 1830s. Italy was another country where the Empire style also outlasted Napoleon's downfall, for the restored rulers, though they were notorious for their reactionary policies, continued to patronize the style of the man who had previously overthrown them. Elsewhere the style usually lasted only as long as the French occupation, as was the case with Portugal. The style took root in Germany because the French were at first welcomed there as sympathizers with nationalist aspirations, and it flourished for a time in Austria, in spite of Franco-Austrian hostilities, after the diplomatic arrangements for Marie Louise's marriage to Napoleon. It was welcomed in Russia by Alexander I (1801–25), who continued Catherine the Great's tradition of admiration of French craftsmanship, but both in Russia and in Poland, where Napoleon was regarded as a liberator and his style adopted with some enthusiasm, a compromise style was developed between French and English influences.

The trade figures for 1812, analysed in part above, reflected the current military and political situation and the strength of the English connection. Russia and Poland could be temporarily excluded from serious consideration owing to Napoleon's campaigns in those countries. Spain and Portugal and their dependencies remained good customers of English furniture, the former in spite of her cultivation of the Empire style. Norway, an old and well-tried friend, was the best market in northern Europe. Holland, Denmark, Italy and Germany were of little account, though Italy may have been supplied via England's Mediterranean contacts. A surprisingly large amount went to Sweden, traditionally a country where French taste prevailed. This may be explained by changes in the political climate when Marshal Bernadotte was elected heir to the Swedish throne in 1810.

Reference has been made to the renewal after 1815 of English interest in French furniture, illustrated, for instance, by George IV's purchases from France and the development in England of the Louis Quatorze style. The trade figures show the other side of the picture, for by the beginning of Victoria's reign France had completely reversed her policy of two centuries and had emerged as the most important single importer of English furniture on the Continent, a lead which she was to retain for the rest of the century. There was a rapid interchange of ideas. English firms employed French craftsmen, some of whom reached England – continuing another tradition – as immigrant refugees after the political upheavals of 1830 and 1848. On the other hand, as early as 1824 J. B. Papworth wrote home from Paris that 'there are a great many things copied from my designs and things executed'.[65] The report on the Paris Exhibition of 1834 comments that the spring-upholstered chairs (*confortables*) shown by Dervilliers compared favourably in appearance and price with chairs of the same kind which were first imported into France from England and Germany.[66]

Elsewhere on the Continent in the decades after 1820, in the period when the *Biedermeier* style competed with historicism and eclecticism as Neo-Classicism reached its final stages, English furniture designs continued to be pervasive, though with some change of emphasis. North Germany was particularly open to English influence. This was the area designated 'the Hanseatic Towns' in the Customs records. It received more English furniture than any other part of Germany through the great port of Hamburg and, to a lesser extent, through Bremen. In the north *Biedermeier* furniture followed closely the simpler and more elegant pieces which were being produced in England. It was frequently made of dark mahogany and upholstered in black horsehair. Like the French, Germans had a fondness for comfortable English seating furniture, and established English types of furniture, such as china cabinets and cabinet-bookcases, were imported or adapted. But such simplicity as remained in this kind of furniture tended to be lost in the Gothic and Rococo revivals current from 1840 onwards.

In spite of the figures for 1812 the pattern of recorded trade with the Scandinavian countries changed after 1815; less furniture than previously was imported from England until about 1850 (Norway was an exception, just prior to 1850). For this state of affairs events during the war were responsible. Denmark, estranged from England after the two bombardments of Copenhagen by the British navy and her forced cession of Norway to Sweden as a punishment for her support of Napoleon, persisted with her versions of the French Empire style until after the mid-century. She was also influenced by German furniture. Nevertheless she received some English influence at second hand through German designs, and her craftsmen retained in their work much of the simplicity inspired by English furniture of the Sheraton period. Danish chair design of the 1830s, for example, showed a close affinity with English design of two decades or so earlier. Danish influence was strong enough for Norway also to cultivate what was known as the 'Late-Empire' style. Sweden reacted earlier than Denmark against Neo-Classicism and took up historical revivals of many kinds. Both Sweden and Denmark preserved a remarkably high standard of hand craftsmanship, a factor which may well underline the renewed interest in English furniture during the handicraft revival towards the end of the century.

In Portugal English influence rapidly returned after the liberation from French rule in 1811. Regency furniture was popular and Trafalgar chairs were special favourites. There was, however, strong *Biedermeier* influence after about 1820, and the value of recorded trade of English furniture dropped in the next three decades. Spain proved a better customer than Portugal and remained so for the rest of the century. In Italy English furniture, in competition with French influence, continued its appeal to the middle classes, many of whose tables and chairs were indistinguishable from contemporary English and French examples. Dutch interest in English furniture was soon resumed after the Napoleonic period, to be retained for the rest of the century, as her record of imports, rising steadily, clearly proves. Belgium, in 1814 part of the newly-formed Kingdom of the Netherlands, then from 1831 an independent kingdom, had close ties of friendship with Britain and was to be, like Holland, a regular importer of English furniture during the century. Her interest was no novelty for, as the Austrian Netherlands, she was importing from England in the late eighteenth century. Further east, English and French furniture continued to influence Russian and Polish design. In both countries chair design—lyre backs, for instance, in Russia—showed English inspiration. Turkey was another country with a long tradition of trade in English furniture. Much of this had gone to English factors in the Levant, and had formed a distinct pattern of trade in return for considerable imports by England of carpets. Before 1850 many of the English exports were doubtless distributed among Turkey's Balkan dependencies. The Letter Book of the fashionable London upholsterers and cabinet-makers, Miles and Edwards of Oxford Street, shows that in 1834 Lord Palmerston introduced the firm to the Turkish Ambassador in London who arranged for a large assortment of furniture chintzes to be sent to Turkey for the Sultan's approval. This firm also had business contacts in the 1830s with the British Ambassador in Paris and with the Empress of Russia.[67]

CHAPTER 8

MATERIALS AND METHODS

TIMBERS

Furniture-makers had an ever widening choice of timbers available for them in this period, particularly after the end of the Napoleonic Wars in 1815.[1] Imported timbers were now coming from distant parts of the globe as the expansion of oceanic trade routes began to tap the enormous resources of Africa, the Far East, Australia and New Zealand. Woods from the last-named became available in the 1840s when, under the auspices of the New Zealand Company, J. M. Levien set up business in London to make furniture with imported supplies. He soon met with success, gaining the medal of the Society of Arts in 1848 for 'the introduction and application of New Zealand woods to furniture', and winning an honourable mention at the Great Exhibition of 1851 for a carved sideboard of New Zealand wood. A table made up of a number of timbers from this country can still be seen at Osborne House, Isle of Wight.[2]

Existing sources of supply in North America, both in the United States and Canada, in South America and in the West Indies continued to be exploited. The war years had also encouraged the use of English timbers, as regular imports could not always be relied upon. The fashion for painted furniture had greatly increased the demand for beech. Home-grown substitutes were sought to replace expensive foreign woods. In spite of the vast extension of world trade after 1815 this demand for native timbers was strongly maintained, following the fashion, as has been seen, for native plants as models for decoration, and in accordance with the belief that English woods were essential for such national styles as the Gothic, Tudor and Elizabethan. The *Repository of Arts* in February 1816 expressed the prevailing sentiment on this point: 'there are no woods more beautiful, or better suited to the purpose of cabinet embellishment, than those indigenous in our own country'. The increase in the number of timbers for cabinet-making between 1800 and 1850 can be gauged by comparing the furniture woods listed in Sheraton's *Cabinet Dictionary* of 1803 with the much greater number described in Charles Holtzapffel's *Turning and Mechanical Manipulation* of 1843 and in Blackie's *Cabinet-Maker's Assistant* of 1853.[3]

The fashionable Regency taste for glossy, marbled and dark-coloured woods, which set off the generally low straight lines and plainer forms of pieces in Neo-Classical style, as well as acting as an admirable foil for

A good example of the use of the fashionable striped woods of the Regency: a calamander davenport, second quarter of the 19th century.

Writing desk, *c.* 1830, decorated with marquetry and geometrical designs in
parquetry in rosewood, maple, kingwood and other woods on a mahogany carcase.

Library pedestal table, *c.* 1810, mahogany veneered with sabicu, cupboard doors flanked by caryatid figures.

Pinewood cupboard, floral decoration, the cupboard doors with brass trellis flanked by Classical terms.

Tripod table of mahogany and amboyna, mid-19th century.

bright brass inlay and mounts, encouraged the demand for mahogany, rosewood, kingwood, and distinctly marked woods such as calamander, zebra wood and amboyna. Where woods of a lighter colour were used, such as satinwood, decoration in lines of ebonized wood ('stringing') was found. For the revived national styles of the post-1815 period oak was the obvious first choice followed by walnut. Mahogany was considered the most suitable medium for the Italian or Renaissance style. Whitaker in 1847 is quite explicit about the most suitable material for the Elizabethan style. A design for a hall table in that style, he writes, is 'best calculated for oak or walnut-tree; mahogany not being, at any time, at all suitable for Elizabethan furniture'.

The various rooms of the house were invested with special characteristics which could be invoked by their furniture and furnishings. In Whitaker's opinion libraries, which 'should have an air of quiet and repose', ought to have green as their predominant colour, and were best fitted with furniture of wainscot, 'that being the most quiet wood'; dark oak for crimson furnishings, maple or rosewood were also recommended and light mahogany, with gold ornaments, was suitable for bookcases. For the dining-room, 'generally still more unassuming than the library', mahogany furniture was best. For drawing-rooms, 'where fancy and fashion have hitherto held undisputed sway', the owner's taste was left to seek as much elegance as possible, but Whitaker's own preference seemed to be for the Renaissance and Italian styles, which were then, according to him, dividing the fashionable world, and for which mahogany was the obvious choice.[4] To others the drawing-room was essentially a 'cheerful' apartment, just as the bedroom was a 'happy' one, and for both rooms light woods were recommended to emphasize the curved and rounded surfaces of their furniture.

In fact the most notable trend of the time was the increased use of light-coloured timbers. The darker mahogany ('Spanish wood'), rosewood, calamander, etc. of the early years of the century were of course not entirely superseded. They continued to be used by well-established firms, notably by those with royal appointments, as the Lord Chamberlain's accounts show.[5] But after about 1815 there was undeniably a growing preference for lighter varieties of walnut, kingwood and satinwood, and especially for woods with knots or 'bird's eye' figures, such as thuya, amboyna and maple, for burrs and pollarded woods such as oak, yew, elm, and for bright, clear birch. Instead of contrasting bright ornaments against a dark background, it was now fashionable to use marquetry of darker woods against the lighter surface. This process was in fact well established before Victoria's accession, for G. A. Siddons's popular trade manual, the *Cabinet-Maker's Guide*, first published in 1825 and running into its fifth edition in 1830, states that 'according to the present fashion of furniture, that process which is most calculated to

Painted decoration remained in fashion: satinwood chest of drawers of the mid-century with floral and ribbon decoration.

Occasional table in calamander, second quarter of the 19th century.

Above Parcel gilt amboyna cabinet *c.* 1850, with Wedgwood medallion.

Right Early 19th-century bureau with cylinder top, decorated with amboyna wood veneers with the fashionable 'bird's eye' figure.

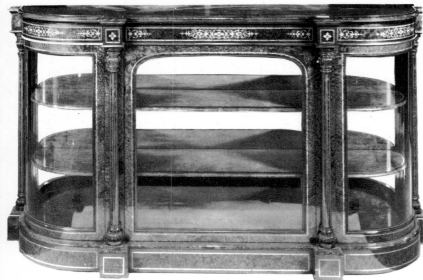

The round forms of the mid-century; a thuya cabinet with gilt brass inlay.

preserve the light appearance of the wood is preferred', and describes how the edges of inlaid holly, 'now lately revived in our cabinet work', were darkened with hot sand for their backgrounds of satinwood and maple.[6]

When the rounded curve in furniture became universal in the early Victorian period, there was even more emphasis on light woods for, as the *Cabinet-Maker's Assistant* explained in 1853, 'any light-coloured wood . . . to show the full beauty of its grain, requires broad and rounded surfaces'.[7] There was also the natural advantage of having these light woods to brighten up small and dimly lit rooms as well as reducing somewhat the heavier scale and coarse carving of furniture. Craftsmen, of course, still prized mahogany as the best material for their skill; it was matchless, as Holtzapffel writes in 1843, for 'its comparative size, abundance, soundness and beauty'.[8] Lighter tones of mahogany were much sought for, especially in the Honduras variety known as baywood. But Siddons's manual makes it quite clear that 'good Spanish wood', i.e. the dark, rich, close-grained type from San Domingo and Cuba, was still the beloved material of many craftsmen, and the book gives directions for closing the grain of more porous varieties so that 'common soft Honduras mahogany will have a face equal to the finest Hispaniola'.[9] Already before 1850 so-called mahoganies were being imported from Africa, but craftsmen were comparing them unfavourably with the genuine species.

This use of light wood means that the traditional view of the early Victorian household as full of dark furniture is inaccurate. Birch was particularly popular at this time, especially the American variety which was reddish-brown and close-grained and almost indistinguishable,

Opposite
Left Cabinet, *c.* 1850, veneered with burr walnut crossbanded with thuya wood; gilt bronze mounts.
Right Bureau of pedestal form, amboyna and ebony, mid-19th century.

when coloured and polished, from Honduras mahogany. Many crafts-men, however, disliked the practice of colouring the wood, so that many rooms of the time were entirely furnished with this bright and gay wood, used in the solid or as a veneer. Maple was also much sought after, and for the same reasons. The best variety was considered to be that from Prince Edward Island, because it could contain both the bird's eye and mottled figures, sometimes on pieces cut out in circular sweeps, such as those used on chair backs. Bedrooms were favoured places for birch furniture, as it was 'suggestive to the fancy of purity and happiness'.[10]

STAINING, GRAINING AND MARBLING

The techniques of staining, graining and marbling had in common the object of imitating the more costly woods and marbles with cheaper sub-stitutes. Graining and marbling differed from staining in using painted decoration. All three were well-known and established processes, but they came to be more widely practised in the first half of the nineteenth century. Staining was an essential part of the craft of the seventeenth-century marquetry craftsman, who used various kinds of vegetable colouring matter and other materials, such as oxide of iron that gave sycamore (which after treatment was known as 'harewood') the greenish-grey colour needed for floral and foliate designs.

Peter Nicholson in 1823 (*The New Practical Builder*) defined grain-ing as 'the imitating, by means of painting, various kinds of rare woods; as satin-wood, rose-wood, king-wood, mahogany, etc., and likewise various species of marble'.[11] This widespread revival of graining seems to have originated at the time of the French Revolution and the subse-quent Anglo-French Wars, when the timber trade was liable to serious interruption and valuable foreign woods were, for a time, very difficult to obtain. Cabinet-makers made considerable use of beech, which was particularly suitable for painted decoration. Even when regular supplies were assured in the later stages of the war, and of course after the peace of 1815, it remained obviously worth while to imitate in native woods the striped, mottled, knotted and bird's eye figures of the fashionable Regency woods. Rosewood, obtained from Brazil during the war years, had already caught the fashion and was being imitated before 1815. The *Respository of Arts* in August 1813, referring ot light chairs 'intended for best bedrooms, for secondary drawing-rooms and occasionally to serve for routs', pointed out that 'these chairs may be stained black, or, as the present taste is, veined with vitriol, stained with logwood, and polished to imitate rose-wood'. Maple was in favour in 1817. In June of that year George Morant, the cabinet-maker of New Bond Street, sent J. B. Papworth, who was making many designs for decoration for him, a specimen of imitation of maple.[12]

Adjustable gout stool in three sections; beech, grained to simulate rosewood. Probably made by Bantings, *c.* 1830.

The trade manuals naturally took up the revived processes with enthusiasm. George Siddons's *Cabinet-Maker's Guide*, first published in 1825, described the equipment as follows:

'The chief tools necessary are common brushes, as used by house-painters, sash tools of different sizes, camel hair pencils with long and short hair, camel hair flat brushes in tin for softening off; graining tools, which are flat brushes of a few hairs in thickness, and of different widths, fastened into wooden handles, and, lastly, horn combs made on purpose for graining; and these are chiefly used for imitating oak, or wainscot, though they will be found often useful for other purposes; they are sometimes fixed into a wooden handle, in the same manner as a graining tool, though generally in the form of a common comb; they should be very thin and elastic, so as to adapt themselves to the several mouldings they are drawn over, in order to produce the grain so peculiar to oak or wainscot.'[13]

The general method for graining (and the procedure was much the same for marbling) was to prepare the work by application of a priming, rubbed down well when dry with pumice stone. The colour of the ground, matching the wood to be imitated, was then painted on and finished by graining. This could be done with oil colour or distemper; the former was preferred as it was more durable, though more difficult to execute. It was best to mix the oil colour with japanner's size to expedite drying, to thin it with turpentine for smooth application and to blend the different shades of the grain together. The pencils, brushes and combs were used to obtain the various dark and light streaks, veins, grain, etc. A knot or curl could be imitated by turning or twisting a piece of bladder or thin parchment on the ground. Siddons concluded that 'these few rules, if joined with a close attention in studying from nature, will enable the ingenious mechanic soon to make himself master of an art which adds so much to the beautifying of our apartments, and which has lately become so much in vogue, that a modern room can scarcely be said to be finished without these decorative embellishments'.

The most comprehensive trade manual devoted to the subject appeared in 1827 with the publication of Nathaniel Whittock's *The Decorative Painters' and Glaziers' Guide*.[14] For full technical instructions, with illustrative material (including coloured plates of timbers) and additional data on the imitation of marbles and stained glass, this book had no precursor in English. It was quickly acknowledged by the trade, and new editions followed in 1828, 1832 and 1841. Interior decoration in all the prevailing styles, panelling, shop fronts and interiors were all dealt with in addition to furniture. There were special sections on the imitation of all varieties of mahogany, rosewood, bird's eye maple and pollard oak ('the lower end of the trunk of the oak tree, near and under the surface of the earth . . . is now become very fashionable for furniture, paneling [*sic*], etc.'). Walnut, incidentally, did not have an engraved representation in the book, as it was 'not much used as a fancy wood'.

The popularity of stained furniture inevitably encouraged the mass production of cheaper varieties. Whittock, who wrote of the excellent imitation of rosewood chairs so commonly sold at every broker's (i.e. second-hand dealer's) shop, declared that staining could not be used to great advantage unless it was carried out in large manufactories, and he described the method thus:

'*At the principal manufactories they are dipped in a large copper containing the boiling red stain and then taken out and allowed to dry before they are dipped again; nor does this standing to dry cause any delay where great quantities are to be stained, as that which is first dipped will be dry before the whole have been dipped once into the stain.*'

The bright red stain used for these chairs was made up of 'a strong infusion of Brazil chips in water impregnated with pearlash' (i.e. potassium carbonate); one ounce of pearlash in a gallon of water being sufficient for one pound of the Brazil wood. For more durable (and more expensive) work Whittock recommended the prevailing method of graining in oil colour which, unlike staining, could stand up to repeated cleaning and washing. Chairs, tables, backs of sofas, bookcases, etc., thus grained to resemble rosewood, were often 'decorated with gilding to imitate inlaid brass'.[15]

In spite of the mass production of cheap stained furniture the imitative methods of the time were regarded as eminently respectable. Loudon in his *Encyclopaedia* of 1833 came out enthusiastically in favour of the fashion. He gave detailed instructions for preparing colours for staining and strongly recommended graining for the woodwork of cottages in a rather curious interpretation of the current notion of the association of ideas:

'*All woodwork, avowed as such, should, if possible, be grained in imitation of some natural wood; not with a view of having the imitation mistaken for the original, but rather to create allusion to it, and, by a diversity of lines and shades, to produce a kind of variety and intricacy, which affords more pleasure to the eye than a flat shade of colour.*'[16]

Staining, by obliterating the natural colour of the wood, spoiled the effect of French polish, which, as the pattern books and royal accounts show, was universally adopted as a surface finish for furniture after 1815, replacing the old method of finishing with beeswax and turpentine. Original French polish (lac dissolved in spirits of wine) achieved a lust-

Three examples of papier mâché chairs of *c.* 1850 with painted and mother-of-pearl decoration.

rous surface, but inferior substitutes, little better than varnishes, led to the whole process being questioned after 1851.

Marbling seems to have owed its revival largely to its use by Henry Holland at Carlton House and Southill. The Library at Southill has marbled woodwork on the bookcases round the room in imitation of the dove-grey marble on the commode bookcases. Marbling received special impetus from the fashion for using British marbles and stone on furniture, and was much in evidence, as was graining, at the Exhibition of 1851. The height of fashion for marbling and graining was probably reached at the Paris Exhibition of 1855, at which the exhibits of T. Kershaw and Charles Moxon were praised by Matthew Digby Wyatt for the 'excellence of their imitation of woods and marbles'. He claimed that foreign workmen queued up to examine them.[17] After this date the whole practice became subject to increasing criticism as being spurious. Gilbert Scott was among the first to condemn the fashion in 1857 (*Remarks on Secular and Domestic Architecture*, p. 76), and Mrs Orrinsmith in 1878 (*The Drawing-Room*) echoed prevailing sentiment in denouncing this 'mere dissimulation . . . no material should be other than it is'.[18] By this date imitative skills had lost their prestige and were associated with cheap low-grade furniture, particularly bedroom suites which were often grained to simulate oak.

PAPIER MÂCHÉ

The first half of the Victorian period, from about 1835 to 1870, marked the heyday of English papier mâché furniture.[19] As in so many other instances papier mâché was not a Victorian innovation but a material with a long history behind it. The term requires some definition. The earliest substance of this kind, originating in Persia and the East, and reaching England in the seventeenth century from France (whence its name), was a mixture of pulped paper, glue, chalk and occasionally sand which, after being pressed, moulded and baked, formed a very hard substance that could be sawn and polished like wood. As early as 1672 it is found employed in England in picture frames. A century later, in 1772, Henry Clay of Birmingham, generally credited with the foundation of the English papier mâché industry, took out a patent for the manufacture 'of panels from paper of several thicknesses dried in a hot stove for furniture, etc'.[20] Clay's patent was not strictly speaking papier mâché in the original sense, and in fact Clay himself called his product 'paper ware' (it was also known as 'Clay's ware') to distinguish it from the true papier mâché produced by contemporaries from pulped paper. Clay's product, in highly varnished panels, was used in coach-building as well as for parts of bookcases, cabinets, screens, tables, trays, etc. Some of his smaller objects were decorated with Wedgwood cameos.

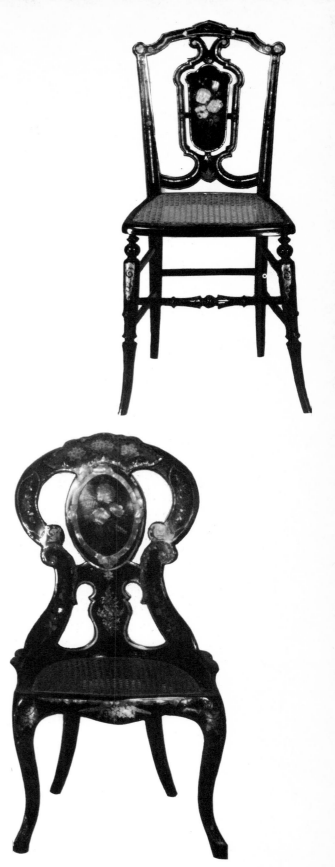

[271]

Clay's successors, Jennens and Bettridge, abandoned niceties of terminology and marketed their paper ware indiscriminately as papier mâché. This firm, who took over Clay's old factory in 1816, were responsible, far more than any other, for the great increase in the production of papier mâché furniture which, with new shapes and decorative methods, made a distinctly original Victorian contribution to English furniture, adding flourishes to the Naturalistic style. There were now two distinct methods of manufacturing papier mâché, one (Clay's method) by pasting sheets of paper on moulds, the other by pressing pulped paper between dies. The two varieties, both given the original name, are summarized in the *Official Catalogue* of the Great Exhibition of 1851:

'There are two varieties of papier mâché; the best is produced by pasting together, on an iron or brass mould, a number of sheets of paper of a spongy texture, allowing them to dry between each addition. In the common variety, the paper is reduced to a pulpy substance, and the form is given by pressure into matrices of metal. Papier mâché may be formed into any desired article by means of the lathe, the plane or the rasp; it is several times varnished; and the irregularities of surface are removed by scraping and rubbing with pumice-stone. The artist then introduces the design; it is again varnished and polished with rotten-stone; and its final brilliancy is given by rubbing with the palm of the hand.'[21]

The main areas of manufacture were Birmingham and Wolverhampton, which by 1860 were employing between 1,000 and 2,000 workers in this particular trade. Jennens and Bettridge made the bulk of all the papier mâché furniture of the period, but the two towns contained many other important manufacturers, including Henry Clay (the name under which Clay's descendants exhibited in 1851), Benjamin Walton, McCallum and Hodson and Alsager and Neville. The main production of most of these firms consisted of popular small articles such as trays, tea caddies and letter-racks. They decorated their own pieces, but a number of smaller establishments specialized in producing 'blanks' (i.e. plain, undecorated pieces), which they sold to similar workshops specializing in decoration. Outside Birmingham and Wolverhampton, the only firm of note that produced work of this kind, Spiers and Son of Oxford, seemed to have decorated blanks (which, however, they marked with their name) supplied from the two main centres.[22] It is essential to note that the term 'japanning' which is normally applied to English imitation of oriental lacquer, was at this time used in the Birmingham area generally to describe work in papier mâché.

Another well-known manufacturer, Charles F. Bielefeld of 15 Wellington Street North, Strand, London, was not a producer of 'paper ware' but of the original type of papier mâché or pulped paper which was widely

Papier mâché chair in the favoured rounded forms of the mid-century, painted with floral bouquets and inlaid with mother-of-pearl.

Far left Papier mâché chair by Jennens and Bettridge *c.* 1850, inlaid with mother-of-pearl.

Left This papier mâché chair combines the balloon-back of *c.* 1850 with legs which still suggest the sabre form of the Regency; mother-of-pearl decoration.

used for architectural decoration. His material was also intended for use by cabinet-makers. A volume of 1840 in the British Museum contains two publications by Bielefeld, the first entitled *On the Use of the Improved Papier Mâché in Furniture in the Interior Decoration of Buildings and in Works of Art*, the second, *Ornaments in Every Style of Design . . . intended for the Assistance of the Architect, Builder, Upholsterer and Decorator*.[23] The complete work formed the firm's catalogue, which was reissued in a much enlarged version in 1850. This second edition illustrated 1,100 different articles, ranging from leaves and rosettes to Corinthian capitals and tables, each piece with its measurements and price. The firm had executed ornamental work for the rebuilt House of Lords, St James's Palace, the Pantheon, Grocers' Hall, several London clubs and the British Museum. Bielefeld's material, it was claimed, was strong enough for ships, bridges and houses. It was used for shop fronts and even for a ten-roomed villa and a village of ten cottages shipped to Australia in prefabricated form.

In the first of Bielefeld's publications mentioned above, a special section addressed 'To the Cabinet-Maker and Upholsterer' shows clearly how extensively the material could be used by furniture-craftsmen, particularly in executing the historical revivals then in vogue. The appropriate text is worth quoting:

'*Papier mâché is applied to the enriched cornices of bookcases and cabinets, to the mouldings and corners and centre ornaments of panel-ing* [sic] *on their doors and sides; to the enriched scroll legs of cabinets and pier tables in the old French style; to ornamental brackets for clocks, busts, vases, etc.; the ornamental parts of picture and glass frames, no matter how carved and elaborate; also to window-curtain cornices, the canopies of bedsteads, etc. It has been very advantageously used for the latter purpose in the state bed at Chatsworth; and also to the canopy of the Royal Throne in the present House of Lords. . . . For the enrichment of bookcases it is admirably adapted, affording opportunities, if in the Gothic style, of introducing elaborate pinnacles and pendants and rich corbels and pierced frets of open work, deeply undercut rosettes, and spandril and mitre or intersection ornaments, etc.*'[24]

No doubt close examination of some of the grander pieces of furniture made at this time in the Rococo and Gothic styles would reveal more use of Bielefeld's material than is at first apparent. Bielefeld stresses that the material was to be treated 'exactly as if it were wood. It is to be cut with the saw and chisel, and may be bent by steam or heat, planed and cleaned up with sandpaper to the smoothest face and to the first arris, if required; it is to be fastened with brads, needle points or glue.' He adds that large objects, such as brackets, could be made either with a wood core or wholly of his material, and claimed that the surface was more suited for gilding than that of any other material. Mirror frames were among Bielefeld's exhibits at the Great Exhibition.

Gothic ornament in this form of papier mâché was also designed by John G. Grace, who used it for simulated Gothic carving on the walls and doors at Abney Hall, Cheshire, while a similar material, *carton pierre*, was extensively used by the prominent firm of George Jackson and Sons of Rathbone Place, London, house decorators and furnishers, who have survived to the present day.[25]

The papier mâché furniture produced in the Birmingham and Wolverhampton areas reflected in general terms contemporary trends and remained very much the same until the 1870s. It is the decorative methods which provide a reasonable guide to chronology, for although several methods could be in vogue at any one time, it is generally true that the more varied and involved the design and ingredients, the later is the piece of furniture likely to be.

The appeal of papier mâché to the Victorians was obviously in its cheapness and durability. Articles made from it could be mass produced; its hard surface made an ideal ground for painted decoration; while its plastic quality lent itself to inlays. Japanners eagerly took up the material, which was superior in many ways to the metals which they had been using. 'The most brilliant effects of gold and colour'—so stated

Papier mâché wall clock of *c.* 1850, painted and mother-of-pearl decoration.

the *Art-Journal* of 1 October 1849, describing the papier mâché exhibits at the Birmingham Exhibition–'are produced with comparative ease and economy'.[26] Gold leaf or gold powder was used to good purpose or, where cheaper work was carried out, the gold was imitated by an alloy of various metals, including silver, copper, zinc and brass. Some of the best work in this medium was done by Joseph Booth, an artist employed in the early 1820s by Jennens and Bettridge, who imitated oriental decoration with great skill, raising the surface of his work with whitening and gold size for bridges, pagodas, trees, rocks, etc.

It was another employee of Jennens and Bettridge, George Souter, who in 1825 introduced the celebrated mother-of-pearl inlay.[27] The very thin mother-of-pearl was first stuck on the article and then painted with varnish to the required design or pattern. Acid was applied when the varnish had dried and the portions of the mother-of-pearl that were not needed–these had been left unprotected by the varnish–were eaten away. The final appearance was of an attractive insertion into the surface, though it had not actually been inlaid. Birds, butterflies and flowers could be worked in this way, and squares of white mother-of-pearl, or

Above Papier mâché occasional table, *c.* 1850; inlaid with mother-of-pearl vase of flowers.

Left Papier mâché cabinet, *c.* 1850, with mother-of-pearl inlay, the top painted and inlaid with a panel showing Warwick Castle.

squares with a mother-of-pearl outline and a floral decoration in their centres, could form the chess board for the top of a games table. Instead of mother-of-pearl simulated gems could be used for inlay in the form of coloured glass stones or paste, in the process known as 'gem-enamelling'.

A very fashionable method was to paint brightly coloured floral and fruit designs on a black japanned ground. This was particularly popular in the 1830s and 1840s. Coloured prints were sometimes pasted on the article and varnished over. Painted panels and boards were also incorporated into a papier mâché frame on, for instance, the back of a chair, on a tray or on a pole-screen. Spiers and Son were famous for the views of Oxford and its neighbourhood with which they decorated their wares. As for the types of furniture and of goods generally which the principal manufacturers turned out, a full account of these appears in the issue

Above Set of papier mâché quartetto tables, *c.* 1850, inlaid with mother-of-pearl; the tops decorated, in order of size, with scenes of a ruined abbey, a chequer board, a floral wreath and a bouquet of lily of the valley.

Right Papier mâché centre table, *c.* 1845, with painted decoration.

Papier mâché chiffonier, *c.* 1850, painted
decoration and mother-of-pearl inlay.

Papier mâché canterbury, *c.* 1850, painted floral
decoration.

mentioned above of the *Art-Journal* of 1 October 1849, most of which is devoted to a description of the Birmingham Exhibition of Manufactures and Art of that year. Among the exhibitors of papier mâché, pride of place, as can be expected, went to Jennens and Bettridge, 'whose works have become famous not only in England but throughout Europe and the Indias' and who were then employing between 300 and 400 workers. The list of goods produced by the firm shows an amazing variety of pieces of furniture and of the numerous knick-knacks scattered about the mid-Victorian home:

> 'Cabinets, cheffoniers, secretaires and writing desks; folding screens, cheval-screens, pole-screens and hand-screens; loo-tables, sofa-tables, occasional-tables and coffee-tables; tea-poys, tea-chests, tea-caddies and tea-trays; portfolios, envelope-cases, card-baskets, card-boxes and card-racks; inkstands; netting-boxes, glove-boxes, work-boxes, snuff-boxes and cigar-boxes; pen-trays, wafer-trays, quadrille-pools; paper-weights, memorandum-cases, brooches, paper-knives; needle-cases, ladies' companions, etuis, chairs, couches, ottomans, stools, mirror-frames, panels for decoration, door-knobs and plates.'[28]

The *Art-Journal* illustrates three of Jennens and Bettridge's furniture exhibits: a tripod flower stand with a Gothic quatrefoil beneath the top; a dressing ('toilet') table with serpentine front, cabriole legs and swing mirror on top; and a chiffonier with double concave front decorated with flowers, fruit and a peacock, sloping sides and a surmounting shelf on scroll supports backed by a mirror.

But already in 1849 the exuberant decoration that was to be a feature of the papier mâché furniture at the Great Exhibition was all too apparent, and the *Art-Journal* added a note of cautious criticism: 'a little less redundancy of ornament might recommend them (i.e. Jennens and Bettridge's exhibits) more strongly to persons of refined taste; but in articles of this class brilliancy of effect seems to be more looked for than delicacy of ornament'. The same criticism was voiced about the brilliant gold and colour effects in the exhibits of another firm, Foothorape, Showell and Shenton, for in 'possessing so many facilities for the most enriched and beautiful effects, the difficulty is in curbing the love of gaudiness which will occasionally peep forth in works of this class'. 1851, of course, would take the criticism much further. Richard Redgrave, reporting on papier mâché products at the Great Exhibition, wrote of 'a mass of barbarous splendour that offends the eye' and of the urgent need for a thorough revision of ornamentation.

Jennens and Bettridge, who impressed their name on their commodities and later added 'makers to the Queen', held appointments as japanners to George IV and William IV as well as to Victoria. At the Great Exhibition they were awarded the prize medal for their pianoforte case.

The notorious 'Day Dreamer' armchair in papier mâché, exhibited by Jennens and Bettridge at the Great Exhibition, 1851, decorated with numerous emblems symbolical of sleep and dreams.

Their other papier mâché exhibits included the 'Victoria Regia' cot, de-signed by the sculptor, J. Bell; a music stool and canterbury; a loo table ('*multum in uno*') adapted for a variety of games; a lady's work table; a sideboard; a chaise longue; an Elizabethan chair with strapwork back; a '*légère*' chair of balloon-back form with cabriole legs; and an inkstand with deer and hounds in oxidized silver. But their subsequently best-known piece, the most widely quoted and illustrated example of mid-Victorian taste (or tastelessness), was their 'Day Dreamer' armchair. This piece marked the end of the road on which Thomas Hope had set tentative steps in 1807. 'The chair is decorated on the top' we are told, 'with two winged thoughts—the one with bird-like pinions, and crowned with roses, representing happy and joyous dreams; the other with leathern bat-like wings—unpleasant and troublesome ones. Behind is displayed Hope, under the figure of the rising sun. The twisted supports of the back are ornamented with the poppy, hearts-ease, convolvulus and snowdrop, all emblematic of the subject. In front of the seat is a shell, containing the head of a cherub, and on either side of it pleasant and troubled dreams are represented by figures. At the side is seen a figure of Puck lying asleep in a labyrinth of foliage, and holding a branch of poppies in his hand.'[29]

Most of the pieces of furniture made from papier mâché, or partly in-corporating it, have long since disappeared, and surviving articles are mainly small ones, such as trays and letter-racks. There are, however, small tables (usually circular tripods), chairs and pole-screens to be

Papier mâché pole screen, *c.* 1850, painted glass screen backed with mother-of-pearl.

Left A fine papier mâché pedestal table, *c.* 1850, painted decoration inlaid with mother-of-pearl.

Below Papier mâché stool, *c.* 1850, inlaid with mother-of-pearl.

[279]

found. Such surviving pieces normally have wood or metal frames to support their papier mâché panels or applied decoration; only chair backs are made solely of the material which is clearly unsuitable for structural purposes in general. An unusual survivor, the well-known half-tester bed now in the Victoria and Albert Museum, has a structure of japanned metal and only the applied panels of the head- and foot-boards are of papier mâché.

Lady's worktable in papier mâché, c. 1850.

Papier mâché writing desk, c. 1850.

Papier mâché half tester bedstead of c. 1850. The bed has an iron structure to which papier mâché head and foot boards have been added.

CAST IRON AND BRASS

Cast iron became a widely used material for furniture during the second quarter of the century. Its relative cheapness and ease of mass production, achieved through improved technical processes, and its durability were all advantages which recommended it. It could also be produced in elaborate ornamental forms and be painted to imitate wood or stone. An early leading firm in the field was the Coalbrookdale Iron Company of Shropshire, a fitting role for one of the great pioneering concerns of the Industrial Revolution. In 1834 this firm began the production of ornamental iron castings, which were chiefly employed at first for garden furniture and hall stands.

Loudon in his *Encyclopaedia* of 1833 was already enthusiastically taking up the cause of iron furniture, particularly recommending cast iron for lobby (or porch) and inn chairs. He illustrates a chair in 'Etruscan' style, suitable for a cottage porch, which could be cast in two pieces. This type could also be made in wood, but whatever the material, it was recommended that it be painted to imitate oak. Another illustration shows a cast- and wrought-iron chair with arm supports and legs made of gas tubing; in this case the seat is made of wood, resulting in a strong, durable, cheap and (with the aid of cushions) comfortable chair. Yet another illustration shows an 'exceeding light yet stable' chair with a circular wooden seat supported on a frame cast in one piece, with tubular legs. All three types of chair were designed by an architect named Mallet. In a section on the introduction of iron into the furniture of farm houses, Loudon maintains that 'this would be attended with considerable economy, at least in the articles of dining-tables, sideboards, bedsteads, and hall, lobby or porch chairs'. He illustrates a circular table, with a top of mahogany or any other firmly grained wood, and supports of cast iron bronzed. Sideboards could have marble or slate tops surmounting enriched cast-iron feet or brackets, of massive architectural effect, and such pieces could be used for 'all houses whatever', especially villas.[30]

Loudon's advocacy of metal beds has been quoted in the section on patent furniture. At the same time he admits that the idea of iron beds would no doubt shock those who had always been accustomed to consider mahogany as essential for this piece of furniture. Iron and brass beds now became universal, their manufacture centred in Birmingham, and it was not until the end of the century that Heal began his campaign, ultimately successful, to bring wooden ones back into fashion. By 1849 Winfield, the Birmingham patentee of 1842, was employing some 400 workers in his factory.[31] Peyton and Harlow, the patentees of metal tubes for beds in 1847, were also prominent producers and their work at the Great Exhibition has already been discussed.

The earliest bedsteads were of cast iron and were somewhat crude in

An unusual piece of metal furniture: a drawing-room aviary, *c.* 1850, with brass and tin dome and wrought-iron legs.

Brass bedstead with canopy, *c*. 1850; an example of the material used with taste and discretion.

character; elaboration came with improved techniques. The strong force of medical opinion behind the hygienic advantages of metal bedsteads over wooden ones had an effect on production for the mass-market, in which cheapness, the overriding consideration, together with increased use of brass, sometimes resulted in simpler and often more elegant articles. But once again the fashionable Victorian insistence on the ornate in preference to the simple, and on making a material look like something else—as the Great Exhibition all too clearly emphasized—stifled almost all attempts of designers to come to terms with the technological world. Winfield, for example, included among the many ornate exhibits which he put on show in 1851 a tube rocking-chair, which in simplicity of design and understanding of material was as progressive as the Bauhaus products of the 1920s, yet at the time it did not excite any particular interest and was not illustrated in the *Art-Journal* catalogue. It would have cut a poor figure, presumably, by the side of the angel cot and the four-poster in Renaissance style (the latter being described as 'one of the best objects of its kind ever brought before our notice'). Brass bedsteads grew more and more elaborate, reaching the peak of ornamental splendour in the mid-1880s.

The treatment of a material like cast iron to make it resemble wood, for which the Victorians have been so strongly criticized (along with their fondness for other imitative materials), raises interesting problems of design, for the Georgian period saw similar deceitful practices—composition made to resemble carved wood on Robert Adam's mirror frames, cheap wood grained to resemble expensive varieties or marbled to imitate foreign marble. Is it a question of condoning in the Georgians what we condemn in the Victorians, or recognizing inherent qualities of control in the one and complete loss of restraint in the other?

Cast iron can be appositely quoted here as it earned the condemnation of A. W. N. Pugin in the following terms:

'*Cast iron is a deception; it is seldom or never left as iron. It is disguised by paint, either as stone, wood or marble. This is a mere trick. . . . Cheap deceptions of magnificence encourage persons to assume a semblance of decoration far beyond either their means or their station, and it is to this cause we may assign all that mockery of splendour which pervades even the dealings of the lower classes of society. Glaring, showy and meretricious ornament was never so much in vogue as at present; it disgraces every branch of our art and manufactures, and the correction of it should be an earnest consideration with every person who desires to see the real principles of art restored.*'[32]

Some of Pugin's sharpest criticisms were reserved for unhappy attempts to create Gothic furniture with cast iron, as, for example, an 'abbey garden seat' which was 'a wiry compound of quatrefoils and fan tracery'.

MARBLE

In the early nineteenth century a fashion arose for table tops made up of coloured spars and marbles of English origin.[33] Their manufacture was mainly centred in Derbyshire, where marble is known to have been quarried in the sixteenth century and was used then and subsequently for building, notably at Hardwick Hall and Chatsworth. After 1750 a water mill at Ashford near Derby was working marble into chimney-pieces, pedestals and vases and similar features of the interior, just as iron manufacturers were producing cast-iron railings and balustrades. It was typical of the Victorians to bring these established materials into

Rosewood side table, second quarter of the 19th century, the top decorated with various coloured marbles with central chequer board.

Top of mahogany table of *c.* 1850 decorated with pietra dura.

Top of ebonized centre table, *c.* 1850, decorated with inlaid floral and foliate designs in marble.

furniture-making. *The Report of the Juries of the Great Exhibition* (1852) explains that the earliest kinds of marble tables were known as 'scrap' tables as their tops were made of 'coloured spars and marbles of irregular shapes embedded in cement and afterwards rubbed down and polished', and that these were followed by slabs embodying spar and marble cut into definite patterns. These tables, however, 'were rudely finished as the workmen were not skilled in the art of making accurate joints and the forms selected were simple and geometrical'. There was a great improvement in decorative standards when the Duke of Devonshire permitted local craftsmen to use his fine collection of Florentine mosaics (*pietra dure*) at Chatsworth as a model, and a boom followed in the industry in the 1840s and 1850s, mainly in Derbyshire, but with other firms at work in Devon and Cornwall.

In 1840 T. Woodruff of Bakewell made a table top introducing groups of flowers, fruit and birds, which was bought by the Duke of Cambridge, and he subsequently gained the patronage of the Queen, the Duke of Devonshire and many other members of the aristocracy. Woodruff and two other Derbyshire firms, G. Redfern (Ashford) and J. Vallance (Matlock), received medals for their tables at the Great Exhibition and all earned commendations in the Jury reports.

These marble tables remained expensive and their high cost, as has been noted, encouraged the use of substitute materials. In 1851 a score of firms exhibited methods of imitating marble. Of special importance as a substitute for marble was slate, in the development of which the outstanding pioneer was E. G. Magnus of 40 Upper Belgrave Place, London SW1. In 1839 Magnus patented, after repeated experiments, a process of enamelling (i.e. japanning) slate. He did not patent his other method of marbling slate by floating mineral colours on pre-pared water, with the result that this process was widely, and often badly, copied. He was, however, awarded a medal by the Society of Arts in 1848 and gained a number of medals at Exhibitions, one in 1851. Loo tables, chiffoniers, consoles, washstand tops and billiard tables were all found with slate tops, though the material was very liable to breakage. Their cheapness was a death-blow to the marble industry which gradually went out of existence by the end of the century. Examples of marble tables that have survived are in the Buxton, Manchester and Sheffield City Museums.

TUNBRIDGE WARE

Tunbridge ware has a long history.[34] The term is used in a general sense to describe the specially decorated wooden articles, usually small ones, which were produced, mainly as souvenirs for visitors, in the neigh-bourhood of the fashionable spa of Tunbridge Wells, Kent, from the seventeenth to the nineteenth centuries. Over this long period the character of the decoration of the ware has changed considerably and this has caused some confusion, for the use of a general term to cover quite different forms of decoration and finishing has obscured the dates at which the various changes occurred. Early decoration on the best work no doubt followed the forms currently in fashion.

During the seventeenth and eighteenth centuries, for instance, forms of marquetry, parquetry, japanning, and painting were probably employed in patterns of floral, geometric, arabesque, scenic and oriental character. Articles thus decorated had a wide appeal, and well before 1800 they were also being sold by London shopkeepers, who were almost certainly retailers and not manufacturers. From about 1775 until the end of George III's reign particularly favoured decorative patterns for Tunbridge ware of the best quality were of cubic, vandyke (i.e. elongated triangular) and mosaic forms, all applied as veneers.[35]

It is this mosaic decoration which is associated today by most people with Tunbridge ware, but here again there is a source of confusion, for veneered mosaic is quite different from the end-grain mosaic familiar in its elaborately minute and repeated patterns. This end-grain mosaic, which marked a radical change in method, was certainly in vogue in the

An example of the Victorians' love of unusual materials: hall chair made of coal, *c.* 1850.

Opposite Top of circular table of black marble inlaid with coloured marbles and other stones by J. Randall; the table made by Samuel Birley, 1862.

Occasional table, *c.* 1845, decorated with Tunbridge ware.

second quarter of the nineteenth century, but the exact date of its introduction and the identity of its inventor are unknown. Contemporary evidence points to the decade 1810–20 as the period when the new patterns began to emerge, and to the brothers James and George Burrows, members of an old-established Tunbridge Wells firm, as the originators. The trade card of the two brothers, dated 1839–40, announces them as 'Inventors of the Mosaic Inlaid Ware', a claim that does not appear to have been challenged by their rivals.[36]

Other distinguished manufacturers in the new technique were Edmund Nye and William Fenner (both these men came from established families in the trade and were partners at one time before separating about 1825), Thomas Barton (Nye's later partner and successor) and Robert Russell.

The method of making and applying the end-grain mosaic was as follows. A large number of very fine hardwood sticks (or slips) of the same length, but of varied colours, were assembled in blocks according to patterns worked on a chart on graph paper. When the sticks were glued together the pattern not only showed on the ends but ran right through the blocks in identical design. The blocks could then be sawn into strips of veneers of end-grain mosaic and glued to the objects selected for decoration. Round blocks were sliced to decorate the lids of boxes, while rectangular blocks could be used to form continuous strips of mosaic. These blocks seem in general to have been from six to eight inches long; rectangular blocks for borders and bandings were about $3\frac{1}{2}$ in across.

At first geometric patterns were in favour. After 1840, and until about 1860, patterns followed those of Berlin woolwork. Then, as skill advanced, at the mid-century and later, floral designs, buildings and landscapes were all worked in mosaic. In some cases the blocks were not sawn but were turned on the lathe to make boxes and similar articles and also structural members for small stands (e.g. watch stands). This process was known as stickwork.

End-grain mosaic was, of course, eminently suitable for decorating the very large number of small objects which have traditionally made up the bulk of Tunbridge ware. Edward and Eva Pinto, responsible for one of the finest collections of the ware, have listed over a hundred categories of these small objects which they have collected or seen, most of the categories containing many varieties.[37] Many of these smaller objects, such as coin cabinets, desk boxes, jewel caskets, medicine chests, picture frames, tea caddies, candle stands, toilet boxes, etc., come properly within the range of small furniture. But larger pieces of furniture are rare and their decoration is usually a mixture of marquetry, veneered mosaic and end-grain mosaic. Such mixed decoration has been used on tables of various kinds, fire screens, teapoys and

Games table, *c.* 1850, decorated with Tunbridge ware; top inlaid with view of Muchross Abbey.

Worktable decorated with Tunbridge ware; made by Edmund Nye, *c.* 1840–50.

chairs. About 1845 Fenner and Co. made a games table thus decorated for the Prince Consort.

The celebrated pieces of Tunbridge ware exhibited by Nye at the Great Exhibition consisted of two round tables, a book stand and a lady's work box.[38] The vast number of pieces of wood employed and the enormous amount of labour thereby required made a special appeal to visitors. The tables contained respectively 110,800 and 129,540 pieces. The book stand was decorated with two mosaic butterflies, one made up of 11,000 pieces, the other of 13,000. The work box had a representation of Bayham Abbey in 13,000 pieces. Nye was also responsible for a fine lady's work table of the mid-century, now in the Tunbridge Wells Museum, which is entirely decorated in end-grain mosaic.

Interior of the Medieval Court, Great Exhibition, 1851, Pugin's well-known
cabinet is seen far right.

CHAPTER 9

THE GREAT EXHIBITION, 1851

The furniture from the British Isles that was shown at the Great Exhibition came within Class 26 (officially described as Furniture, Upholstery, Paper Hangings, Papier Mâché and Japanned Goods). In this class 528 exhibitors, representing companies, partnerships, private firms and individuals, are listed in the Official Catalogue.[1] There were also exhibitors of furniture, including Pugin and Crace, in the Medieval Court. Some carved furniture, among which was the cradle made by W. G. Rogers for the Queen (and exhibited under her name), was shown in the Fine Arts section, Class 30 (Sculpture, Models and Plastic Art, Mosaics, Enamels, etc.).

Naturally enough the most illustrious names in the fashionable furniture and upholstery world were well represented, for obviously their prestige was at stake. Among the London firms with royal appointments who exhibited were J. G. Crace, Johnstone and Jeanes, Holland and Sons, G. J. Morant, Snell and Co., Gillow and Co., Jackson and Graham, H. and A. Arrowsmith, Jackson and Sons and Hindley and Co. Most of these firms have already been referred to in connection with developments in furniture in the generation or so before 1851, and all

Engraving of the cabinet designed by A. W. N. Pugin and made by J. G. Crace for the Great Exhibition, 1851 (*see also* p. 140) Described as 'one of the most important pieces of furniture in the Medieval Court'— *Art-Journal Illustrated Catalogue.*

had examples of their work shown in the *Art-Journal Illustrated Catalogue* as makers of 'decorative furniture', except Crace, who was a producer of 'ornamental furniture' and Jackson and Sons ('papier mâché ornaments'). There were plenty of other prominent London firms among the exhibitors as well as rising English provincial firms, including Trapnell and Son (Bristol), H. Eyles (Bath), G. Doveston (Manchester) and, inevitably, Jennens and Bettridge (Birmingham). The last named, whose London showrooms were also given in the *Official Catalogue*, were very much in the public eye and the *Art-Journal* devoted a good spread of three pages to them. To all the above names could be added those of numerous firms and individuals from Scotland and Ireland.

Side by side with the famous, and forming a significant element in the display, were the exhibits of hitherto obscure men and women of humble station whose work represented the results of what must have been long-drawn-out and wearisome labour. This kind of work, the

General view of the furniture section at the Great Exhibition, 1851.

fruits of the toil of unlettered genius, now given universal recognition in a blaze of publicity, made special appeal to the the strong streak of romantic sentimentality so rife in the mid-Victorian period. The following few random extracts from the *Official Catalogue* tell the story:

'No. 44   Bates, T. H., St. Albans, Herts. Des. and Manu. Rustic loo-table composed of upwards of 4,000 pieces of English wood—oak, maple, hazel, willow and crab. The exhibitor a labourer.

No. 45.   Abbot, J., Horse and Groom, Crouch St., Colchester. Inlaid pentagon table. Inlaid table, with carved pedestal, the sole work of the exhibitor, a blacksmith.

No. 104.   Barrie, J., Edinburgh, Des. & Prod. Carved book-tray, executed by a ploughman, in the evening, by candle-light, without the aid of any model or design, and solely with a penknife.'

A similar random selection, taken from almost any group of consecutive entries in the *Catalogue*, will show the extraordinary variety of types, styles, materials, ornaments, methods of decoration and their imitations, which make up Exhibition furniture. Entries 48 to 54 will suffice:

'No. 48.   Garthwaite, W., Darlington. Imitations of various woods, in painting.

No. 49.   Riddett, G., Ryde, Isle of Wight. Inv. & Manu. Patent reading-table; music-stand, table, or screen, for an invalid.

No. 50.   Eyles, H. 31 Broad St., Bath. Des. & Manu. An English pollard-oak table, with porcelain star, manufactured by Chamberlain and Co., of Worcester. English walnut-tree easy chair, and English walnut-tree drawing-room chair, with porcelain panels.[2]

[No. 51 not entered in the *Catalogue*].

No. 52.   Heasman, W., 60 Middle St., Brighton, Inv. Model of a circular roller-blind of improved construction.

No. 53.   Palmer, R. Brighton, Manu. Specimens of mahogany and oak staining on deal.

No. 54.   Nye, E., Mount Ephraim, Tunbridge Wells, Manu. Two round tables, book stand, and work-box, ornamented with devices in wood mosaic.'[3]

Exhibition furniture reflected completely the assertion of opulence and faith in mechanical progress which, coupled with nostalgia for the past, made up the temper of 1851. Visitors came to wonder and to be impressed, reluctant to let anything mar their romantic preoccupations. An acute contemporary observer, Charles Babbage, saw this at the time of the Exhibition: 'In questions relating to taste, the subject matter is so idealized that the enthusiastic and the timid equally dread

An American exhibit, awarded a Prize Medal, at the Great Exhibition, 1851: rosewood piano in Renaissance style by Nunns and Clark of New York.

its contact with the more sober powers of reasoning, lest the process of analysis should disenchant its visionary scenes, and dissolve the unreal basis of their delight.'[4]

This passage should be set next to the quotation from Wellesley's article in the *Quarterly Review* of October, 1844 (Introduction *supra*, pp. 7–8). Wellesley's superb self-confidence assumed that England's leadership in the arts and architecture could be as readily acknowledged as it was in industry, for he continued:

'*In architecture the age is doing for London what Augustus did for Rome ... We have the finest street and the finest bridges in Europe and the Corso is brought into Pall Mall. In painting and sculpture it is the same ... All the fine arts are on the advance.*'

Yet English furniture-makers were prepared to acknowledge the supremacy of French design and craftsmanship. This is seen in the awards, open to all exhibitors, British and foreign, which were made by the Jurors and their Associates.[5] The Jurors were required to 'reward

Mid-Victorian functional simplicity: rocking
chair of strap brass made by R. W. Winfield,
Birmingham, 1862, based on his rocking chair in
tube brass shown at the Great Exhibition, 1851.

excellence in whatever form it is presented, and not to give induce-
ments to the distinctions of a merely individual competition', and with
this in mind, the chief considerations were 'improved beauty of form
. . . accuracy and certainty of performance . . . beauty of design in form
or colour, or both, with reference to utility'. In the context of 1851 these
considerations could only spur the search for novelty.

Medals were of two kinds. The 'Council Medal' was given for
'important novelty of invention or application, either in material or
process of manufacture, or originality combined with great beauty of
design,' but not, it was stressed, for 'excellence of production or workmanship alone'. Of the five Council Medals awarded in Class 26 not one
went to a British firm; four went to France and the fifth to Austria. The
'Prize Medal' was awarded for reaching a 'certain standard of excellence
in production or workmanship'. Of the seventy medals awarded in this
category forty-six went to foreigners, mainly French. The more prominent English firms who gained the prize medal were Cookes (for their
Kenilworth Buffet), Doveston, Dowbiggin, Gillow, Holland, Jackson

and Graham, Jennens and Bettridge, Johnstone and Jeanes, Morant, Moxon, Trollope and the two billiard-table manufacturers, Burroughs and Watts and Thurston. Among the foreign winners were the Austrian firm of Thonet, whose bentwood chairs were thus recognized by the Jurors but largely ignored by everyone else. There was also a category of 'Honourable Mention' for which sixty-seven exhibitors qualified; here British awards (twenty-seven) outnumbered those of the French (fourteen).

It is likely that the background of the four eminent London firms who appeared among the Jurors—an honour that excluded them from awards, though they could exhibit—had an important influence on the final assessment for medals. They were Crace (Pugin's colleague in the Gothic style), Snell (specialist in French furniture), Jackson (papier mâché and *carton pierre*) and John Webb (a royal craftsman, like the other three, who had worked for Barry in the new Houses of Parliament in the Gothic style, and for the Duke of Atholl at Blair Atholl in the florid 'old French style').[6]

It must be re-emphasized that the Exhibition of 1851 by its very nature exaggerated the mannerisms adopted by the interpreters of the various fashionable styles, as it exaggerated the products of workers in new materials. That the furniture on view was not typical of normal everyday pieces was clear to the compilers of the main (three-volume) *Catalogue*, for they write that 'many of the decorative objects appear better to become apartments of a palace than those of persons in the ordinary walks of life'. They add that 'the amount of ingenuity, of contrivance and arrangement which has been expended upon furniture is scarcely conceivable and it has been applied to the most common objects of domestic utility'.[7] The ornate and anecdotal in furniture decoration were inevitably a legacy of the Exhibition, retaining a market value through the misleading impression of fashionable furniture which thousands of visitors took home to the provinces. But in many directions 1851 signalled important changes.

The exhibitions that followed 1851 were witness to the changes. The Paris Exhibition of 1855 re-affirmed the supremacy of French furniture.[8] But by the time of the International Exhibition in London in 1862, which can be regarded as an attempt to remedy the worst features of 1851, the British had improved their design so much, according to the French, as to become dangerous competitors.[9] Designers were beginning to move away from the domination of upholstery. Seat furniture revealed more of the wooden framework, with greater emphasis on form. As a finish to furniture, the ubiquitous French polish was challenged by coloured surface decoration. The curve, the predominant feature of pre-1851 furniture, was gradually being replaced by the straight line. Eighteenth-century styles, both

French and English (with special attention, in the case of France, to Louis XVI taste), were revived with interest in elegant forms and the use of light-coloured satinwood and of marquetry decoration. Comfort was still an important element in design, but now increasingly subordinate to theory, not its dictator—a change for which professional designers may claim credit.

It is, of course, a fortunate coincidence that 1851 makes so useful a dividing line in the century, but a good case can be made out for giving it a special emphasis in the study of furniture, even though to establish 'landmarks' of this kind is fraught with many dangers, however convenient a method it may be for clarifying stages in development. 1830, the concluding date of most histories of English furniture, is too conveniently tied to the end of the Georgian period and too exclusively related to the winding up of the Classical tradition. All the arguments that have been marshalled to justify the importance of 1830 could be equally well applied to 1840 had George IV died a decade later. The first half of the nineteenth century is an age of transition in English economic and social history, and one of momentous implication. It is against this background as a whole that we have considered the furniture of the time. The Exhibition of 1851 set before the world the initial attempts of designers and craftsmen to tackle the problems of an emerging industrial society, and demonstrated how inadequate their results were.

REFERENCES

INTRODUCTION

1 *The Library of Entertaining Knowledge. A Description and History of Vegetable Substances, used in the Arts and in Domestic Economy. Timber Trees: Fruits*, 2nd edn 1830, pp. 173–4.

2 *Quarterley Review*, vol. LXIV, October 1844, p. 447. This is a review of a publication on fresco painting.

3 This point is emphasized in S. Giedion, *Mechanization Takes Command*, 1955, p. 334, referring to an illustration (fig. 191) of a secretaire-bookcase by Percier and Fontaine, 1801 (in their *Receuil de Décorations Intérieures*).

4 The authoritative work is C. Hussey, *The Picturesque: Studies in a Point of View*, 1967.

5 Price's *Essay* is in Sir T. D. Lauder (ed.), *Price on the Picturesque*, 1842. See also N. Pevsner, 'The Genesis of the Picturesque', *Architectural Review*, vol. XCVI, November 1944, pp. 139–46, and Pevsner's essay on R. P. Knight in vol. I of *Studies in Art, Architecture and Design*, 1968.

6 G. A. Sala, *Notes and Sketches of the Paris Exhibition*, 1868, pp. 319, 325.

7 J. Steegman, *Consort of Taste 1830–70*, 1950, chapter IV, pp. 95–101. On Ruskin, see S. Jervis, 'Ruskin and Furniture', *Furniture History* (the Journal of the Furniture History Society) IX, 1973.

8 P. Floud, 'Victorian Furniture', *The Connoisseur's Guide to Antique Furniture*, (eds. L. G. G. Ramsey and Helen Comstock), 1969, p. 107.

9 H. Schaefer, *The Roots of Modern Design: Functional Tradition in the Nineteenth Century*, 1970, chapter 6 on Furniture, pp. 131–60.

10 For Gruner's relationship with the Prince Consort see W. Ames, *Prince Albert and Victorian Taste*, 1967.

11 For a general account of the activities of an antique dealer of the period see E. T. Joy, 'John Coleman Isaac. An Early Nineteenth Century London Antique Dealer', *The Connoisseur*, December 1962 also G. de Bellaigue, 'Edward Holmes Baldock', *The Connoisseur*, August and September 1975.

12 Giedion, op. cit., pp. 364–88, 'The Reign of the Upholsterer'.

13 E. J. Hobsbawm, *Industry and Empire – An Economic History of Britain since 1750*, 1969, makes this point (p. 53) about clothing (except hosiery), footwear and building as well as furniture.

14 For the Louis Quatorze revival see Chapter 3.

15 M. Girouard, *The Victorian Country House*, 1971. Patronage is dealt with in the Introduction, esp. pp. 8–10.

16 Morel and Hughes are referred to by C. Musgrave, *Regency Furniture 1800–30*, 2nd edn, 1970, p. 94, quoting C. Hussey in *Country Life*, 14 April 1950.

17 Loudon's furniture sections are reprinted in *Loudon Furniture Designs from the Encyclopaedia of Cottage, Farm and Villa Architecture and Furniture, 1839*, 1970, with an introduction by Christopher Gilbert. See also John Gloag, *Mr. Loudon's England*, 1970.

18 The paragraph references to the points mentioned in the text are as follows (1839 edn): Fashionable styles, 2072; Louis Quatorze, 2072; chairs, 2078; bed pillars, 2134; Gothic drawing-room, 2165, fig. 2021; Gothic library, 2161, fig. 2012; staining, 577; Etruscan chair, 638, fig. 640; sofa, 650; 'right of enjoyment', 2172; adapting old fragments into modern furniture, 2072 and 2174; Americans and Australians, 2174.

19 The *Art-Journal Illustrated Catalogue* has been reprinted as *The Crystal Palace Exhibition Catalogue, London (1851)*, 1970, with an introduction by John Gloag.

20 The appropriate page references in Wornum's essay to the main points raised here are as follows (Wornum's pages are marked in the Catalogue by three asterisks which are omitted for brevity): page iv, Louis Quatorze gilt stucco; page v, Cinquecento, lack of Classical ornament, Medieval Court; page vi, Hollands' bookcase; page vii, the English (comfort) and French (luxuries); page xi, deficiencies of carving; page xiii. Kenilworth buffet; page xxi, 'principals, not accessories'; page xxii, national styles. See also section *infra* on The Renaissance Style.

21 For the Warwick school of carving: E. Aslin, *Nineteenth Century English Furniture*, 1962, p. 53, and chapter 7, *infra*, note 25.

22 R. Redgrave, *Reports on the Paris Exhibition (1855)*; Part III, *On the Present State of Design as Applied to Manufactures*, 1856, para 101.

THE REGENCY

1 A. Alison, *Essays on the Nature and Principles of Taste*, 2nd edn, 1810, pp. 54, 82–3.

2 For reprints of Sheraton's works: *The Cabinet-Maker and Upholsterer's Drawing Book* (3rd edn, 1802), eds. C. F. Montgomery and W. P. Cole, 1970; *The Cabinet Dictionary* (1803), eds. Montgomery and Cole, 1970. For a general study: R. Fastnedge, *Sheraton Furniture*, 1962.

3 For general reference: Musgrave, op. cit.; M. Jourdain, *Regency Furniture 1795–1830*, revised and enlarged by R. Fastnedge, 1965; and B. Reade, *Regency Antiques*, 1953.

4 For the best study of Holland: Dorothy Stroud, *Henry Holland; his Life and Architecture*, 1966. See also the *Illustrated Catalogue* of the Henry Holland Exhibition at Woburn Abbey, 1971.

5 Daguerre and Lignereux: *Wallace Collection Catalogues: Furniture. Text with Historical Notes and Introduction* by F. J. B. Watson, 1956, pp. 144–5; and H. Clifford Smith, *Buckingham Palace*, 1931, pp. 102–3.

6 Beckford: quoted by Musgrave, op. cit., p. 30. Oberkirch: *Mémoires de la Baronne d'Oberkirch publiés par le Comte Léonce de Montbrison son petit-fils*, n.d. (1841?), 2 vols., p. 44. (English translation, 3 vols., 1852, vol. 2, p. 221).

7 H. Clifford Smith, op. cit., p. 103 and passim.

8 David: F. J. B. Watson, *Louis XVI Furniture*, 1960, p. 98, fig. j.

9 Watson, ibid., p. 145 and fig. 192; also the Arts Council of Great Britain Catalogue, *The Age of Neo-Classicism*, 1972, p. 747.

10 Windsor Castle, George IV Accounts: Furniture, Lustres, Lamps, etc., Clocks, Linen, Gaslighting. RA 25050–25501, particularly 25052. By gracious permission of Her Majesty the Queen.

11 (ed.) Mrs Paget Toynbee, *The Letters of Horace Walpole*, 1903, vol. 13, letter of 17 September 1785. H. Clifford Smith, op. cit., pp. 101, 103, 147, 151.

12 Wyatt Papworth, *J. B. Papworth, Architect to the King of Wurtemberg*, 1879, p. 11.

13 H. A. Colvin, *A Biographical Dictionary of English Architects 1660–1840*, 1954, pp. 595–7. D. Udy, 'The Neo-Classicism of C. H. Tatham', *The Connoisseur*, August 1971.

14 Architectural Publication Society, *Dictionary of Architecture*, 8 vols., 1853–92. Section on Furniture in vol. 3, E–G.

15 For Tatham chimney-piece at Wilson Park: D. Watkin, *Thomas Hope 1769–1831 and the Neo-Classical Idea*, 1968, p. 209, pl. 91.

16 In addition to the Holland notebooks in the Library, R.I.B.A., P. Ward-Jackson, *English Furniture Designs of the Eighteenth Century*, 1958, pp. 26–7, 63–4, and figs. 298–300.

17 Stroud, op.cit., p. 111, and D. Stroud, 'Woburn Abbey, Bedfordshire, The Last Phase–I', *Country Life*, 8 July 1965, pp. 98–102.

18 G. de Bellaigue, 'The Furnishing of the Chinese Drawing Room at Carlton House', *Burlington Magazine*, September 1967, pp. 518–28. This argues convincingly that the pier tables are French, a conclusion suggested by Musgrave, op.cit. Dorothy Stroud (*Henry Holland*) argues that they are English.

19 *Southill: A Regency House*, 1951. 'The Furniture and Decoration' by F. J. B. Watson, pp. 19–41. Expenses, p. 19; Mrs Whitbread's room, pp. 23–4; Drawing-room, pp. 28–32; Johnes, p. 23; boudoir, pp. 25–8.

20 Reprint of *Household Furniture*, 1970, with preface by C. Musgrave. The most complete study of Hope is by Watkin, op.cit. Also C. Musgrave, 'In search of Thomas Hope', *Antique Collector*, August–September 1972.

21 Louis Simond, *The Journal of a Tour and Residence in Great Britain during the Years 1810 and 1811*, 2 vols., 1817, vol. II, p. 194.

22 Watkin, op.cit., chapter IV, 'The Duchess Street Mansion', pp. 93–124.

23 Smith's review appears in vol. x of the bound series, 3rd edn, 1810, pp. 478–86.

24 Hope's collection is described in Westmacott, p. 211.

25 *Household Furniture* (subsequently *H.F.*): Picture Gallery, Plate 2, p. 21; Drawing-Room, Plate 6, p. 24; sideboard, Plate 9, p. 26 and pp. 27–8. The Flaxman Room was reconstructed at the Victoria and Albert Museum for the Age of Neo-Classicism Exhibition, 1972; see *Catalogue*, pp. 776–7.

26 *H.F.*, Plate 7, pp. 25–6.

27 Ibid., Plate 13, p. 30.

28 Ibid., Plate 50, p. 45.

29 Ibid., Plate 9, pp. 27–8.

30 Ibid., Plate 8, pp. 26–7.

31 Ibid., p. 33.
32 Watkin, op.cit., p. 200.
33 *H.F.*, pp. 12, 15.
34 Ibid., p. 53.
35 The *Compositions* were republished as *Compositions of John Flaxman, R.A.: Homer, Hesiod, Aeschylus*, 1882.
36 *H.F.*, p. 15.
37 *H.F.*, p. 35.
38 Ibid., p. 29.
39 Ibid., p. 2.
40 Giedion, op.cit., pp. 338–43.
41 J. Britton, *The Union of Architecture, Sculpture and Painting; exemplified by a Series of Illustrations, with Descriptive Accounts of the House and Galleries of John Soane*, 1827, pp. 22–3.
42 J. T. Smith, *Nollekens and his Times; Comprehending a Life of that Celebrated Sculptor; and Memoirs of several contemporary Artists*, 2 vols., 2nd edn, 1829, vol. II, p. 240.
43 *Quarterly Review*, vol. XXXVII, No. LXXIV, March 1828, p. 318; review by Sir Walter Scott of Steuart's *The Planter's Guide*.
44 The designs in Smith's *Household Furniture* of 1808 are reprinted in J. Harris, *Regency Furniture Designs 1803–26*, 1961.
45 *H.F.*, p. 11.
46 G. Smith, *The Cabinet-Maker's and Upholsterer's Guide, Drawing Book and Repository*, 1828.
47 Colvin, op. cit., pp. 102–3, for Brown's career.
48 R. Brown, *The Rudiments of Drawing Cabinet and Upholstery Furniture*, 2nd improved edn, 1828. Preface p. x. For other references: 'purity of ornament', p. xi; 'harmonizing metals', p. xii; 'wholly Grecian', p. xiii; Dr Thornton, Plate xxii; Dr Johnson, p. 39; 'gramen caninum', p. 38, Plate xii; cheval glass, p. 44, Plate xvi; 'running fig leaves', p. 41, Plate xiv.
49 *The Practical Cabinet-Maker* reissued as fascimile reprint of 1826 edition, with introduction by Christopher Gilbert, 1973. References are to this reissue.
50 Ibid., introduction, p. x.
51 Ibid., Plate 24.
52 C. Musgrave, *Regency Furniture*, p. 84 for reference to Whitaker's *Designs*, 1825. See also Harris, op. cit., p. 26, Plate 260, and Jourdain, op. cit., p. 36, fig. 61.
53 George Smith, 1828: 'wholly obsolete', p. vi; Mr Hope, p. vii; necessity of economy, p. 187; '*mélange*', p. 187; 'perfection of Greek architecture', p. vi.

THE GRECIAN, EGYPTIAN AND CHINESE TASTES

1 Loudon, op. cit., para 2072.
2 Holland and Sons Day Book, 1835–40, O–S (V&A Museum).
3 H. Whitaker, *Practical Cabinet Maker and Upholsterer's Treasury of Designs*, 1847, includes some designs of the furniture made for the Conservative (now the Bath) Club, e.g. Parts 2, 4, 6, 18, 19. Whitaker's sideboard for the Club is illustrated on Plate 23 (B) in P. Floud, *The Complete Connoisseur Period Guides: Early Victorian Furniture*, 1968, p. 1,303.
4 Macquoid, P. and Edwards, R., *The Dictionary of English Furniture*, 3 vols., 1954, vol. 2, pp. 233–4. N. Pevsner, *Studies in Art, Architecture and Design*, 2 vols., 1968, vol. I, 'The Egyptian Revival'.
5 Mary Russell Mitford, *Our Village: Sketches of Rural Character and Scenery*, 2 vols., 1839; Rosedale. pp. 259–79.
6 Simond, op. cit., vol. II, p. 196.
7 C. A. Busby, *A Series of Designs for Villas and Country Houses, adapted with Economy to the Comforts and to the Elegancies of Modern Life*, 1808, p. 11.
8 Hugh Honour, *Chinoiserie. The Vision of Cathay*, 1961. For Chippendale's japanned furniture at Nostell Priory see the fully documented account by Lindsay Boynton and Nicholson Goodison, 'Furniture of Thomas Chippendale at Nostell Priory–II', *The Burlington Magazine*, June 1969, pp. 351–60, esp. p. 359 (25).
9 Musgrave, op. cit., pp. 64–6; also Musgrave, *Royal Pavilion: an Episode in the Romantic*, 1959. For the Chinese Drawing-Room, Carlton House: *supra* Regency, note 18.
10 Loudon, op. cit.; bedroom chairs, for instance, retain this appearance in front legs and stretchers, e.g. fig. 655 (cottage parlour chair).
11 Alison, op. cit., pp. 82–3.

THE HISTORICAL REVIVALS

1 N. Pevsner, 'Good King James's Gothic', *Architectural Review*, February 1950, pp. 117–20.
2 The two views by Hearne are between pp. 14 and 15 in *The Landscape*.
3 Quoted by Robert C. Smith, 'Gothic and Elizabethan Revival Furniture, 1800–50', *Antiques* (N.Y.), March 1959.
4 C. Hussey, *English Country Houses: Late Georgian 1800–40*, 1968; Mamhead, pp. 193–205; Scotney Castle, pp. 220–29.

5 The plates in Hunt's *Exemplars* are dated 1829; the observations on the furniture of the Tudor period, pp. 120–6.

6 Loudon, op. cit., para 2072.

7 *Quarterly Review*, vol. XLV, no. XC, July 1831, pp. 502–4.

8 *Report from the Select Committee on Arts and Manufactures*, 2 vols., 1835–6. Cockerell's evidence on the Elizabethan style in vol. 2, p. 193. For Cockerell see Colvin, op. cit., pp. 144–7.

9 Information on Watt's collateral descendants from Patricia Butler.

10 Shaw engraved 22 of the 25 signed plates (the rest of the 60 plates were unsigned) in Bridgens's *Furniture with Candelabra*. The relationship between Bridgens and Shaw is discussed in Weinreb's *Furniture Catalogue*, 1965, in a short summary under 'Bridgens'. Little is known at present about Bridgens; Colvin, op. cit., p. 97, has only eight lines on him. Bridgens's book apparently had a first (undiscovered) edition in 1833. See Simon Jervis, 'Cottage, Farm and Villa Furniture', *Burlington Magazine*, December 1975.

11 Fildes, p. 34.

12 J. Gwilt, *Encyclopaedia of Architecture, Historical, Theoretical and Practical*, new edn revised by Wyatt Papworth, 1867. Nash's *Mansions*, 1838–49, more than any other source was responsible for the current popularity of 'Olden Time'; see Steegman, op. cit., chapter IV, 'Architectural Critics and the Olden-Time', pp. 75–101.

13 Sala, op. cit., p. 325.

14 L. Gruner, *The Decorations of the Garden-Pavilion in the Grounds of Buckingham Palace, Engraved under the Superintendence of L. Gruner. With an Introduction by Mrs. Jameson*, 1846. The furniture in the three rooms of the Pavilion (Octagon, Pompeian and Scott rooms) is illustrated at the end. Further details in Steegman, op. cit., pp. 202–4.

15 H. W. and A. Arrowsmith, *The House Decorator and Painter's Guide; containing a Series of Designs for Decorating Apartments, suited to the Various Styles of Architecture*, 1840, note to Plate 13.

16 T. King, *Original Designs for Chairs and Sofas*, n.d. (1840?), has examples of chairs (e.g. Plate 23) in Elizabethan style with distinctly Carolean features. King remains a very shadowy figure. John Gloag, *The Englishman's Chair*, 1964, p. 210, considers him to be a publisher, not a designer. *The Upholsterer's Accelerator*, n.d. (1833?), by King has on the title page 'by an upholsterer of forty-five years experience (many years at the head of some of the first London establishments)'. This seems to indicate his standing, as does the list of twelve works by Kind published at the end of the *Accelerator*, including the second edition of the *Modern Style*. But much more needs to be found out about him.

17 Whitaker, *Treasury of Designs*, refers to the unsuitability of mahogany for Elizabethan furniture in his notes to Part 10, and to the 'bosting' of carving in notes to Part 8. In his Introduction, Whitaker includes (p. 6) 'General Instructions for Furnishings', containing suggestions for appropriate woods for the furniture of rooms. There is emphasis on upholstery and general decoration.

18 Henry Wood. Little seems to be known about him. He published works on (a) *Cheval and Pole Screens, Ottomans, Chairs and Settees, for Mounting Berlin Woolwork*, n.d., (b) *Designs for Furniture and Draperies in the Styles of Louis XIV, Francois Ier, Elizabeth and Gothic*, n.d., (c) *Designs for Settees, Sofas, Ottomans and Easy Chairs*, n.d., (d) *Designs for Furniture*, n.d. Wood's designs obviously had Berlin woolwork in mind. This was introduced from Germany early in the century (traditionally in 1810, though it has been traced to an earlier date) through patterns printed on square paper and copied stitch by stitch on square-meshed canvas in coloured wools.

19 *Furniture from Broughton Hall made by Provincial Firms 1788–1909*. Catalogue of an Exhibition at Temple Newsom House, 1971, with an introduction by Christopher Gilbert. The Elizabethan furniture is detailed in item 36.

20 The Gillows' records (formerly at Waring and Gillow Ltd., now in Westminster Public Library, photocopies in the Victoria & Albert Museum, Department of Furniture & Woodwork) referring to the Elizabethan furniture for the Richmond-Gale-Bradyll family of Conishead Priory are dated 1841 (sections 5188–5621, December 1837–April 1849). The sketches in the records show a great deal of spiral and bobbin turning on the supports of chairs and a fly table (no. 5335), and strapwork and bulbous legs on an oak writing table (no. 5339). The oak carved bookcase (no. 5340) is reproduced in Aslin, op. cit., plate 21.

21 Information concerning the Elizabethan dining-room suite at Charlecote Park, purchased in 1837, was kindly supplied by Mr O. J. Pattison, Curator. The reference (L6/1118) is among the Lucy papers in the County Record Office, Warwick.

22 For the general background see K. Clark, *The Gothic Revival*, 2nd edn, 1950.

23 *Gentleman's Magazine*, vol. LXX, part 2, November 1800, p. 1,069; and vol. LXII, June 1802, p. 491.

24 Colvin, op. cit., Papworth, pp. 436–43; Robinson, pp. 507–8.

25 Ibid., A. C. Pugin, pp. 479–81.

26 For Pugin's career and work: M. Trappes-Lomax, *Pugin: a Medieval Victorian*, 1932; Phoebe A. Stanton, *Pugin*, 1971; Stanton, 'Welby Pugin and the Gothic Revival', (Ph.D. thesis, University of London, 1950); A. Bøe, *From Gothic Revival to Functional Form: a Study in Victorian Theories of Design*, 1957, chapter 2, 'Gothic Reform'; C. Wainwright, 'A. W. N. Pugin's Early Furniture', *The Connoisseur*, January 1976, pp. 3–11.

27 A. W. N. Pugin, Notes for an uncompleted autobiography 1812–31 with slips of uncopied memoranda. V&A Museum Library, 86 MM 13.

28 G. de Bellaigue and Patricia Kirkham, 'George IV and the Furnishing of Windsor Castle', *Furniture History* VIII, 1972, pp. 1–34.

29 H. Clifford Smith, op. cit., p. 103.

30 A. W. N. Pugin, *The True Principles of Pointed or Christian Architecture: set forth in Two Lectures delivered at St. Marie's, Oscott*, 1841, pp. 40–1.

31 The letters are dated 17 June 1830–1 September 1831 and are addressed to Mrs Gough, Perry Hall, Handsworth, Birmingham.

32 Clark, op. cit., chapter 7, 'Pugin', pp. 122–49.

33 *True Principles*, opening paragraph.

34 Pegs securing mortise and tenon joints are clearly marked on some designs, e.g. on a state chair in *Gothic Furniture*, and on the triangular base to a circular table (A. 146) in a drawing dated 1849.

35 Lewis Nockalls Cottingham: Colvin, op. cit., pp. 153–4. The drawings in the Department of Prints and Drawings, V&A Museum are among the Crace papers. All are signed, but not all are dated; the dates are 1842–3.

36 19 November 1836. Coleman Isaac to his wife from Venice: 'Before I left I ordered one of those large Gothic Arm Chairs out of Pugin's Book it is to cost £2. 7s.' In 1840 A. Welby Pugin paid an account to Coleman Isaac. See note 11 to Introduction *supra*.

37 See *A Report by the Victoria and Albert Museum concerning the Furniture in the House of Lords*, 1974.

38 Some houses in which Pugin and/or Crace saw to the furnishings are described in the following *Country Life* articles: Lismore, County Waterford–II, 13 August 1964; Taymouth Castle, Perth–II, 15 October 1964; Leadenham House, Lincs–I, 17 June 1965; Easthor Castle, Heref.–III, 21 March 1968.

39 M. D. Wyatt, *The Paris Universal Exhibition. Report on Furniture and Decoration*, 1856, pp. 297–8.

40 J. G. Crace, *On Furniture, its History and Manufacture*. In this paper read to the R.I.B.A., session 1856–7, Crace praises Pugin as 'one of the greatest artists of his age'.

41 For the Wyatt family: Colvin, op. cit., pp. 717–40.

42 The decoration of the interior of Crockford's Club, 1827, was taken to mark the exact date of the Louis Quatorze revival in P. Floud, 'The Early Victorian Period: Furniture' in *The Connoisseur's Period Guides*, eds. R. Edwards and L. G. G. Ramsey, 1968, p. 1,320.

43 de Bellaigue & Kirkham, op. cit.

44 *Select Committee*, 1835–6; Papworth's evidence, vol. I, p. 95.

45 Arrowsmith, op. cit., Plate 16, 'Salon in the rich and fashionable style of Louis Quinze'.

46 J. Pye, *Patronage of British Art, an Historical Sketch: comprising an Account of the Rise and Progress of Art and Artists in London, from the Beginning of the Reign of George II*, 1845, pp. 296–7.

47 For Thomas King see note *supra*, 16.

48 Wyatt, op. cit., passim for praise of French technical excellence.

49 R. Trevelyan, 'An English Palace in Palermo. Villa Malfitano–I', *Country Life*, 13 July 1972. This villa, begun in 1887, had a Louis XV drawing-room and a Louis XVI drawing-room, demonstrating the longevity of French eighteenth-century styles.

50 Wornum, p. iv in *Art-Journal Illustrated Catalogue*.

51 Ibid., p. xxi on 'this naturalistic, or, as we may call it, horticultural school of ornament'.

52 The *Shorter Oxford English Dictionary* gives 1840–5 for the earliest use of the term in the modern meaning.

53 Whitaker's designs in Renaissance style can be seen in his Parts 3, 5, 6, 7, 8, 9, 13, 14, 22, 27.

54 Wornum's definition of Renaissance periods is on p. iv of his Essay.

55 Redgrave's analysis of the Renaissance is noted in N. Pevsner, *High Victorian Design: a Study of the Exhibition of 1851*, 1951, p. 69.

56 Wornum, p. iv.

57 Ibid., p. v.

58 Ibid., p. vi.
59 Ibid., p. xiv.
60 Holland and Sons Day Book 1852, E–I.
61 For Bullock see Reade, op. cit., passim, esp. pp. 63–71; also E. T. Joy, 'A Modernist of the Regency. George Bullock, Cabinet-Maker–I', *Country Life*, 22 April 1968, and 'A Source of Victorian Romanticism. George Bullock, Cabinet-Maker–II', *Country Life*, 29 August 1968.
62 Brown, op. cit., refers to Bullock in his description of Plate xxv.
63 Reade, op. cit., p. 22.
64 *The Life and Letters of Maria Edgeworth*, ed. A. J. C. Hare, 2 vols., 1894. Vol. I, pp. 275–6 for Bullock's tables at Aston Hall.
65 Reade, op. cit., p. 101, fig. 60.
66 A. Coleridge, 'The Work of George Bullock, Cabinet-Maker in Scotland–I', *The Connoisseur*, April 1965, pp. 249–52; and do.–II, May 1965; pp. 13–17.
67 Simond, op. cit., vol. I, pp. 409–10.
68 My thanks are due to Dr James C. Corson, Honorary Librarian of Abbotsford, for considerable help with information about Bullock's furniture at Abbotsford.
69 J. G. Lockhart, *Memoirs of the Life of Sir Walter Scott, Bart.*, 2 vols., 1878, vol. I, p. 337.
70 For Oakley: R. Edwards & M. Jourdain, *Georgian Cabinet-Makers*, 1955, p. 111. Parker, and Town and Emanuel: Sir Ambrose Heal, *The London Furniture Makers 1660–1840* (Dover Reprint), 1972; Le Gaigneur: H. Clifford Smith, op. cit., pp. 120–1.
71 G. A. Siddons, *The Cabinet-Maker's Guide; or, Rules and Instructions in the Art of Varnishing, Dying, Staining, Japanning, Polishing, Lackering and Beautifying Wood, Ivory, Tortoiseshell and Metal*, 5th edn, 1830, pp. 120–9.
72 Musgrave, op. cit., pp. 128–30 for techniques of buhl-work.
73 Siddons, op. cit., p. 125.
74 Trollope & Sons, 15 Parliament St, Westminster, no. 162, Class 26, p. 132 in the *Official Catalogue of the Great Exhibition*, 1851.
75 For a general account: E. T. Joy, 'A Versatile Victorian Designer–J. B. Papworth', *Country Life*, 15 January 1970.
76 Wyatt Papworth, op. cit.
77 Ibid., p. 95 for Cockerell's speech.
78 *Select Committee* 1835–6, op. cit., vol. I, pp. 92–5.
79 Papworth, op. cit.: Snell, pp. 51–2 and 83; Morant, p. 21; Blades, pp. 37–8; Seddon, p. 85.
80 Ibid., p. 54. (gas lamp).
81 Ibid., p. 82. (buhl).

82 Ibid., p. 91. (Chinese room).
83 Architectural Publication Society, *Dictionary of Architecture*, op. cit. The section on 'Furniture', vol. 3, E–G, refers to Loudon's use of designs ('copies, more or less close') by Papworth.
84 P. Coxe, *The Social Day*, 1823, has interior views of a Breakfast Room, Dressing-Room and Dining-Room.
85 See note 77 *supra*.

ROYAL FURNITURE MAKERS

1 C. Musgrave, *Life in Brighton*, 1970, p. 233.
2 E. T. Joy, 'Royal Victorian Cabinet-Makers, 1837–87', *Burlington Magazine*, November 1969, pp. 677–87; this contains an alphabetical list of the royal craftsmen.
3 For Charles Elliott: N. Barton, 'Rise of a Royal Furniture-Maker–I, *Country Life*, 10 February 1966, pp. 293–5; do.–II, 17 February 1966, pp. 360–2; E. T. Joy, 'Charles Elliott, Royal Cabinet-Maker', *The Connoisseur*, June 1959, pp. 34–9.
4 M. H. Port, 'The Office of Works and Building Contracts in Early Nineteenth-Century England', *Economic History Review*, 2nd series, vol. 20, 1967, pp. 94–110. Also, Public Record Office L.C. 1/12 Official Letters, 1827, no. 848, Treasury to Lord Chamberlain, 19 April, about dealing with public offices.
5 Notes on royal craftsmen in the previous century can be found in E. T. Joy, 'Furniture-Makers to the English Court in the Eighteenth Century', *Connoisseur Year Book*, 1961, pp. 14–18.
6 Samuel Pratt in royal accounts, PRO L.C. 9/354, 1832–45.
7 Bailey's 'Sketch of chair approved by H.M.' in PRO Works 21/19, 1838–40.
8 Benjamin Booth's trade card (Guildhall Collection, London), dated 1775, advertises his 'Floor-Cloth and Turnery Warehouse for all kinds of kitchen equipment.
9 Silver and Co., portable trunk-makers in PRO L.C. 9/355, 1846–54.
10 PRO L.C. 11/95–98, Bill Books, 1837.
11 PRO L.C. 9/355, 1846–54.
12 The main Osborne accounts are in the Holland and Sons records (V & A Museum) and these, with the Osborne papers at Windsor Castle, are dealt with in E. T. Joy, 'Holland and Sons and the Furniture of Osborne House', *Antiques* (N.Y.) April 1971. Hollands' identified surviving furniture in the Queen's Drawing-Room at Osborne provides one of the finest examples of the time of the revived French styles. Cubitt's joinery can be seen in the servants' quarters, in cupboards, shelving, moulding, etc.

13 For Osborne's influence at home and abroad:
 Ames, op. cit., p. 64.

14 Holland and Dowbiggin were separate
 organizations until 1852, when Holland took
 over Dowbiggin's address; they seem,
 however, to have worked in close conjunction
 until then.

INTERIORS

1 Giedion, op. cit., illustrates medieval rooms
 with furniture round the walls, e.g. p. 267,
 fig. 142.

2 P. K. Thornton, 'Room Arrangements in the
 mid-eighteenth Century', *Antiques* (N.Y.),
 April 1971, pp. 556–61.

3 Adam Smith, *The Theory of Modern
 Sentiments*, 1759, part IV, 'Of the Effect of
 Utility upon the Sentiment of Approbation',
 p. 205.

4 *The Letter-Books of Sir William Chambers*,
 1769–74, (B. Lib. Add. MS. f. 41133–41136).
 Add. MS. 41133 f. 107, Chambers to Lord
 Melbourne 14 August 1773.

5 M. Tomlin, 'Back to Adam at Osterley.
 Furniture re-arranged to the Original
 Designs–I', *Country Life*, 18 June 1970; and
 'Osterley in the Eighteenth Century–II',
 25 June 1970.

6 Simond, op. cit., pp. 285–6.

7 Jane Austen, *Persuasion*, Everyman edn,
 1949, p. 33.

8 Mitford, op. cit.

9 Gomm: *Sundry Drawings of Cabinet Ware*,
 etc., in the Library, Henry Francis du Pont
 Museum at Winterthur, Wilmington, Del.,
 USA.

10 The Banting sketch is in the Library,
 Ickworth.

PATENT FURNITURE

1 A synopsis of furniture patents is in Patent
 Office, *Abridgement of Specifications
 relating to Furniture and Upholstery 1620–
 1866*, 1869. Also, E. T. Joy, 'Georgian
 Patent Furniture', *The Connoisseur Year
 Book*, 1962.

2 There is a Harlequin Pembroke table, of the
 kind illustrated and described in Sheraton's
 Drawing Book, but with an oval and not
 rectangular superstructure at Temple
 Newsam.

3 T. Martin, *The Circle of Mechanical Arts*,
 1820, pp. 110–11 (1st edn 1813).

4 The population figures (for Britain) are in
 Hobsbawm, op. cit., p. 67. For cramped
 living conditions in London: Dorothy
 George, *London Life in the Eighteenth
 Century*, 1930, chapter II, pp. 63–108.

5 The patent numbers (for specifications) of the
 quoted patentees are (date first): 1771
 Eckhardt, 995; 1772 Gale, 1002; 1774
 Campbell, 1086; 1798 Gunby, 2248; 1802
 Walker, 2657; 1808 Crosby, 3153; 1812
 Figgins, 3539. Extending dining tables: 1800
 Gillow, 2396; 1805 Brown, 2896; 1807
 Remington, 3090; 1814 Doncaster, 3827. For
 metal applied to furniture: 1769 Pickering,
 920; 1777 Marston and Bellamy, 1165; 1812
 Steinhoeuser, 3533; 1813 Bennett, 3677;
 1828 Pratt, 5668; 1828 Day, 5691. It may be
 useful to detail the patents for castors for
 there can scarcely be a clearer witness to the
 growing heaviness of furniture: 1811
 Sturgeon, 3406; 1812 Loach, 3540; 1813
 Jenkins, 3698; 1816 Barron, 3976; 1816
 Steinhauser, 4008; 1827 Winfield, 5562; 1828
 Guthner, 5584; 1833 Lewty, 6478; 1834
 Lutton, 6921; 1838 Handcock, 7835; 1839
 Harcourt, 8240; 1840 Rymer, 8485; 1841
 Loach, 8788; 1841 Pape, 8823; 1841 Stewart,
 9182; 1841 Fourment, 9203; 1843 Charlton,
 9870; 1849 Furlong, 12459; 1849
 Chauffourier, 12695; 1850 Hinley, 13383.
 What is the reason for the concentration
 around 1840? NB Steinhoeuser 1812 and
 Steinhauser 1816; this is probably the same
 man.

6 George, op. cit., chapter I, pp. 21–62.

7 L. O. J. Boynton, 'The Bed Bug and the "Age
 of Elegance"', *Furniture History* I, 1965,
 pp. 15–31.

8 Brass tube etc., patents: 1812 Steinhoeuser,
 3533; 1812 Thompson, 3560; 1817 Day,
 4132; 1826 Thompson, 5403; 1826 Day,
 5410; 1827 Winfield, 5573; 1831 Winfield,
 6206. NB Benjamin Day, 1817; William Day,
 1826 – the latter used tubes, 'kept in position
 by spring catches', to raise and lower the
 backs of chairs, etc. In 1827 Breidenbach's
 metal wire for bed frames 'will not harbour
 vermin'.

9 Loudon, op. cit., para 1376, p. 655.

10 Winfield 1841, metal bedstead patent 8891;
 Peyton and Harlow 1847 metal tubes patent
 11705.

11 *Art-Journal Illustrated Catalogue*, op. cit.
 gives three pages (242–4) to Winfield's
 exhibits including the notorious 'angel cot'.
 There are illustrations of two graceful metal
 beds (p. 144) by Peyton and Harlow.

12 1812 Paxon's bed for invalids, 3597; 1813
 Sam. James's sofa for invalids 3744. The
 latter is illustrated in Giedion, op. cit., p. 410,
 fig. 243. 1830 Minter's reclining chair, 6034,
 is referred to by Giedion (p. 408) and was the
 subject of a lawsuit in 1834 when his patent
 was unsuccessfully challenged by three others
 (W. Carpmael, *The Law of Patents*, 6th edn,
 1860 – 1st edn, 1832).

13 1826 Pratt, 5418, illustrated by Giedion, p. 380, fig. 225 and described as 'this first spring-upholstered chair'; 1827 Evans and King, 5506; 1827 Dickinson, 5537; 1809 Hakewill, 3217.

14 For Butler's trade card: Heal, op. cit., p. 18.

15 1774 Campbell, 1086: Little Marylebone St, Golden Square (Heal, p. 33). 1785 Waldron, 1483: 11 Catherine St, Strand (Heal, p. 190 'patent bedsteads'). 1827 Daws, 5490: 17 Margaret St, Cavendish Square (Heal, p. 48 'recumbent easy chairs').

16 E. T. Joy, 'Pocock's–the Ingenious Inventors', *The Connoisseur*, February 1970. This article is based on documentary information of William Pocock's family history kindly supplied by Mrs Molly Powel.

17 The Banks Collection (British Library) includes two cards (D2. 621 and 623) of 'Pocock's Patent Library or Office Table Warehouse'.

18 The two-page advertisement of Pocock's business, illustrated in the article in note 16 *supra*, was found among Foreign Office papers (PRO FO 185/50, Spain, 1814) dealing with Spain.

19 Morgan and Sanders: trade card in Heal, p. 115. Their trade card in the Banks Collection has on the back a letter addressed to a customer referring to their dispute with T. Oxenham over the succession to T. Butler's business. Their premises were named 'Trafalgar House' after 1805 as they had supplied furniture to Nelson. *The Windsor & Eton Gazette*, 15 August 1812–quoted from issue in the archives in the *Gazette's* office, Windsor.

20 W. Hogarth, *The Analysis of Beauty*, 1753, p. 14.

21 Adam Smith, op. cit., part IV, p. 205 et seq.

22 Alison, op. cit., Essay 2 'Of the Sublimity and Beauty of the Material World'.

23 Giedion, op. cit., develops the theme of American leadership, p. 389, 'The Constituent Furniture of the Nineteenth Century'.

24 Hobsbawm, op. cit., p. 62.

25 *The Pickwick Papers*, nos. xix–xx, chapter LVI, p. 604 in 1st edn.

26 Papworth, op. cit., p. 57.

27 A number of these patents were for roller blinds, e.g. 1836 Guthner, 7206, 'drawing or winding up window and other roller blinds'.

28 Loudon, op. cit., para 665, p. 336.

29 International Exhibition 1862. *Report by the Juries, Class XXX, Furniture and Upholstery, including Paper-Hangings and Papier Mâché*, Introduction.

30 R. Kerr, *The Gentleman's House; or, How to Plan English Residences from the Parsonage to the Palace; with Tables of Accommodation and Cost, and a Series of Selected Plans*, 1864, p. 73.

THE STRUCTURE OF THE FURNITURE INDUSTRY

1 For the structure of the Georgian furniture industry in London: E. T. Joy, 'The Eighteenth-Century London Furniture Industry', *Apollo*, May 1962, pp. 185–88; also the same author's MA thesis, 'The London Furniture Industry in the Eighteenth Century', University of London Library, photocopy in the V & A Museum Library.

2 R. W. Symonds and B. B. Whineray, *Victorian Furniture*, 1962, p. 17.

3 P. G. Hall, *The Industries of London since 1861*, 1962, chapter 5, esp. p. 91.

4 Edwards and Jourdain, op. cit., Introduction.

5 G. Unwin, *Industrial Organization in the Sixteenth and Seventeenth Centuries*, 1904, pp. 4–5.

6 Anon., *A General Description of All Trades*, 1747, p. 49.

7 The Guildhall Collection (London) of trade cards, dating mainly from *c.* 1750, includes many examples of the retailer who 'buys and sells' and does not make furniture, e.g. a receipted trade card of May 1743, of William Tomkins, Upholsterer and Sworn Appraiser, at the Royal Bed, near Little Moorgate in Moorfields, states that 'he buyeth and selleth all Manner of Household Goods . . . New and Old'. These cards refer to the City of London.

8 T. Mortimer, *Universal Director*, 1763, part 2 (list of craftsmen-shopkeepers under the heading 'Mechanic Arts and Manufacturers').

9 Patricia Kirkham, 'The Careers of William and John Linnell', *Furniture History* III, 1967, pp. 29–44, esp. p. 32. With reference to firms losing employees who set up on their own, Benjamin Goodison, royal cabinet-maker, thus lost two capable men, his nephew and partner Benjamin Parran, and his servant Edward Griffiths, the former supplying the royal family and the latter obtaining several important commissions. Edwards and Jourdain, op. cit., pp. 97 and 106.

10 Pryor's trade card in the Banks Collection (B. Lib.), D2, 632, 1797, gives two addresses.

11 Oakley's trade card, ibid., D.2. 627, 1809. Oakley's standing is thus described in P. A. Memnich, *Neueste Reise durch England, Schottland und Ireland*, 1807, p. 136.

12 For the early history of the firm of Gillow: *A Record of a Furnishing Firm in Two Centuries*, 1901.

13 Papworth, op. cit., p. 85.

14 A visit to Seddons's works is described in *Sophie in London, being the Diary of Sophie von la Roche*, trans. C. Williams, 1933, pp. 173–5.

15 PRO 1851 Census. H.O. 107. 1478. I am indebted to Patricia Kirkham for this information concerning Holland and Sons.

16 For Jackson and Graham: Wyatt, op. cit., p. 306.

17 Hall, op. cit., p. 72.

18 H. Mayhew, *London Labour and the London Poor*, 1967 (1st edn 1851). Vol. 3, 'The London Street Folk', p. 221.

19 Lady M. S. Bentham, *The Life of Brigadier-General Sir Samuel Bentham*, 1862, p. 99 (patents).

20 Aslin, op. cit., p. 24.

21 Wyatt, op. cit., pp. 307–8 (Jackson and Graham) and p. 311 (Holland).

22 The slow progress of woodworking machines is noted in M. P. Bale, *Woodworking Machinery*, 1880, which refers (p. 3) to the 'crude state' of such machinery in England 'till within the last thirty years'. This is borne out by J. H. Clapham, *An Economic History of Modern Britain. I, The Early Railway Age*, 1926, p. 445.

23 *Library of Entertaining Knowledge*, op. cit., pp. 171–3.

24 Martin, op. cit., p. 211.

25 Rogers's bill for the cradle is in PRO L.C. 11/134: 'For William Gibbs Rogers. Carver in Box Wood. 10 Carlisle St, Soho Square. A Turkey Box Wood Cradle elaborately ornamented at the Head feet and sides and rockers with various royal insignia, garlands of flowers, etc. . . . £330.' The Warwick school of carving was responsible for some of the most elaborate work of the mid-century. Prominent firms were Willcox, the Kendalls and above all Cookes, whose 'Kenilworth Buffet' at the 1851 Exhibition has been referred to above (Introduction, note 21). Full information can be found in *The Woodcarvers of Warwick*, The City of Warwick Museum, 1966.

26 See G. B. Hughes, 'Mechanical Carving Machines', *Country Life*, 23 September 1954, pp. 980–1.

27 PRO Works 11/8 (4), 1–18, 1845: these documents deal with the Ministry of Works' investigation of carving machines during the rebuilding of the Houses of Parliament. Barry's letter concerning the tests made with Jordan's and Pratt's machines is dated 3 April 1845.

28 Gillows were unique in being in this period an established provincial (Lancaster) and London firm. For the purposes of this chapter they are considered as a London firm.

29 John T. Kirk, 'Sources of some American Regional Furniture', *Antiques* (N.Y.), December 1965.

30 For Christopher Gilbert see note 19 to chapter *supra* on 'Historical Revivals'; also his introduction and notes in the Catalogue of *Victorian and Edwardian Furniture by Pratts of Bradford* (Exhibition, Bradford, November 1969– January 1970); Catalogue, *Oak Furniture from Yorkshire Churches* (Exhibition, Temple Newsam, September 1971); and Catalogue, *Town and Country Furniture illustrating the Vernacular Tradition* (Exhibition, Temple Newsam, July–August 1972). An important study of a Leeds firm is Dr Boynton's 'High Victorian Furniture: the Example of Marsh & Jones of Leeds', *Furniture History* III, 1967.

31 G. Eland (ed.) *The Purefoy Letters (1735–53)*, 1931: letters to King (Bicester) 14 July 1736 and 20 October 1736; to Belchier (St Paul's Churchyard), 11 January 1735, 8 February 1743 and 18 July 1749; and to Baxter (Covent Garden), 11 January 1735 and 1 February 1735.

32 C. Hutchinson, 'Victorian Cabinet-Makers of Leeds', *Country Life*, 9 March 1972.

33 For the Salt family and Kendell see Boynton, note 30 *supra*.

34 Aslin, op. cit., p. 86 (James Lamb, Manchester).

35 Note 30 *supra* for Pratts of Bradford and their use of hand processes.

36 The York directories are all in the City Library, York. The evidence appears to show that cabinet-makers and upholsterers (and all furniture tradesmen, including furniture brokers) reached their numerical peak about 1851.

37 The Catalogue, *Ernest Gimson 1864–1919* (Exhibition, Leicester Museum, 1969) for information about Philip Clissett.

38 J. L. Mayes, *The History of Chairmaking in High Wycombe*, 1960.

39 Daniel Defoe, *A Tour through the Whole Island of Great Britain*, 1928 (reprint of 1724–26 edn). Under 'High-Wickham'.

40 B. North: Mayes, op. cit., pp. 30–2.

41 Loudon, op. cit., para 638, p. 643.

42 A summary of the export trade in furniture from England can be found in the following: E. T. Joy, 'The Overseas Trade in Furniture in the Eighteenth Century', *Furniture History* I, 1965; and 'The Overseas Trade in Furniture in the Nineteenth Century', *Furniture History* VI, 1970; 'English Furniture Exports', *Country Life* –I, 20 June 1952, and –II, 27 June 1952.

43 PRO B.T. 6/187, English ships clearing from the port of London to the United States, 1783.

44 The trade in furniture to the West Indies in the Georgian period is considered in E. T. Joy, 'Furniture for the West Indies', *The Connoisseur Year Book*, 1954.

45 These geographical divisions were those officially employed in the Customs accounts.

46 For Holland: *World Furniture*, ed. Helena Hayward, 1965, p. 166.

47 Roentgen: P. Thornton and D. Fitzgerald, 'Abraham Roentgen "Englische Kabinettmacher"', *V & A Museum Bulletin*, October 1966.

48 English influence on Norwegian furniture and the important role of Ankers are outlined in E. T. Joy, 'Anglo-Norwegian Furniture at Kunstindustrimuseet i Oslo', *Kunstindustrimuseet Årbok*, 1965.

49 Christopher Gilbert, 'Furniture by Giles Grendey for the Spanish Trade', *Antiques* (N.Y.), April 1971, pp. 544–50.

50 English pattern books in Poland are mentioned in *World Furniture*, p. 179.

51 For Morgan and Sanders see note 19 under 'Patent Furniture' *supra*.

52 Hursthouse, vol. 2, chapter xv, 'Domestic Outfit'.

53 Northcote-Bade, p. 16, fig. 1, and p. 36, fig. 12 illustrate emigrants' cabins.

54 Ibid., pp. 58–66 for a full account of Levien's career; also, Michael Levien, 'The Furniture of J. M. Levien', *The Connoisseur*, January 1976, pp. 50–7.

55 Roberts, vol. i, p. 4.

56 For Lannuier: *World Furniture*, pp. 197–9 and p. 247.

57 The statement that nine-tenths of furniture imports were French appears in Felice Davis, 'Victorian Cabinetmakers in America', *Antiques* (N.Y.), September 1943, p. 113.

58 *World Furniture*, p. 197 and p. 247 (Duncan Phyfe) and p. 195 (Seymour).

59 A. J. Downing, *The Architecture of Country Houses*, 1851, p. 410. Section XII in this work, p. 406 et seq., makes interesting references to mid-century furniture fashions in America.

60 Buckingham, vol. i, p. 48; Lady Wortley, vol. i, p. 287.

61 The American pattern books mentioned are in the Library at Winterthur. Stokes's *The Cabinet-Maker and Upholsterer's Companion*, first published in 1829, had Philadelphia editions in 1852, 1872 and 1906. His text is very close to Siddons's. For Hall: J. Down, 'The Greek Revival in the United States', *Antiques* (N.Y.), November 1943.

62 Downing, op. cit., p. 440; his two Gothic bookcase designs are on p. 445. 'Elizabethan' chairs in the Museum of the City of New York are illustrated in *World Furniture*,

p. 250, figs. 958 and 959. For Belter: Clare Vincent, 'John Henry Belter's Patent Parlour Furniture', *Furniture History* iii, 1967, pp. 92–9. Kenkel's *Catalogue of Furniture in Every Style* is in the Library at Winterthur.

63 PRO Customs 9/100 for the value of furniture exports in 1890.

64 S. Grandjean, *Empire Furniture 1800–25*, 1966, pp. 59–65, 'The Empire Style becomes International'. For *Biedermeier*: *World Furniture*, pp. 257–8; also, G. Himmelheber, *Biedermeier Furniture*, trans. and ed. Simon Jervis, 1974.

65 Papworth, op. cit., p. 127.

66 Giedion, op. cit., p. 376, quoting Dervilliers and the Paris Exhibition, 1834.

67 Felicity Mallet, 'Miles and Edwards of London', *Furniture History* vi, 1970, pp. 73–80.

MATERIALS AND METHODS

1 *The Library of Entertaining Knowledge*, op. cit., has a special section on the main furniture woods *c*. 1830. Also, E. T. Joy, 'Furniture Woods of the Victorians', *Country Life*, 6 October 1966.

2 For Levien see note 54, 'Structure of the Industry', *supra*.

3 C. Holtzapffel, *Turning and Mechanical Manipulation*, 1843, vol. i, chapter 6, 'Descriptive Catalogue of the Woods commonly Employed in this Country'. Blackie, *The Cabinet-Maker's Assistant*, 1853, reprinted 1970 with an introduction by John Gloag. See note 7 *infra*.

4 Whitaker's discussion of fashionable timbers is referred to in note 17, 'Historical Revivals', *supra*.

5 Spanish mahogany, exemplifying the best wood, is frequently mentioned in the royal accounts throughout and after this period. In 1854–5, for instance, Francis, Johnstone and Jeanes, Banting, among others, were supplying furniture of best Spanish mahogany to Buckingham Palace (PRO L.C. 11/135 and 11/136). In 1849 Seddon's charged the royal family one shilling each for 'Spanish veneers' (L.C. 11/134).

6 Siddons, op. cit., pp. 5, 6.

7 *Cabinet-Maker's Assistant*, 1853, op. cit., gives details of furniture woods in its second section, 'Practical Observations on Cabinet-Making', pp. 1–48.

8 Holtzapffel, op. cit., p. 92.

9 Siddons, op. cit., pp. 4–5.

10 *Cabinet-Maker's Assistant*, op. cit., second section, p. 21.

11 P. Nicholson, *The New Practical Builder*, 1823, p. 147.

12 Papworth, op. cit., pp. 39–40.

13 Siddons, op. cit., pp. 92–3.

14 Whittock: the title continues 'containing the most approved methods of imitating oak, mahogany, maple, rose, cedar, coral and every other kind of fancy wood'.

15 Whittock: 'walnut is not much used as a fancy wood and therefore no engraved representation is given of it', p. 39. For imitation of rosewood, p. 72; of inlaid brass, p. 73.

16 Loudon, op. cit., para 577, p. 277.

17 Wyatt, op. cit., p. 342.

18 G. Scott, *Remarks on Secular and Domestic Architecture*, 1857, p. 76; Mrs L. Orrinsmith, *The Drawing Room*, 1878, p. 29. See also M. Jourdain, *English Interior Decoration 1500–1800*, 1950, p. 68.

19 Jane Toller, *Papier Mâché in Great Britain and America*, 1962.

20 1772 Clay patent no. 1027.

21 This summary is in the *Official Descriptive and Illustrated Catalogue*, 1851, vol. II, Class 26, p. 742, following entry 131 (exhibits of Halbeard & Wellings, Birmingham. This firm's series illustrated the manufacture from raw material to the finished article.)

22 S. Jervis, 'O Ye Spiers of Oxford', *Country Life*, 23 August 1973, pp. 482–3.

23 Bielefeld. The B. Lib. copy (786 m. 28 [1] & [2]) gives two parts in one volume, the title-page of part I illustrating Bielefeld's works, 15 Wellington Street North, Strand.

24 Ibid. The references to furniture are in part I, p. 6. The prefabricated village shipped to Australia is described and illustrated in the *Illustrated London News*, 6 August 1833.

25 For *carton pierre*: Symonds and Whineray, op. cit., p. 91.

26 The *Art-Journal* issue of 1 October 1849 is devoted to describing and illustrating the Exhibition of Manufactures and Art, Birmingham, pp. 293–321.

27 Souter in Symonds and Whineray, op. cit., p. 90.

28 *Art-Journal*, op. cit., p. 306 for an account (with illustrations) of the Jennens and Bettridge exhibits.

29 *Official Descriptive and Illustrated Catalogue*, op. cit., illustrates the 'Day Dreamer' in vol. II, Plate 30. It is also described and illustrated on p. 345 of *The Illustrated Exhibitor*, 1851.

30 Loudon: Etruscan chair, note 18, Introduction *supra*; iron table p. 655, fig. 1251; chairs ('by Mr. Mallet'), figs 650 and 651, pp. 320–1.

31 S. Jervis, *Victorian Furniture*, 1968, p. 14.

32 Pugin, *True Principles*, p. 30.

33 Aslin, op. cit., p. 43. For Magnus: Wyatt, op. cit., p. 318.

34 The best and most recent study is E. & E. Pinto, *Tunbridge and Scottish Souvenir Woodware*, 1970.

35 R. Edwards, *The Dictionary of English Furniture*, 1954, vol. 3, p. 352.

36 Pinto, op. cit., pp. 40–1.

37 Ibid., pp. 29–30.

38 *Infra*, chapter 9, 'The Great Exhibition', p. 291.

THE GREAT EXHIBITION

1 This official total is misleading in some respects. Several numbers are missing and exhibitors are known to have been entered twice (e.g. Holland, W., St John's Warwick, 62A and 407).

2 These are the pieces, now in the Victoria and Albert Museum, which are described above in the section on 'The Naturalistic Style' (Chapter 3).

3 For Nye, see section *supra* on Tunbridge ware, pp. 285–7.

4 C. Babbage, *The Exposition of 1851; or, Views of the Industry, the Science and the Government of England*, 2nd edn, 1851, p. 132.

5 The considerations for the awards of prizes are set out in the Introduction to the three-volume *Official Descriptive and Illustrated Catalogue*, 1851. A short summary is given in *The Great Exhibition of 1851: A Commemorative Album* (compiled by C. H. Gibbs-Smith), 1950, p. 15.

6 Webb's bills (1841) at Blair Atholl refer to furniture 'in the old French style', 'elaborately carved', and 'in the same florid style'.

7 Introduction to Class 26 in vol. II.

8 'The incontestable pre-eminence of France in many sections of Class XXIV'–Wyatt, op. cit., p. 278.

9 Steegman, op. cit., p. 225.

ACKNOWLEDGMENTS

The author and publishers would like to thank the following for permission to reproduce illustrations:

Reproduced by gracious permission of Her Majesty the Queen, 34, 35, 40*t*, 41, 42*t*, 95, 96*t*, 132*l*, 133, 134, 150*tl*, 182, 188*t*, 188*b*, 189, 190, 191, 197, 248
Ashmolean Museum, Oxford, 55*l*, 59*bl*, 83*tl*
Borough of Brighton Royal Pavilion, Art Gallery and Museums, 42*b*, 47, 52*t*, 64*t*, 92, 96*b*, 98*t*, 203*b*
Bradford City Art Gallery and Museums, 79*bl*
British Library, 38, 51, 53*l*, 53*r*, 54*t*, 54*b*, 55*r*, 56, 59*cr*, 61, 68, 80*b*, 81, 84, 87, 88*r*, 89*l*, 90, 91*br*, 104, 113, 114, 119, 120, 136, 137*t*, 142, 148, 149, 150*r*, 153, 156*t*, 158*bl*, 158*br*, 159, 175*tr*, 207
V. C. Brooke, 210
The Brooklyn Museum 258 (photo: Cooper-Bridgeman)
Christie, Manson & Woods, London, 74*br*
City of Norwich Museums, 237*bl*
Country Life, 44, 45, 46, 106, 107, 109, 169
Design Council, 237*tr*, 238*tl*, 238*tr*, 238*bl*
Raymond Fortt, 13*b*, 20*c*, 20*b*, 21, 27*b*, 83*tr*, 266*tr*
Guildhall Library, City of London, 219, 220, 221, 222, 223
P. R. Hooper, 78*br*, 83*bl*
Angelo Hornak Photographic Library, 97, 115
House of Lords Records Office, 140*l*, 140*br*, 141
Michael Levien, 249
London Museum, 184
Mary Evans Picture Library, 202, 224, 225, 226, 278
Metropolitan Museum of Art, 250 (Fletcher Fund, 1934); 251*r* (Gift of C. Ruxton Love, 1960); 252*tr*, 254*b* (The Friends of the American Wing Fund, 1968); 252*b*, 253*t*, (Gift of the Family of Mr and Mrs Andrew Varick Stout, in their memory, 1965); 253*bl*, (Gift of Mrs Russell Sage, 1909), 253*br* (Gift of Mrs Paul Moore, 1965); 254*tl* (Edgar J. Kaufmann Charitable Foundation Fund, 1968), 254*tr* (Gift of Ronald S. Kane, 1967); 255; 257*l*

(Gift of Mr and Mrs Lowell Ross Burch and Miss Jean McLean Morron, 1951); 292 (Gift of George Lowther, 1906)
Museum of the City of New York, 256*t*, 258 (Gift of Mrs Henry de Bevoise Schenck)
Museum of Fine Arts, Boston, 251*l* (photo: Cooper-Bridgeman)
Douglas C. Morris & Co., 22*l*
National Monuments Record, 161*b*
The National Trust, 16, 57*br*, 58*tr*, 83*br*, 88*l*, 89, 98*b*, 102, 110, 112, 122, 125, 146, 156*br*, 194, 195, 196*t*, 198*br*, 213, 231, 268
Charles Perry, 22*tc*, 100*b*
Public Records Office, London, 208, 209
Science Museum, London (Crown Copyright), 229
Sotheby's Belgravia, 12, 13*t*, 20*t*, 30*b*, 31, 32, 33*tl*, 33*b*, 74*bl*, 78*t*, 78*bl*, 79*l*, 79*tr*, 79*br*, 80*c*, 82, 99*tr*, 99*b*, 100*t*, 105*t*, 111*t*, 123*bl*, 126, 128*bl*, 128*br*, 129*b*, 130*tl*, 130*b*, 131, 132*r*, 143*t*, 151, 152, 154, 156*bl*, 157*tr*, 157*bl*, 157*br*, 158*t*, 174, 175*b*, 198*tr*, 198*tl*, 199, 205, 211, 232, 233, 256*b*, 257*tr*, 262, 264*l*, 265, 266*tl*, 266*bl*, 266*br*, 267, 270, 271, 272, 273, 274, 275, 276, 277*t*, 279*c*, 279*r*
Sotheby's Bond Street, 11, 22*tr*, 22*b*, 23, 24, 25, 26, 28, 29, 30*t*, 52*b*, 58*tc*, 58*b*, 60, 65*t*, 65*c*, 72, 74*tr*, 76, 77*bl*, 85, 86*t*, 91*bl*, 101*b*, 130*tr*, 165, 167, 171*t*, 173, 240
Temple Williams, 116
United Photographers, 293
The University of Reading Museum of English Rural Life, 238*br*
Victoria and Albert Museum, London (Crown Copyright), 8, 27*t*, 33*tr*, 40*b*, 50, 57*tr*, 57*tl*, 58*tl*, 59*t*, 59*b*, 65*b*, 74*tl*, 75*t*, 79*tc*, 80*t*, 86*r*, 91*t*, 99*tl*, 101*t*, 111*b*, 117, 123*t*, 127, 128*tl*, 128*tr*, 137*b*, 138*tl*, 138*bl*, 138*br*, 139, 140*tr*, 143*b*, 147, 151*t*, 155, 157*tl*, 171*b*, 176, 198*bl*, 203*t*, 204*r*, 237*br*, 263, 264*r*, 264*b*, 277*b*, 279*l*, 280*r*, 284*r*, 289, 290
The Wallace Collection, 172
Henry Francis du Pont Winterthur Museum, 252*tl*
Worshipful Company of Goldsmiths, 77*t*, 214

INDEX